THE CHILD OF GULAG

"An intelligent, well-written, informative book about growing up in the Soviet Union and overcoming repression, it brims with history, reference and subtle allusion. Yuri Feynberg is stimulating, adventurous and witty. I highly recommend this book to anyone interested in reading an eyewitness account of life in the Siberian Gulag and one brave man's escape from it.

—Terry Thompson, Professor,
Graduate School of Journalism Columbia University

"A fascinating story of a life in the context of a world changing without end. I felt I was altered in time and living in the history of Eastern Europe. I was particularly moved by the level of historical detail that pieced together events in Russian / European history and the heart felt the impact on Yule's life, family and the salient influence on the practice of medicine and health care. I could not put it down. "

—Andrew F. Laine, D.Sc.

Percy K. and Vida L. W. Hudson Professor of
Biomedical Engineering and Radiology
Chair, Department of Biomedical Engineering
Columbia University, New York, NY

THE CHILD OF GULAG

THE CHILD OF GULAG

YURI FEYNBERG

TATE PUBLISHING
AND ENTERPRISES, LLC

The Child of the Gulag

Published by Tate Publishing & Enterprises, LLC
127 E. Trade Center Terrace | Mustang, Oklahoma 73064 USA
1.888.361.9473 | www.tatepublishing.com

Tate Publishing is committed to excellence in the publishing industry. The company reflects the philosophy established by the founders, based on Psalm 68:11,
"The Lord gave the word and great was the company of those who published it."

Cover design by Rtor Maghuyop
Interior design by Joana Quilantang

Published in the United States of America

ISBN: 978-1-62295-240-3
1. History / Historiography
2. History / Europe / Russia & the Former Soviet Union
12.11.15

DEDICATION

TO ZOYA, THE ANGEL OF THE GULAG

ACKNOWLEDGMENTS

I am grateful to Lukasz Stanczyk for his technical assistance throughout the writing process.

PROLOGUE

16 January 1997. The flying dream was back, remarkably lucid after a twenty-five year absence. Yule was dreaming of flying high above the Hudson River, looking down at the stretch between the Tappan Zee and the George Washington bridges. This flight, however, was different; instead of the characteristic soaring, it was a tailspin, slow at first, then gradually becoming faster and faster until, finally, reeling out of control. This particular dream had another unusual quality—he was dreaming and analyzing the dream at the same time, a strange sensation of adopting both the role of the participant and the observer. The spin had come to an abrupt halt when he hit the water. There was no perceptible pain, just a feeling of cold water on his face. He opened his eyes. The worried face of a Parkway Patrolman floated like a specter above him, almost surreal and intangible. Yule was lying on his back, feeling a pleasantly cool drizzle on his face. He heard the patrolman talking into his police radio. "Male, Caucasian... bleeding out the mouth... looks like serious internal... no other vehicles involved..." Yule was not scared. On the contrary, there was a pleasant feeling of euphoria—the endorphins did their job by making the inevitable transition from life to death painless, as gentle as droplets of rain caressing one's cheeks.

But Yule had opened his eyes again, his body refusing to sink into the respite promised by death. Overhead, he was blinded by very bright and shadowless lamps shining down onto him. A tube was hanging out of his mouth, accompanied by two more thick tubes, one on each side, emerging from somewhere in his body. Only the ends of each tube were visible, eventually terminating inside a pump, which was rising and falling with every breath he took. Perhaps it was the other way around, with the cylinder autonomously going up and down, thereby enabling him to breathe. Yule pondered for a moment. His mind was slowly clearing, struggling to piece together the sequence of events that brought him here. He remembered driving on the Palisade Parkway, passing exit number two, Alpine. There was black ice on the road. An incomprehensible schism, succeeded by the flying dream ending up with him on his back, lying on the hard road. The next thing he remembered was the bright and luminous orbs above him, blinding Yule as he emerged from the cold grasp of death itself.

A Filipino nurse leaned over him and asked, "What is your name?" Yule's mind was surprisingly clear, his memory sharper than usual.

"Yule Fine," he answered.

"Date of birth?"

"Where do you live?"

"Do you take any medications?"

His answers were as short and as clear as the questions.

"Is there anyone you would like to notify?"

"My wife. How long am I going to be here?"

The nurse glanced at the two people standing next to her, deftly manipulating a series of tubes and gauzes, then looked at Yule and asked, "Do you know what happened to you?"

"No, but I have to sign the payroll checks for my staff no later than Wednesday; I have to be in the office before Wednesday..."

All three members of the staff looked at each other and smiled. "He's going to make it," said the older doctor. He looked at Yule, shook his head, and added, "You have fourteen broken ribs, a severe concussion, a smashed right clavicle, a cracked seventh vertebrae, and collapsed lungs. On top of that, you have just received a second blood and plasma transfusion." He was peering at Yule above his steel-rimmed glasses. "Still want to leave?"

"Yes… as soon as I can walk. You can't keep me here against my will. Besides, I feel fine."

"That's because you are pumped with an extra dose of morphine. Patients with just one broken rib go on disability for many months; you have got fourteen, my friend. Not to mention the collapsed lungs and the broken clavicle. After we are done patching you up, you will require months, maybe even years, of therapy." The older doctor, who was clearly annoyed with Yule's stubborn bantering, finished whatever he was doing and walked away.

"What hospital is this?" asked Yule.

"Hackensack University Medical Center," answered the younger doctor. "I am Dr. Cahill, your orthopedic surgeon."

Yule spent the next several days in a seemingly endless cycle of hallucination, dreaming, waking up, and trying to remember where he was only to drift back into a fog of farraginous thoughts. He vaguely remembered his wife sitting next to him, her worried face, eyes brimming with tears. They had a conversation, an argument of some sort, but he couldn't recall afterwards what it was about. He vividly remembered, however, his embarrassment when a nurse's aid, a young Hispanic woman, had emptied his bedpan. Yule couldn't recall asking for a male aid but probably did. From that point on, there was a male aid assigned to him. His name was Ahmed; he was in his mid-twenties, a second-year medical student. He was tall, dark, and handsome with his big, sad eyes and long hair.

On the first day, Ahmed gave Yule a sponge bath and washed his hair. The following day, he brought in a shaving kit and gently shaved Yule's one-week-old beard. He left the mustache intact without even asking Yule for his preference; Ahmed had figured it out due to the fact that the mustache was visibly older than the beard. After the shaving was finished, he pulled out a small mirror and showed Yule the results. An unfamiliarly gaunt face with dark circles under the eyes stared back at Yule. Ahmed read the articulate disgust in Yule's facial expression.

"You have great skin and shouldn't grow any facial hair, not to mention that you'd look at least ten years younger without it," he commented. "You must've been doing something right, because your body is twenty years younger than you are," he added, laughing.

"Is this your Middle Eastern politeness talking, or do you really mean it?" inquired Yule.

"I was actually born in the US," answered Ahmed, still laughing.

"What about your parents?"

"They are from Afghanistan."

"One can't escape one's family culture; my daughter was born here too, but she is more Russian than my wife," said Yule. "But as far as my physique is concerned, it's a combination of good genes and a lot of sports throughout most of my life, not to mention my wholesome way of life; I don't smoke, drink very little alcohol, and never did drugs."

"That's pretty comprehensive," said Ahmed, laughing again. "I will see you tomorrow. Is there anything else you need before I go?"

"No, but thank you for what you did for me." Yule choked up. "You are god-sent, Ahmed."

That was something completely unexpected from Yule, a man who already had a reputation as a "tough customer." Ahmed couldn't find a proper response. He merely waved his hand and, for the second time, said, "See you tomorrow." He went out and closed the door behind him.

The following morning, after a regular visit by Dr. Keys, morphine had been discontinued and replaced by Percocet. Use of the right arm was very limited, almost nonexistent. The right shoulder, without the support of a collarbone, had been pulled closer to the neck by the contracted muscles. The intravenous stand was still there, but the tubes had been removed from his chest. In their stead, Yule was given a small device to blow into in order to exercise his lungs. He had visitors on a daily basis. Tatiana came with their ten-year-old daughter Rebecca, who became visibly frightened by her father's uncharacteristic look. It was, Yule knew, a mistake to bring her into the hospital, but he had missed her very much and insisted on the visit. Yule's staff from work also paid him a visit; they were worried. When the leader of an organization is in trouble, the organization is rendered unstable. Whether they were genuinely concerned or whether it was just an act of pure self-preservation didn't matter. It was still good to see them.

The next day, Yule had received permission to start the arduous endeavor to walk. It was much easier said than done. Simply put, Yule couldn't walk at first. His body, deprived of oxygen due to the decimated lungs, tended to stop obeying his brain after just a few steps. A Physical Therapist Aid had been assigned to help Yule with his rehabilitation. She was a tiny Russian woman in her late-fifties. All four foot ten inches of her attempted to support Yule's body during their walks in the hospital corridors. Her name was Galina. She was a comic, constantly jesting and saying that men, whenever they become ill and helpless, always seek the refuge of a woman. Much to her amazement, Yule had switched to Russian. They continued conversing in Russian throughout their "walks." She was in the country for five years. Once a chemistry teacher in the town of Pripyat, which was built for employees of the Chernobyl Nuclear Power Station, her husband, Vasiliy, was an engineer at the plant who had perished in the infamous nuclear reactor meltdown of 1986. At the time of the accident, forty-five thousand people lived in the town of Pripyat. The explosion had released approximately one hundred times more radiation than the atom bombs dropped over Hiroshima and Nagasaki toward the end of the Second World War. Galina had an interesting approach to her husband's death. According to the official investigation report, the violent explosion instantly killed her husband, who was in charge of turbine operations. Galina thought of his instant death as a blessing because it had spared him from the public humiliation of an open trial and the inevitably guilty sentence. The ultimate verdict would have been years in a labor camp, a verdict that greeted the rest of his colleagues, the unfortunate survivors of the blast.

"I know my husband," said Galina, a detectable trace of pain in her voice. "He wasn't capable of cutting corners, nor compromising the safety of the people."

"I've read a lot of reports regarding the accident. One particular report by Swiss investigators places the blame on the Soviet Nuclear Authority for not passing the relevant information on to the operating crew in Chernobyl."

Galina stopped abruptly and looked up, her glance penetrating deep into Yule's blue eyes.

"What information?" she demanded.

Yule already regretted his previous comment; he forgot the intensity of the Russian character. It was, however, too late and the damage was already done.

"I've read about it more than five years ago," he said. "But, as far as I remember, there was a similar accident with a reactor of the same type in Lithuania, around 1983 or so. It had to do with too many control rods being raised at once and then reinserted simultaneously during an emergency shutdown."

"So that was the information that the government didn't share with Chernobyl?"

"Apparently," said Yule. "At least, that's what the Swiss investigators had found."

There was an ephemeral pause, merely long enough to allow for this new information to sink in.

Quite suddenly, and with much emotion, Galina burst out, exclaiming, "Thank you, thank you very much!" She was ecstatic. "I knew it wasn't his fault. I knew it, but there was no information for the people. We didn't know anything..." She was sobbing, burying her head into Yule's chest and, as a consequence, completely forgetting her responsibility to keep him in an upright position.

"Take it easy," said a passing nurse, shaking her head disapprovingly. "He is about to collapse."

The thirtieth of January: discharge day. Ahmed first wheeled Yule into the elevator, then outside where his wife was waiting in the car. It was an indefinably great feeling, the knowledge of going home accompanied by the anticipation of being with his daughter and, of course, Candy, a seventy-pound pit bull-greyhound mix rescued from the Teterboro animal shelter only one day before she was scheduled for euthanasia. Candy was a strikingly good-looking dog, brindle with white socks and long, muscular legs. She resembled a small horse, trotting with her characteristic and remarkable power, speed, and grace. Candy had very expressive, almond-shaped eyes, not unlike the color of light amber. Whether through some indefinable sense of cognition or by means of congenital instinct, she knew immediately that something was wrong with the master. Sniffing his clothes resulted in a fit of sneezing. Perhaps the smells of a hospital were too potent for her ultra-sensitive olfactory abilities. The most remarkable event, however, had taken place when Yule was in bed attempting, with not much success, to discover the least painful position to lie in. Candy jumped onto the bed, stretched next to Yule, and pressed her body against his—the effect was almost immediate. As soon as Yule embraced her warm body, the nagging pain was greatly reduced.

For the next five days, Candy stayed with Yule whenever he was confined to his bed, leaning against his broken ribs as if she possessed a profound knowledge of her remedial abilities. She got up only out of necessity, to eat or to go outside for a few minutes. Yule had always attributed his relatively quick recovery to the healing power of his dog.

It had been more than a month since the accident, yet the events that occurred on that sixteenth of January were no more clear than they were immediately following the incident. The brain was obviously blocking the memories of the traumatic event, erecting an impenetrable barrier. The defense mechanism was doing its job. Yule, however, couldn't just leave it at that and thus refused to rest in that naturally induced respite of ignorance. He was constantly searching for the answer. Was it an animal that crossed the Parkway and made Yule step on the brakes? Perhaps he simply fell asleep behind the wheel, as some suggested? The former was a logical possibility; Yule could never run over an animal, regardless of how large or small. The latter was simply out of the question; after thirty years of driving, including long-distances and mountainous terrains, just falling asleep wasn't even comprehensible. What was it then? Yule began to suspect that there was a possibility of him becoming unconscious, thus causing him to lose control over the vehicle. It happened too quickly—he remembered his last thought right before he opened his eyes and saw the cloudy sky above, feeling the cold drops of rain on his face. Did the Radiologist miss anything in the X-ray or in the other tests? Although Hackensack Medical Center had an excellent reputation, one can never rule out the distinct possibility of a not-so-diligent person who cut some corners in his daily routine. Yule didn't have to go far for an example of this very lack of diligence: his broken right clavicle was never fixed and remained shattered into four separate bones which, as a result, became fused into an odd and unnatural shape, making Yule's right shoulder a few inches shorter and greatly reducing his range of motion. The logical explanation for this oversight was that they were too busy with keeping their critical patient alive to deal with a non-essential fractured collarbone. Yule picked up the phone, dialed the Medical Records Department, and asked for his records.

"You have to come in and sign a release form, sir," said a pleasant female voice. "We need at least one day to prepare your records."

"Thank you, I will see you tomorrow."

Yule still couldn't drive; he couldn't fully use his right arm, and every change of body position, regardless of how minute, resulted in a shot of sharp pain. Walking with a cane was admittedly odd but substantially less painful. Tatiana had taken a leave of absence from work and was driving him to work and back every day. Yule, being right-handed, had to learn how to write with his left hand. His signature didn't look right and, in some cases, certain documents and several checks had been rejected.

The following day, Yule finally had the opportunity to go over his medical records. They were contained within a thick manila envelope, ominously sealed with a large *confidential* designation. Yule broke the seal and spread the pages out over his desk. It was rather painful to go over the details of his injuries, medical procedures, and the lengthy trauma nursing notes: *multiple fractured ribs including a flail segment, pulmonary contusion, and bilateral thoracostomies.* Yule began to feel pain in every part of the body mentioned in the discharge record, a testament to the remarkable connection between one's physiology and psychology. He started skipping most of the records, specifically looking for the head X-ray report. He located the page-long document: *without contrast administration.* Yule scanned the report and went all the way down to the *impression.* There it was, the possible answer to the question that had eluded him for so long: *mass enlarging of the sella turcica, probably representing a pituitary adenoma.* The radiologist did indeed do his job. It was the attending physician who didn't read the report and thus discharged Yule without an appropriate follow up.

The next step was to retrodict the accident. Was this tumor responsible for his loss of consciousness? Taking into consideration the size of it (two centimeters in diameter) and the fact that it compressed the *optic chiasm*, the answer was a very probable *yes*.

It was time to take the matter into his hands. Yule decided to have an MRI done as soon as possible, and if the radiologist's finding was confirmed, surgery would be in order.

The MRI came back showing a substantial adenoma growing out of the pituitary gland, right next to the optic nerve. Yule opened his laptop, the faint glow of the screen partially illuminating his face as he typed *neurosurgeon, pituitary adenoma* into the search engine. The search had resulted in several names. One in particular, Dr. Kalmon Post at Mount Sinai, caught Yule's attention. A pause followed, the silence broken only by the subtle hum of the laptop. Yule slowly picked up the phone and dialed Dr. Post's office.

"Mount Sinai, Dr. Post's office."

"I would like to schedule a consultation visit with Dr. Post."

"Who is your referring physician?"

"I don't have one."

"How do you know that you need a neurosurgeon?"

"I have an MRI film that shows a pituitary adenoma."

"Are you a doctor?"

"Yes, but not of medicine."

"Of what, then?" The receptionist was slowly losing her cool.

"I have a Ph.D. in Health Administration."

The answer had satisfied her to some extent. "What insurance do you have?"

"I will pay for the consultation myself."

That had apparently appeased her, completely.

"Next Wednesday at 11:30," she said.

"Thank you." He hung up.

Dr. Post was very matter-of-fact. Without exhibiting any manifest curiosity toward Yule's story, he informed Yule that this type of adenoma is not uncommon, usually benign, and that he had performed hundreds of similar procedures. The tumor, Dr. Post explained, is removed through the nose, and the consequential stay at the hospital is usually two days, in what is known as a "short-stay unit." The doctor's confidence was both reassuring and comforting. The day for the surgery was set, the procedure to be performed in six weeks.

Meanwhile, his Percocet addiction took a violent stranglehold. Yule knew that the medication contained traces of Oxycodone. The withdrawal symptoms, Yule also knew, are similar to those of morphine withdrawal. Tatiana had suggested the more conventional route of a detox clinic or support group, but Yule had a different idea. He had a family history of morphine addiction that resulted in tragedy. No, the conventional and safe treatments would not suffice. The only true solution was to go cold turkey. He would tackle the monster head-on, confront the demon that was the cause of such unfathomable lament in his life with true resolve and determination. It was a risky experiment, to be sure, but Yule had decided to go through with it to test the strength of his character one more time, and to prove (if not to anyone but himself) that it is quite possible to stop using drugs without any external help or pampering. The following week, Yule had reduced the dosage to half. After seven days, he had stopped taking it completely. He decided to do it on Friday, so that by Monday the withdrawal symptoms would dissipate.

Yule didn't take his usual morning dosage on Friday. In the beginning, it wasn't so horrible. About two hours after he had arrived at his office, however, the symptoms slowly but surely began to creep in. Initially, the symptoms were limited to frequent spells of yawning every few minutes, light tremors, as well as some palpitations. It was uncomfortable but still manageable.

The worst came at night: the agitation, the sleeplessness, the endless cycle of sweat and chills. Worst of all were the muscle spasms, so severe that Yule, as he later characterized it, felt like Regan MacNeil being thrown up into the air by her shaking bed. By the following morning, the worst was over with, and Yule finally fell into an almost merciful slumber.

He woke up five hours later, feeling substantially weaker but great at the same time. He did it. The feeling of success was remarkable, something akin to the amalgamation of relief and physical accomplishment felt by a mountain climber as he scales the final peak of his long and arduous journey.

As it often occurs in life, however, the ephemeral euphoria of success was quickly replaced by the infinitely more numerous concerns of the future. The next thought was about the upcoming surgery. The surgery itself was just a matter of logistics. The nagging concern was about the origins of the adenoma. How did he get it? The history on both sides of his family contained no records of cancer or cancer-related ailments. The main killers in his family were war and heart failure. Was there something in his own life, something apart from his genetic composition—perhaps some event, or maybe a specific environment where he had been exposed to carcinogens, which had corrupted his genes and triggered the growth of an adenoma? Yule commenced a mental playback of past events, searching desperately through the vast records of his mind for some abnormality. But what was it? A large quantity of X-rays? The mercury vapors from the coal mine in Gorlovka, where he had worked for a short time? Something in his military service? Perhaps the trip to Baikonur Kosmodrom? The Launch Pad—Area Fifty-four?

Memory is a truly remarkable phenomenon—information lies dormant for thirty years without any associations or virtually any need to be pulled out until a life-changing event spawns a recollection, and here they were, the memories of the R-36 launch pad in Baikonur, Kazakhstan in 1965, as lucid and as detailed as the day of the event itself. The R-36 (also known as 8K67 with heavy warhead) was an intercontinental ballistic missile, the most advanced second-generation missile of that time. The warhead had the capability to enter into orbit around the Earth on its way to the target. This missile was not declared operational yet; this particular launch was conducted as a seemingly innocent test.

As a member of the Eighth Airborne Corps of the 103rd Guards Airborne Division, Yule was assigned to provide security during the transportation and the launch of the 8K67. After the convoy had arrived at the launch site and the one-hundred-twenty-ton missile had been up-righted on the launch pad, Yule's special unit had secured the perimeter and taken cover in the trenches encircling the launch pad. It was a quiet, rainy day. Yule could hear the voices of technicians testing the ratters. "*Vtoroy i chetvertiy k tretyemu*," *second and fourth to third*, they were shouting, reporting the movement of the ratters to the technicians stationed in a van parked next to the missile. The tankers containing UDMH, the main component of the rocket fuel, had arrived. The full name of this fuel was Asymmetrical Dimethylhydrzine, a highly toxic, volatile, and clear liquid with a characteristically sharp, fishy smell. The fuel was not sensitive to shock, but its vapors were highly flammable. Russians mixed it with an oxidizer to propel the 8K67 rockets.

The fueling went according to schedule; all fifty tons of UDMH were pumped into the rocket without so much as a hitch. The next step in the complex sequence was to bring a tanker with nitrogen tetroxide, an oxidizer that was to be mixed with the UDMH in order to create a concoction powerful enough propel the advanced rocket. That was when the inexplicable and calamitous chain of events had commenced, events that scarred themselves into the deepest recesses of Yule's mind. The tanker, carrying one hundred twenty tons of oxidizer, didn't stop at the designated fueling bay. It continued, moving at a relatively high rate of speed, onwards toward the rocket that stood sentinel over the launch site. The event played itself out in an illusory slow motion, almost surreal, as if misplaced from some strange and cruel nightmare. The tanker smashed against the umbilical structure under the rocket, which immediately started to slowly tip toward the direction of the tanker. The total height of the 8K67 rocket was about one hundred ten feet; thus, its fall took a good few seconds to terminate. The height of the rocket, the rate of its fall... none of that seemed to matter. The end result was inevitable, delayed only by the laws of physics. After a few seconds, the rocket smashed on top of the tanker, breaking in half and spilling the volatile fuel onto the ground. There was no fire or explosion. The spilled liquid almost immediately turned yellow as a strong ammoniac smell filled the air. It took just a few seconds for the dangerous stream of yellow liquid to reach the trenches, seconds that were not enough for anyone to react in time. The fuel spilled into the space where Yule and his six men were watching the calamity unfold. Toxic fumes filled the air. Gasmasks were donned as quickly as possible. Whereas the fueling unit had their HAZMAT suites on, the technicians wore nothing but their regular uniforms.

"The crew!" yelled Yule as he pointed toward the launch pad where the technicians were scrambling to get away from the fumes. Two of them were already unconscious, lying on the concrete platform next to the tanker. Yule and his men picked up the two technicians and carried them to safety; the rest were running away, anticipating an explosion of epic proportions. The sound of ululating sirens pierced the air—an ambulance followed by a fire truck. There were no immediate casualties (at least no announcements had been made). The entire incident had been kept secret, facilitated by the lack of any explosions to be detected by the monitoring seismic stations. Thus, it went largely unnoticed by the rest of the world. The driver of the tanker was killed on impact, and it's anyone's guess as to why he failed to stop. Was it an act of sabotage? Perhaps drunkenness or a technical malfunction? The world had never found out and neither would it ever unravel the mystery. Yule's unit of the Eighth Airborne Corps had been flown back to their base in Western Ukraine. His demobilization came soon afterwards. Four months later, he was honorably discharged and had returned to his home in Leningrad.

The symptoms had manifested themselves years later: the heat intolerance was one of them, but Yule had rationalized it as being the result of spending his childhood in an extremely cold climate. Some other symptoms weren't so easily explainable. For instance, Yule would become nauseous while on a boat or a plane. That was embarrassing for a former paratrooper with more than one hundred sorties under his belt. He kept the condition to himself, trying to avoid any uncomfortable situations or confrontations, but now, thirty years later, the pieces of the puzzle had finally fallen into place. It was quite probable that the pituitary gland (which controls the endocrine system) had been affected by the slow-growing adenoma, thereby altering its normal functions such as thermoregulation and body equilibrium.

There is an old adage which states that things happen for a reason. Had it not been for a dreadful auto accident, Yule would've likely harbored the tumor for years to come, possibly losing sight and suffering from all kinds of hormonal imbalances as a consequence. Although there was a remote, outside possibility that the adenoma came to be as the result of a heredity disorder known as *multiple endocrine neoplasia* (or MEN I), Yule had dismissed it. Until the age of twenty-five, he had never experienced any symptoms. Thus, the only logical explanation was his exposure to the dangerous fuel. It felt as if a great burden had been lifted off of Yule's shoulders. His findings made perfect sense, and with a great degree of certainty he was convinced that he was correct.

The next and (hopefully) final chapter of this medical mystery was to be the surgery.

The twelfth of August, Mount Sinai Hospital in Manhattan: the day of the surgery. The operating room was small and equipped with state-of-the-art tools. It looked quite different from the large and bustling ICU at Hackensack Hospital. Dr. Post hadn't arrived yet, but the anesthesiologist was there, a woman in her fifties with soft, tired eyes. It was only eight o'clock in the morning. She must've worked the night shift like most of the physicians in New York, moonlighting at the emergency rooms and pulling a lot of overnight shifts. She once again confirmed Yule's weight and his medications, put a mask over his face and emptied the syringe into his arm. Before Yule fell asleep, he had a fleeting image of a vast expanse of snow-covered Siberian Tundra; a chain of small hills and two gray wolves were in the distance. They were light gray with a touch of red on their faces. One of them, the larger one, had a black spot on his back, right at the base of the tail. As Yule faded away into the darkness, he caught a fleeting glimpse of their ponderous, amber eyes. They were seared into his mental vision as the darkness came over him, not unlike the gentlest and most delicate of blankets being slid over his tired, blue eyes.

THE WHITE MUTENESS

"MAN—THE MOST CRUEL OF ALL ANIMALS."

NIETZSCHE

19 April, 1949. Still cold, even by Siberian standards. Negative thirty degrees Fahrenheit was simply too cold for this time of year. Luckily, if any luck was to be found in the desolate cold, there was no perceptible wind. It made breathing, at the very least, much easier. A crudely made, prickly woolen scarf, tightened in a large knot behind his neck, covered the tip of Yule's nose, completely engulfing his mouth and chin. Without that scarf filtering and warming the air, breathing would be next to impossible—the freezing air, if left to its own devices, could easily burn the trachea and paralyze the lungs. The flops of the Russian *ushanka,* a signature fur hat, were also knotted under his chin. One could tell that it was Yule only by the pair of inquisitive bright blue eyes peering through the mounds of wool and fur. That, and his distinctive dark brown, bear fur coat without buttons. The coat was held in place by a wide leather belt with a large bronze buckle featuring an equally large *red star and anchor* welded onto its surface, the ubiquitous insignia of the Soviet empire. It was his stepfather's, Vladimir's, naval belt from the time that he was a commanding officer on board one of the Soviet battleships during the war, a time seemingly as distant as the vast, endless expanses of the Siberian Tundra.

The German naval campaign in the Baltic Sea was one of their most successful military operations of the Second World War. Soviet naval losses in 1941 were devastating: approximately 126 military and eighty-nine civilian ships in total. Among the casualties was the Soviet battleship *Marat*, sunk on September 22, 1941. The crewmembers, those who survived the torpedo blast, had been "rescued" by the Germans and sent to one of their POW camps in Poland. Yule's stepfather, Vladimir, a naval officer, was among the captured. In the March of 1945, after being liberated by the Soviet Army, Vladimir found his naval belt in the camp's warehouse among thousands of waifs. He saw it as a good omen, but he could not have been more wrong. After he was returned to the USSR, all commanding officers were court-marshaled for treason, and thereby sentenced for three to twenty-five years in Siberian Labor Camps, popularly known as "GULAG." Yule's stepfather was among the lucky ones; he received only four years. Since he was wounded and captured while unconscious, the court had shown some leniency in their sentencing. Vladimir had a piece of shrapnel embedded in his head for the rest of his life. That shrapnel was responsible for his occasional uncontrollable bouts of anger and severe drinking, problems that plagued Yule's stepfather throughout his entire life. But that was a different chapter altogether, another story authored by another life. Since officially there were no political prisoners in the Soviet Union, former prisoners of war were labeled "criminals," akin to and equated with murderers, rapists, and thieves. That was Stalin's Law, and everyone understood that. Understanding meant no questioning. This form of punishment was considered fair. After all, the impervious and infallible dictator, Comrade Joseph Vissarionovich Stalin, had refused to negotiate the release of his own son, who was also a prisoner of war and who had later perished during an escape attempt. How could a man who refused to negotiate for his own son's life grant mercy and forgiveness to others? Well, that was the official version, but the Second World War's history had been re-written numerous times, especially the parts concerning Stalin. "Official" and "fabricated" were two words that shared a close and intimate relationship during Stalin's reign.

Vladimir was eventually released in 1949 and, since he really had no place to go, stayed at the camp, eventually becoming employed as an artist/photographer. There was a section within the camp for non-prisoners, called the "free settlement," where he had settled down. Vladimir was a very talented individual, a true Renaissance man in virtually every sense of the term. He was a musician, a painter, a photographer, and an excellent hunter (a skill naturally invaluable to residents of Siberia). Naturally, most of his oil paintings depicted the glorious achievements of the Communist Party and its immortalized leader, Joseph Stalin. Soon after his release, he and Yule's mother Zoya got married. Since Zoya was a medical doctor who enjoyed the highly privileged status of the medical staff, the couple was granted a special accommodation in the form of a separate three-room log cabin with a small fenced property to keep a pig named Masha. The pig was complimentary.

It was almost eight o'clock in the morning and still very dark. Beneath the cloudless sky lay the tundra, illuminated by the pale touch of the moon overhead. The moon's natural light granted an almost surreal touch to the desolate landscape, an eerily anemic overlay that distorted and metamorphosed the surrounding environment. Over the valley of snow was a glowing halo of navy blue light, nothing more than a feeble attempt by the landscape to reflect itself against the dark heavens. Feeble it was, as it only succeeded in pushing its glow dimly against the black velvet blanket of the night sky, penetrating nothing more than a petty fraction of its infinite expanse. Aside from the immeasurable specks of stars and the pregnant moon, lights flickered faintly from countless lanterns, glowing atop watchtowers that stood like behemoths over the landscape. The changing of the guard was about to take place on all of the watchtowers. Every morning, while on his way to his daily lessons, Yule would stop for a few minutes to watch this remarkable, almost hypnotic routine. The current guards had spent the last two pre-dawn hours, the coldest hours of the night, atop a thirty-foot watchtower, pacing or circling the five-by-five-foot landing with virtually no heat to grant them any respite. Despite their long and heavy fur coats, fur hats, and huge mittens, the guards would climb down shivering and audibly rattling their teeth. On an unusually cold night like this one, a person who was not familiar with the guards' routine would have been amazed by the elaborate warm-up dance that took place on top of the towers. Normally, the dance consisted of an unusual succession of quick jumps, sit-ups, handclaps, and chest and leg slaps with both hands to get the blood circulating. The Ministry of Internal Affairs had equipped the guards with long-range Mosin-Nagant rifles with scopes. The rifles were about six feet in length, not to count the bayonets. Despite the fact that this particular model was invented at the end of the 1800s, it could potentially hit a target a mile away. The unofficial name for this type of rifle was *tryechlineinaya vintovka,* the three–line rifle. There was no escaping its long, cruel reach.

Since Yule's arrival at the camp three years ago, those rifles had rarely been fired. No one runs away. No one is stupid enough to attempt to. After all, there was no place to go; similar camps guarded by the NKVD, the KGB's predecessor, were the closest shelters. Otherwise, there was nothing around but hundreds of miles of wilderness, full to the brim with wild animals notably hungry in the long, cold winter. The Kolyma River, along with an infinite chain of mountains permanently covered with snow, were impassible most of the year, as effective as the towers that stood sentinel over the bleak surroundings and the barbed wire that encased the camp.

The shadow of the northern watchtower reached the tree line—it was a quarter past eight o'clock, and Yule was late for his lessons. The distance between Yule's *izba* (Russian bungalow) and his teacher's *izba* was approximately half a mile, and the path connecting the two consisted of well-compressed snow on the top of a ridge, rising about six feet above fresh snow on both sides of the path (not unlike a bridge flanked by water on both sides). The width of this path varied. It some places, it was as narrow as one foot, and in the widest sections, the path spanned approximately three feet in width. It was, needless to say, crucial to stay on the path; otherwise, a wrong step would lead to a tumble down the slope, into the soft snow seven to ten feet deep that flanked both sides of the path. For an adult, it would not present any serious problems, but for a seven-year old such as Yule, it could potentially spell disaster. The snowstorms in this part of the Kolyma River Basin could come without warning, as sudden and as unpredictable as the strike of lightning. A person could easily be overcome by the snow and perish in what Russians called a *purga,* a whiteout. During those all-too-frequent whiteouts, a person could lose any sense of direction after walking just a few short yards, but on a day like this one, with not a cloud in sight, there was absolutely no reason to worry. Yule was very wrong. He had severely underestimated the fickleness of the Siberian weather.

The compressed snow was crunching audibly under the weight of Yule's boots, the only sound penetrating the deathly silence of the world. The sound was rhythmic, almost captivating. After just five minutes of walking, Yule noticed, with growing consternation, that the sky was becoming darker as a heavy, thick, and led–colored cloud crept in. The sound of crunching ceased as Yule stopped to consider his next course of action. After just a few more minutes, he considered going back. He did enjoy his lessons, to be sure, but the boy found his life to be significantly more valuable. As soon as he turned back, however, the snow started to fall. It always started gently at first, kissing and caressing the surrounding world not unlike a lover in an amorous embrace. The flakes were large and soft at first, winding their way down toward the permafrost with a grace only inherent to the flight of a snowflake. As the wind picked up speed, however, the falling snow became more aggressive, transitioning from a soft embrace to an angry quarrel. It took only a minute for Yule to lose his forward site, and only a few seconds after that to lose his sense of direction. Out of desperation, he stepped sideways—bad idea. Yule tumbled all the way down the slope and into the deep river of snow beneath. After his body finally stopped sinking, he couldn't determine whether he was upright or upside down—the sensation was one of near weightlessness. His fur coat and many layers of clothing underneath, normally so invaluable to one's struggle to survive the cold winters of Siberia, were severely restricting his movements. After a few minutes of struggling, Yule was completely exhausted and disoriented. The scarf had fallen off of his mouth, no longer protecting him from the brutally cold and merciless air, which was now scraping and grinding his trachea and lungs with each breath. Yule decided to take a little rest and closed his eyes, attempting to regain some strength and to slow his racing heart. It took just a few minutes for his body to lower the temperature and for the mind to start wandering aimlessly. Is that what death feels like? Does it come so gently, so peacefully? Yule drifted into sub-consciousness.

He dreamt about the train ride that brought him and his mother from Moscow to Vladivostok, a trip covering six thousand miles of what is now known as the Trans-Siberian Railroad. That trip took more than a month and ran along the Chinese border, the south shore of the Great Lake Baikal, the Mongolian boarder, and the Chinese border again. The train winded through the majestic landscape like a slithering snake, dwarfed by the sheer magnitude of the surrounding environments. The frequent stops, due to the snowdrifts, were used by the passengers as an opportunity to get out and see the sky. Occasionally, the stops were abrupt, accompanied by the screeching of brakes piercing the air. It usually meant that there was a body under the train, perhaps a suicide or a drunk who fell into a final slumber on the tracks. Zoya made sure that Yule wouldn't see the dead bodies. Once, however, he got away and managed to look at the torso of a killed man, separated from his lower body by a wheel. Another poor soul lost to the icy wilderness.

The train, carrying mostly prisoners destined for Gulag, had traversed Manchuria and re-entered Russian territory before arriving at Vladivostok, where the prisoners had to wait for two weeks until the waterway was free of ice. Yule and his mother then took a ship called the *Dalstroy* and sailed to the city of Magadan, the capital of the Kolyma region, reputedly the coldest inhabited place on the face of the planet. Prisoners sarcastically spoke of Kolyma as a place where winter reigned for twelve months, while the rest was given to the summer. From Magadan, Yule and his mother took the infamous "Road of Bones," named as such because of the hundreds that had perished while building the road. The name, however, was given to the road in a figurative sense—the dead could not be buried in the frozen earth and were therefore routinely dumped into the snowy banks of the Kolyma River. The corpses washed away with the spring runoff. The "Road of Bones" connected Magadan to Yakutsk, stretching over a span of approximately nine hundred miles. Building it was incredibly hard work because Kolyma was covered with permafrost and taiga, the primeval form of forest that covers most of Russia. It was full of swamps, as the water couldn't penetrate the ever-frozen ground. The severity of the climate comes from Kolyma's complete geographical isolation from the warm Pacific currents. Instead, the region is exposed to the severely cold Arctic air. The Arctic cold air currents are, in turn, blocked by the surrounding mountains and thus cannot escape toward the ocean; instead, they are continuously circulating within this "ice cauldron."

They pulled out of Magadan with the engine of a Japanese Diamante tractor humming in front of them, laboring at a dizzying speed of ten miles an hour. After about three days of a torturous three hundred mile ride up and down *sopki* (snow and rocks), they arrived at the place of destination—a *pryisk*, gold mining camp, appropriately called *Ledyanoy*, Icy. Most of the neighboring *pryisks* had similar names, such as *Shturmovoy*, Stormy.

Still semi-conscious, Yule saw his mother leaning over him and felt her soft hand on his forehead. "I think he is waking up," she said. Yule forced himself to completely open his eyes. He was in his bed. Both his mother and his stepfather were standing over him, concern etched clearly upon their faces. The first thought that came to Yule's mind was that he overslept, oblivious to all that occurred during the violent and sudden storm.

"Am I late for school?" he asked.

"No, today is Sunday," said Vladimir.

Yule's mind started to grasp the situation, albeit slowly at first. Much of it was still a blur. He distinctly remembered leaving the house on Friday morning; the rest was completely indistinct.

"You have been sleeping for two days," said Zoya. "Do you remember what happened to you?"

He didn't.

"Well, you got lost in the blizzard and were buried under ten feet of snow. We formed a pretty large posse to find you. Luckily, we did," said Vladimir, looking at Yule disapprovingly, as if the sudden and unexpected onslaught of violent snow was his fault alone. That did not bother Yule. He was used to being blamed for everything. The sole regret he had was that he missed his time with his teacher. Since Yule was the only child at the camp, his mother had made an arrangement with Ivan Lensky, a former professor at the Moscow State University, to give Yule private lessons in reading, writing, math and history. Very few knew the professor's real name, so virtually everyone called him just that: Professor. The name carried a hint of sarcasm and Yule, despite his tender age of seven, sensed it acutely when adults spoke of his teacher. Yule also addressed him as Professor, but with the respect that this remarkable man deserved.

In 1936, Professor Lensky had published a scientific article in which he argued with the official Marxist Doctrine that a member of any society is formed by the rules of that society and that genetics play no role in this process. Professor's contention was that the genetic makeup of an individual is more or at least equally important in the formation of individuality. That alone was enough to earn him ten years of hard labor in the GULAG, to be labeled as an intellectual enemy of the state and a danger to the USSR. At the time of his arrest, Ivan Lensky was fifty-five years old. By Russian standards, he was ancient. Russian men, on average, did not live very long, especially in Siberia; alcoholism and the lack of medical care were the contributing factors. When Professor was asked by Zoya to start teaching her son, he was already sixty-eight. He was not supposed to live that long, especially not in a GULAG located deep within the gelid prison of Siberia. If he continued working in the goldmine, he would certainly have been long dead, perhaps from malnutrition or from some work-related accident. Physically frail he may have been, but Professor was in complete possession of his faculties. He had intelligence and an encyclopedic knowledge of the history of the world, its religions, and the sciences that was second to none. Professor belonged to a category of prisoners known today as the "Cream of the Crop of Russian Intelligencia." Due to his improbable age and declining health, Zoya was able to free him from the morbid clutches of the goldmine, so that, in its stead, he could give Yule a good and proper schooling. Zoya was a "free-hired" doctor. In other words, she was not a prisoner, but rather a professional who came to the GULAG to work and to get paid. As a general practitioner, she treated not only the prisoners, but also the prison guards and NKVD (The Soviet "Secret Police" and Intelligence Gathering Agency) officers. The latter were the source of her significant influence within the *Zona* (territory surrounded by barbwire). She could assign prisoners to less strenuous work or, in the most extreme cases, free them from work altogether. That influence, along with her coveted access to medical supplies and narcotics, made her position secondary only to the commander himself. This remarkable power of hers played a crucial role in Yule's future.

During the winter months, all of the GULAG labor camps within the "Golden Ring" become completely cut off from the rest of the world, encompassed by a deadly sea of snow, ice, and mountains; a few of the mountain passes were covered with up to twenty to thirty feet of snow, at least until late March. The camps would normally stockpile the supplies necessary to survive the brutal winter. Bread, canned food, frozen milk, frozen meat, kasha, and macaroni were the main staples of the camp diet. Fruits, vegetables, and other perishable goods were non-existent. Yule was lucky that his mother was a doctor who had access to a vast array vitamins and supplements. His growth and development would have been seriously impaired if it wasn't for a daily intake of polivitamins, gematogen (blood supplement), garlic powder, and condensed milk.

The following Monday, Yule made his usual trip to Professor's hut, thankfully without any problems in the form of storms. He knocked on the door and, after a brief pause, he heard a raspy voice respond, "Enter." Yule slowly opened the door. It was dark inside of the *izba*. Professor, who had suffered from chronic insomnia for many years, most likely dozed off just prior to Yule's arrival. Professor had a mane of long white hair and an equally white beard. He reminded Yule of a picture of Poseidon from one of his illustrated books. Despite Professor's age and declining health, he still looked dignified and proud, indeed like Poseidon reincarnate. An insuppressible intellect and uncanny strength of character shone in his bright eyes, windows to a remarkable and incomparable personality.

"Where are your books and your note pad?" asked Professor.

"I lost them in the blizzard three days ago," said Yule, and then described what happened to him that morning.

Professor had a very philosophical attitude toward life. "I guess it wasn't your time," he said. Yule did not quite understand what he meant by that, but decided not to ask, for some reason, fearful of the answer that might be given.

"Well, since you have no textbooks, or any supplies for that matter, we will skip our algebra and grammar lessons and start with the history of Russia."

Despite being just a few months short of his eighth birthday, Yule was a well-read child who started his education at the age of four. He was a voracious reader. By the age of six, Yule had already read every single book he could get his hands on. The titles ranged from some ponderous reads such as "The Big Soviet Encyclopedia" to his mother's complex and fascinating medical books. Yule's vocabulary and his comprehension of complicated and multifaceted subjects were at college levels. Professor was understandably proud of the fruits of his labor. He loved to teach, and his passion for sharing the knowledge manifested itself in Yule's expeditious progress. Having no peers to play with and surrounded by intellectuals and the books, Yule was, almost by necessity, plunged into the convoluted world of adults and their ideas. He witnessed ubiquitous conflicts between those who still believed in Stalin's omnipotence and those who already came to the realization of Stalin's paranoia, manifested in his purges and unwarranted arrests. "Why did you come here?" asked Yule. "And how come you don't have any family, like my mother?"

"Your mother came here voluntarily; I was brought here against my will."

"Why?"

"Because I wrote a book that our government did not approve."

"You mean Stalin did not like it?"

"That too. Did Vladimir tell you anything about why he is here?"

"He did not tell me, but I always listen to grown-up conversations and know a lot about Stalin and the war."

"Well, after I published my book about genetics versus environment, I got a visitor who asked me to make 'some corrections' which would have turned my entire theory upside down. I told him that I have to think about it. The man advised me not to think too long. Two months later, one early morning in the November of 1936, two black government cars, charmingly referred to as 'Black Ravens,' pulled up to the entrance of my apartment building. Two NKVD agents knocked on my door. Two more agents were waiting downstairs. I knew immediately that it was my turn to disappear, just like many of my friends and colleagues did, never to be seen again. All of them had been labeled Enemies of the People. Two agents turned my entire apartment upside-down while a third one was summoned from downstairs to be a witness and to record a search protocol. I asked one of the agents why I was being arrested. He answered that I can make a formal inquiry in writing at the Office of the People's Commissar of Internal Affairs. The same agent, the more talkative one, told me to take some warm clothes with me, and I knew then where I was going… I turned around and looked at my wife. She was crying silently, wiping tears with a white handkerchief, and looking at me with horror in her eyes. I told her that I have done nothing wrong and that this misunderstanding will somehow be resolved.

"The ride to Lubyanka, the NKVD Headquarters in Moscow, was silent. The Black Raven passed through the massive gates and into the courtyard of the notorious Lubyanka Internal Prison. Prisoners were routinely shot in this courtyard while automobile engines were revved up to drown out the noise. I was taken to a basement deep under the building, perhaps two or three stories below, and put in a cell with a concrete floor and no windows. There was no toilet either, which meant that I was not going to be there long. I was right—a few hours later, I was taken to an interrogation room on the same floor. It was a fairly large room with no windows, furnished with a metal desk along with two metal chairs that were positioned on both sides of the desk. A metal gooseneck lamp stood on top of the desk. The same two agents who searched my apartment brought me in and told me to sit down. I chose the chair facing the door, but I was told to take the other one, with my back toward the door. The interrogator was a very young man, perhaps in his mid-twenties, with very light, penetrating eyes and very light, receding hair. He introduced himself as Constantine and then proceeded to read out the charges. The accusations against me were ridiculous. In summary, I was accused of being a foreign agent who promoted a number of anti-Soviet theories aimed to undermine the structure of the Soviet Union from within. In the course of numerous daily interrogations, I learned that a number of colleagues, as well as my students, made absurd claims against me. I refused to admit any wrongdoing. I was punched in the face, stomped on, soaked with cold water, and left wet in a cold room. On several occasions, I was made to stand in my cell until I collapsed. All of these sessions ended up with the same request to admit my participation in anti-Soviet propaganda activities. The 'preliminary interrogation' continued for eight long months. Finally, in the July of 1937, the NKVD finalized its case against me. Without participating in a trial, the special collegium of the Supreme Court of the Russian Federation sentenced me to ten years of collective labor in a camp, for 'participation in anti-Soviet propaganda.' A week later, together with dozens of people like me, I was stuffed into a railroad car and my journey to Kolyma began. And here I am."

"Where is your wife now?"

"She died three years later."

Yule was silent; although he lived next to the prisoners ever since he could remember, no one told him why they were here. People around him, the prisoners, the guards, and the civilian workers, never bothered to explain anything to Yule. In general, the culture of the labor camps promoted silence—a wrong word could result in a lot of misery for a person at worst or death for the person at best. Yule always took for granted that this was the way of the world, that this was how it should be. The only person who treated him not as a child but as an intelligent human being was Professor.

After a pause that lasted for perhaps a minute, Professor continued with his intended lesson. "There will be no examination on this subject; your main test will come as you go through your life. The understanding of your country, her peoples' characters, and the knowledge of her history will be invaluable." He paused for a moment and added, "I hope that your world will be different from that of mine—but enough of sentiments, we have a lot of material to cover. I do not know if you have any idea of how huge Russia is. In fact, Russia is the largest country in the world in terms of geography. You probably remember how you and your mother had spent a month in a train to get here? You crossed only one corner of the land. If you look at a map, you will see that that the train ride was along the border of China. If that train were to make a turn and head north, toward the Arctic Circle, it would have taken another month to cross the country south to north. The cradle of Russia is the wide strip of rich land that lies between the forests of the North and the steppe of the South. For many centuries, the steppe was the home of nomadic people. Russia became a part of world history in the seventh century B.C. when the nomadic Scythians moved from the southern steppes to Hither Asia. The first written account of this invasion comes from the 'Father of History,' a Greek by the name of Herodotus, who visited southern Russia in the fifth century B .C." Professor reached out and pulled out a large, leather-bound volume from under his makeshift desk. He opened it where a piece of paper denoted the needed page. "Listen to the words that came to us from twenty-five-hundred years ago. Us Russians have a lot of Scythian blood in our veins." He started to read:

"The Scythian soldier drinks the blood of the first man he defeats in battle. Whatever number he slays, he cuts off their heads and carries them to the king; he is thus entitled to a share of the booty, whereto he forfeits all claims if he does not produce a head." He finished reading and closed the book with an audible *thump*, looked at Yule, and added, "The very name 'Scythian' comes from the old Slavic word *skit,* wanderer, describing their nomadic lifestyle. Now do you believe that these barbarians were our ancestors?"

"Yes, I do, but we don't do those kinds of things to people."

Professor laughed, saying, "You are right, we don't cut human heads off, but we do things that are much worse. You will find out for yourself as you get older. Meanwhile, I will give you one more example of how the character of a nation, once formed, survives for thousands of years. According to the already-familiar-to-you Herodotus, Scythians were very suspicious of foreigners. He recorded cases of two famous Scythians who were murdered by their own people for adopting Greek customs. When the xenophobic side of their nature rises to the surface, Russians sometimes call themselves Scythians. Even traditional Russian dress owes much to Scythia."

Professor paused, peered at his wristwatch, and said, "It is already two o'clock. You better go home. Tomorrow, we will do the usual math and the grammar, and then we will continue with the history of Russia—if you like, of course."

"I like it very much; it is so interesting, even more so than Greek Mythology."

"Then there is even more fascinating material for tomorrow. Bring all your gray cells with you, you will need them."

"Can you tell me what tomorrow's lesson will be?"

"You will learn how the Russian religion became what it is today. Good-bye now. I am hungry and tired, and you must be too."

Yule decided not to take the usual treacherous path, the same one where he was caught in the blizzard last time. Instead, he elected to go around the perimeter of the camp, following the circumference of the barbwire fence. On the inside of the fence, there was a path left by the perimeter watchmen who were making their occasional rounds, checking the integrity of the fence for any gaps or breaches. Although it was a much longer way home, Yule was in no hurry to get there. He enjoyed being alone, oftentimes giving into imagination as he walked atop the crunching snow. Most of the guards on the watchtowers knew him as "the doctor's boy." They also knew him by his distinct brown-fur coat. Once, a new guard took a shot at Yule when he climbed through the fence onto the other side. Luckily, the guard was not an especially sharp shooter. After this incident, the commander had issued an order to use binoculars before shooting.

The first signs of spring were ubiquitous—there was this special, almost imperceptible smell in the air, the harbinger of change and life. It was still cold though. Yule passed through the section of the fence where he made his usual (as the prisoners called it) "breaking free" maneuver. That particular section had unusually wide spaces between the horizontal wires, wide enough to let Yule's small physique slip through. He did just that, as he had done countless of times before, and started walking toward the edge of the susurrus forest. In about three hundred yards, he reached the edge of the forest. For some reason, Yule felt compelled to explore it a little further. He was always fascinated with the myriad of signs denoting the rich wildlife of the area. The footprints of the white hare, spaced about five feet apart, indicated a chase, a desperate dash for survival from a wolf whose footprints were lined up with those of the hare. For the wolf, it was a matter of survival. Perhaps there were wolf pups that were waiting in a den. Pups were usually born during this time of year, near early spring. A little further down were tracks left by a *kuropatka*, a white bird that resembles a small chicken. Next to them, Yule noticed a strange-looking, continuous groove left in the snow by an unfamiliar animal. He traced this groove with his eyes and found, at the end of it, an object that looked, at least from a distance, like a lost fur mitten. But that didn't make any sense. Why would anyone venture out here? Yule moved closer, his unquenchable curiosity getting the better of him. To his amazement, he discovered that the object was no mitten but, rather, a tiny wolf pup. It still had its eyes closed, and its tiny triangular ears were flat against its head. The pup was obviously just a week or two old and, somehow, was left alone in the open snow. Yule knew perfectly well that wolves never abandon their young; most likely, the mother was trapped or killed by a local hunter. Although wolves don't normally leave their pack's territory, their territories could range up to one hundred square miles in size. No other packs would dare approach the border, even to hunt or observe. Yule took one mitten off, kneeled down, and scooped up the little, orange fur-ball. It was warm to the touch. He started gently massaging the little body, imitating how the mother-wolf would do it with her tongue. The pup made an insignificant squeaking sound and stuck his tiny pink tongue out. Very rarely do wolves have just one pup; it only happens before a notably bad winter or when the pack leader has a premonition of some cataclysmic event in the near future. Thus, Yule turned around and followed the groove back to the den. He knew that there was a remote possibility that the mother could still be in the den. He also knew that he stood no chance against her. A Siberian wolf is a very tall, powerful animal—it stands about four feet tall and close to six feet long. With its long legs, it could outrun almost any animal in the deep snow. Yule decided to take the chance anyway. He stuck his ungloved hand into the opening, his heart racing and thumping against his chest. Yule immediately felt the touch of a tongue. He slid his hand deeper, palm-up under the little creature, and pulled it out. This one was in better shape than the first but was also deaf and blind. Yule put both pups under his coat in order to warm them up. After some thought, he headed back to the camp. He decided not to go home but to bring the pups to Professor's bungalow, instead. Professor, like Yule's parents, also owned a pig that just had three piglets born a week before. The two wolf pups were quiet under Yule's coat, enjoying the warmth of his body.

Yule knocked on Professor's door and immediately heard the hallmark voice rasp, "I don't expect any one, go away." That was a traditional Russian joke, ironically an acknowledgment of a guest.

"It's me, Professor," said Yule. "I have two more guests with me."

The door swung open. "What is it?"

Without uttering a single word, Yule opened up his coat, revealing the wolf pups beneath.

"Oh my God," exclaimed Professor. He fell silent for a few seconds. For just a split second, one uncharacteristic moment, his eyes became soft and lost their usual steeliness. All of a sudden, Professor sprung into action; without saying a word, he snatched the pups from Yule's chest and carried them through a small door into an adjacent room (a small barn rather than a room) where his pig Chukcha was lying in a layer of hay, three piglets at her teats. He gently placed one pup next to a free teat. The pup immediately moved toward the smell of milk and the warmth of the underbelly. The same procedure was followed with the second pup. The result was identical; Chukcha just looked at the new arrivals but did not move. Professor and Yule stood there, looking at the peaceful scene like the proudest of parents. Professor turned to Yule. "Now, tell me where you got them."

Yule described the events in detail, starting from his decision to circumnavigate the camp instead of cutting through the usual path. When he finished, Professor paused to consider the information.

"I am glad that you rescued the pups, but you have to promise that this is the last time you venture outside the Zona." He paused and added, "They can shoot you and there is no court to convict them. Understand?"

Yule nodded, looked at Professor, and switching to the clearly more important subject, asked, "Are they going to survive?"

"Of course. They have a much better chance to survive than you, crawling through the perimeter fence." Yule kept quiet, looking at the pups that were vigorously sucking the teats—they were obviously really hungry. He never saw an orange-colored wolf before. The tops of their heads were sprinkled with red-orange, gradually changing into a more characteristic light gray toward the lower jaw. The eyes also had light gray circles around them, not unlike human eyebrows.

"Are these red wolfs?"

"No, this is just baby fur; it will change into all gray and black. Most likely the tips of their tails will turn black, possibly along with the paws."

One pup stopped sucking and immediately fell asleep. A minute later, the second one followed suit. One was slightly larger than the other, with a black round spot near the base of the tail.

Naturally, it was the pup found outside the den, the more adventurous of the two. According to their size, they were approximately ten to twelve days old and, under the circumstances, in surprisingly good shape. The disappearance of the mother, possibly the entire pack, must have happened very recently.

"We have to give them names," said Yule.

"How about Chook and Cha?"

"Is it from Chukcha's name?"

"That's right."

"Okay. The one with the spot will be Chook."

Professor nodded, stating, "Now, you have to hurry home. I don't need any problems with your stepfather."

Yule looked at the peacefully sleeping pups one more time and left. This time, the trip home was relatively uneventful.

"We were worried already," said Zoya. "Where have you been all this time?"

"The material was so interesting that I did not want to stop."

"What kind of material?"

"We were reading about Russian history and how Russian character and lifestyle go back to the Scythians."

"And what is it that we have in common with the Scythians?" asked Vladimir.

"Unbelievable cruelty," said Yule, getting annoyed with this curt questioning. He was also alluding to the whippings he occasionally received from Vladimir's famous belt.

Vladimir pretended not to understand the hint and cut the questioning short. "Let's eat."

Despite a smack to the forehead via a wooden spoon that Yule received for chewing with his mouth open, dinner went unremarkably.

"I told you many times to keep your mouth closed when you chew," said Vladimir.

"How can I talk with my mouth closed?"

"You swallow first and then talk."

"Sorry."

That night, Yule couldn't sleep at all. He kept thinking of the wolf pups and the destiny of the entire wolf pack that vanished without a trace. When he finally dozed off in the morning, his fleeting thoughts gave way to dreaming as he transitioned from the worries of the real world to the fantastic realm of the subconscious. His dream was not about the wolf pups but rather his usual, recurrent dream. The flying dream, where he would fly away from a danger that he could not see. The danger, however, was always there, omnipresent and ever-approaching, invisible yet somehow tangible. The events of this dream were the same nearly every night: Yule would strain every muscle in his body and lift off about ten to fifteen feet above the ground. Occasionally, he could go higher and land atop a tree. That usually made him feel much safer. When the danger was gone, he would descend and walk away. The danger was always big, black, and amorphous.

Yule woke up and jumped off the bed, his heart full of happiness and anticipation. He was, after all, going to see the wolf pups! Zoya was still at home, getting ready to leave for work. "Your breakfast is on the table," she said, "and don't forget the polivitamins."

"Thanks, Mom. By the way, how come Masha doesn't have babies like the professor's pig?"

"She will, soon. We have only one male pig here, and it belongs to the commander. It is not easy to coordinate a special rendezvous to start a 'pig family.'" With that said, she closed the door, leaving Yule to ponder whether she was serious or merely making fun of his naïveté. Maybe she knew that Yule read enough medical literature available to him around the house to understand these basic facts of life.

Carried on the wings of excitement, Yule did not even remember how he got to the professor's hut. The door was unlocked. Without knocking, he burst in and looked around. The very first thing he saw was a pair of dark blue eyes peering inquisitively at him from the corner. It was Chook (the one with the black spot) who opened his eyes first.

"Aren't you going to say hello?" asked Professor, smiling.

"I am sorry, I just—"

"Never mind, I understand."

"My God, he has blue eyes… I never saw a wolf with blue eyes."

"Wolf pups are always born with the blue eyes," said Professor. "The color will gradually change to amber. By the way, both pups are boys."

By the time they finished talking, Cha woke up and also opened his blue eyes. "We are the first things they saw," said Professor. "They have accepted us as their family and, of course, Chukcha, as their mother. We also have to decide what to do with them. While they are on Chukcha's milk, we have no problems, but in a few weeks they will need solid food and a lot of it."

"Can't they eat what the pigs eat?"

"No, the pigs are omnivorous; the wolf pups need meat to develop properly."

"I know where to get meat! I pass the kitchen every morning, and they always dump little piles of bone, cartilage, and sometimes pieces of bear meat that are too tough for people to eat."

"Settled then. I will let you know when to start bringing the meat. Meanwhile, I will tell my friend Semion, who hunts almost every day, to save some raw meat for the pups."

Semion was released recently, after an eight-year sentence for the horrible crime of being too kind to prisoners. He was once a prison guard in Lubyanka where he was caught brining food to a prisoner in solitary confinement. Since his release, he became an official hunter for the camp and, being an excellent marksman, significantly increased the meat supply for the camp personnel.

Yule went into the barn and took Chook into his arms. The little triangular ears were almost in a vertical position; only the tips were slightly bent forward. His face was still orange, but the ridge on his back looked dark gray. The pup made a growling sound while attempting to jump off. Yule eased him down to the ground and set him on the floor next to the other pup.

"This is a much better way to interact with them," said Professor. "They are not your house pets to be carried around all over the place. Besides, some day they will have to be released and must become independent."

The pups were still unsteady on their legs. The piglets, which were older by only one week, looked much larger and were knocking the pups down in a playful manner. The pups did not seem to mind.

"Let's get to work," said Professor. "As I promised, we will learn about the history of religion in Russia." And without any further delay, he started to speak, pacing back and forth as if he were in front of a large audience in a lecture room. Yule loved these lectures; he clung to Professor's every word, though sometimes he did not know its meaning. He would write down the word to look it up later in Ozegoff's Dictionary.

"By the end of tenth century," Professor continued, "the Russian state was already one of the largest kingdoms in the world, but the Russians were still uncivilized pagans. At the same time, Greek missionaries had invented an alphabet for Slavonic writing. The western Slavs were already Christian, with their own literature. It was high time for Russia to choose one religion and to join the civilized world. There were several choices: Christianity, Islam, and Judaism, but as Russians liked to say, all roads lead to Byzantium, the second Rome. Baghdad was civilized but distant, and the West was distant and not very civilized. The

Russian chronicle of that period tells us that ambassadors were sent to neighboring states to observe the religions in action. The laws of Islam practiced by the Bulgarians were judged 'not good,' the Latin Mass of the Roman Empire reportedly had 'no beauty,' but those who were sent to Constantinople said that they had never seen such beauty, and that they had a feeling that God was present during the service. The Liturgy of the Orthodox Church has not changed since that time. My personal opinion, however, is that it was unfortunate for Russia that it took its Christianity from Greece, not Rome, because the future, of course, lied with the West." Professor paused, stopped pacing, and looked at Yule. "Are you with me so far; any questions?"

"Didn't you say before that Greece was more civilized, and that the West was wild?"

"Yes, I did, but there is no contradiction because, by attaching themselves to Greek Christianity, Russians excluded themselves from any share in future Western achievements for many centuries. Granted, at that time no one could foresee that the friction between the Eastern and Western Christians would become so intense that it put a wall between them."

"I understand now," said Yule.

"Well, I think that it's enough for the beginning. Let's do some math and grammar."

They took a little break to play with the pups, whose legs were still wobbly. The pups, Yule noticed, were already revealing different personalities. Chook was definitely more aggressive, exhibiting the traits of a future alpha-male. Cha, on the other hand, was more submissive and spent most of his playtime on his back, allowing Chook to bite (or rather gum) the scruff of his neck. They had no teeth—yet.

The rest of the lesson went well. When they finished with grammar, Professor said, "Since we just learned of the roots of Russian religion, I would like you to know that from the very beginning, the language of the Russian Church was easily understood by the people. Old Slavonic was not a rich language but strong and warm. It had a lot of similarities with Greek. Modern Russian emerged from Old Slavonic but, because of numerous language reforms, including the integration of the language of the Mongolian Hordes who occupied Russia for centuries and some Western influences, it has become what it is today: one of the most beautiful, poetic languages in the world. The turning point in this transition from a mixture of naïve and foreign was the work of Mikhail Lomonosov, a man whose great talents met his country's needs. He took Old Slavonic and the mixture of all foreign languages used by Russians at that time and set them in a modern syntax through which all the resources of spoken Russian became available."

The last minute of Professor's lecture flew over Yule's absent mind. He was politely looking at the speaker, but his mind was with the pups. When Professor, suspecting a lack of audience, stopped speaking, Yule decided to change the subject.

"Do you know any other languages, Professor?"

"Greek and Latin."

"Do they teach these languages in the mainland schools?"

"Not any more. Don't forget, my dear boy, I was born and educated before the Revolution of 1917 in the St. Petersburg Czar's Gymnasium, from which I had graduated. These languages were mandatory then. We will talk about it next time. See you tomorrow."

"I won't come tomorrow; my stepfather will go to the goldmine with the prisoners in the morning and will take me with him."

"Why?"

"He will be taking photographs of them working. Some central newspaper needs the pictures to go with an article about productivity."

On the way home, Yule had a strong urge to visit the pups' old den, but the thought of the possibility that their mother had returned stopped him. He was not willing to take the risk this time around.

The following morning, Yule was awakened by an alarm clock at five. Vladimir was already in the kitchen, making breakfast.

"Why so early?" Yule asked.

"I need to start taking pictures of the workers as they are getting ready to leave for the mines. They leave at six."

"Are we going to ride with them?"

"No, I will have a sleigh with a horse. The laborers will carry a lot of ammonal with them… it is not safe."

"What's an ammonal?"

"It's an explosive to blow up the rocks to get to gold. It is a mixture of ammonium nitrate, TNT, and aluminum powder. Doesn't your professor teach you about these things?"

"Not about explosives; we are going through Mendeleev's Periodic System."

"I am just kidding," said Vladimir with an unusual alacrity. "You don't need to know about explosives. Let's go."

They walked together toward the main gate; it was wide open, the large snowfield immediately beyond it was already bustling with activity. This was the time of morning when Yule was normally fast asleep, unaware and ignorant of the daily mass exodus of prisoners leaving for the goldmine. The scene was overwhelming and was marked by about a dozen huge sleighs with wide, greased skids, loaded with prisoners twenty or so apiece, and numerous large crates full of supplies, equipment, and explosives. Large horses, three to five per each sleigh, were snorting loudly, nostrils flaring and releasing large clouds of white vapor into the freezing air. The horses looked healthy and well-fed; they had side blinds over their eyes to allow them to see only the road ahead. They were impatiently pounding on the snowy ground with their massive hooves, ready to forge ahead. The entire scene was surreal.

The sleighs had massive tracks reinforced with steel strips underneath. Yule and his stepfather were assigned to a two-seater drawn by a relatively small horse, quiet and obedient, with her tail tied into a knot. At the commander's signal, the entire cavalcade, led by a sleigh occupied by the guards, moved forward. The last sleigh, similar to first, was also full of guards. Surprisingly, the ride was comfortable, even soft—the fresh snow was very forgiving and the reinforced sleigh tracks slid effortlessly along. Yule's sleigh was placed right before the last one. Vladimir handled the reigns with expertise, and the little horse trotted rhythmically and smoothly. The sky was beginning to brighten up. The first rays of the sun reflected off the snow and the glare made it difficult to see ahead.

Despite this minor inconvenience, the mood was great—the majesty of the surrounding snowy mountains and the vast expanses of the tundra had made everyone forget the misery of their circumstances: *joie de vivre* in hell.

It took about twenty minutes to reach their destination. The mine looked like a small rocky mountain with an open mouth etched onto its face, a narrow railroad track penetrating and disappearing deep into the darkness inside the tunnel. In front of this opening, the tracks diverged, going in several different directions. There were metal pushcarts, fitted with sheet metal containers, on each track. As Yule found out soon enough, the containers would be filled with broken ore, pushed manually outside and, finally, dumped of their contents. At that point, the ore would be sorted out by hand in search for gold. This form of gold mining (when the lode deposit was located beneath the surface) required a shaft to be drilled at an angle into the ground to access the lode. There were, therefore, long vertical tunnels that connected the top of the rock with the ore block at the bottom. Now Yule understood what the ammonal was for; a "special brigade" of prisoners who dealt with explosives climbed on top of the rock and inserted bricks of ammonal into the predrilled holes within the vertical tunnels. The long Bickford cords were lowered to the ground. The brigade members climbed down and ignited the cords. About thirty seconds later, a series of muffled explosions shook the mountain, followed by the noise of ore falling down the tunnels and into the shafts. As soon as the noise subsided, the hauling brigade began loading the pushcarts. One at a time, almost rhythmically, pushcarts full of ore emerged from the tunnel and were emptied at the end of a designated track where the next brigade immediately started sorting the ore, meticulously separating the pieces that contained gold. The guards closely supervised each stage of this operation.

Yule noticed that not all of the prisoners were working; a half dozen of them had congregated behind the ore-sorting station, smoking, talking, and seemingly enjoying the sunny day while their colleagues labored strenuously around them. The guards were paying no attention to the group, pretending not to see them.

"Who are these people?" asked Yule. "And why doesn't the *Bugor* make them work?"

"Sh-sh-sh," answered Vladimir, "keep your voice down. These are *vori v zakonye,* thieves-in-law. They don't work."

"Why?"

"I will tell you on the way back, when we are alone."

Yule just stood there, watching the goldmine with rapt attention. He was completely mesmerized by the uncannily synchronized activity of this human ant colony. He realized, at this one moment of utter fascination, that spelunking was not a career for him. Vladimir was taking photographs of each stage of production. An hour later, he waved to Yule from a distance and pointed toward their sleigh. The little horse was standing there with her head lowered into a burlap bag hanging around her neck, melancholically chewing on the oats within. The day was still beautiful, and an anticipation of the warm weather made it even more pleasant. During the ride home, Vladimir explained that a *thief in law* is a criminal who obeys The Code of Thieves and who, thus, has a higher standing among other criminals. According to The Code, *vori v zakonye* must refuse to work or to help prison guards in any way. Any violation of this rule could lead to severe punishment, including death. The guards understandably preferred not to get involved with them; the daily production quota was divided among political prisoners and low ranking criminals.

Yule fell asleep as soon as his head touched the pillow, exhausted from the visit to the goldmine. In his dream, he took flight again, only this time he was able to soar very high above the rocky tops of the black mountains, looking down at the tiny humans below. Surprisingly, there wasn't the usual amorphous danger in this dream, just the pleasure of flight.

The joy, however, was short lived. By the next morning, a strong northern wind brought thick winter clouds, while close to a foot of fresh snow accompanied them. Yule spent the next two days at home, reading profusely as he was wont to do. During heavy snowstorms, life at the Zona went on as usual, with the exception of cancelled trips to the goldmine for the prisoners. As far as the camp's personnel were concerned, the work continued. Everyone had a form of snowshoes called "snow-steppers." They resembled very short, wide skis that were attached to one's boots. Occasionally, Vladimir brought Yule with him on a hunting trip, an excursion into the Tundra. Wearing snow-steppers and carrying several shotguns, they had to walk less than a mile beyond the main gate. Then, the hunting was on. Vladimir had a special custom-made three-barreled shotgun. Each barrel was of a different caliber: the smallest had cartridges loaded with very small round led pieces designed to hunt kuropatka, whereas the larger one was engineered to accept large cartridges stuffed with round pieces of led called *zhigan.* These larger cartridges were designed for bears. A professional gunsmith, who was doing his time at the camp and was maintaining the guards' arsenal, was the mastermind behind this invention. The same gunsmith built a child-size shotgun for Yule. His gun had a short barrel and small stock; otherwise, it was as deadly a weapon as a regular shotgun. They did not, however, go hunting this time. Vladimir was busy developing and printing photographs of the glorious labor force fulfilling the USSR's need for "metal." After all, the huge sign above the main gate read: *Strane Nuzen Metal*, the Country Needs Metal. The word gold wasn't used; it was an ambiguity by design.

Four days later, on a sunny Monday morning, Yule made his usual trip to Professor's *izba*. The wolf pups greeted him by sniffing at his boots and sneezing several times from excitement, recognizing his smell. Yule kneeled down and petted them, feeling their new milk teeth dig into his skin; the little teeth were as sharp as needles.

"Yes, my friend," said Professor lovingly, as if it were his merit alone that the pups grew so quickly. Maybe it was. "You have to be careful now. They are wolves, after all."

"Do they still play with the piglets?"

"Not really. The piglets play differently, though the pups try."

"What are the piglets' names?"

"They have no names, considering they are food. You wouldn't want to have, say, a Boris for dinner, would you?"

"I guess not."

"Soon, the pups will be eating solid food in addition to Chukcha's milk."

"Should I start bringing leftovers from the kitchen? They have a lot of farrago left daily."

"In a few days. I already have a mountain goat, skinned and frozen outside, courtesy of my friend Semion, the hunter. And now, let's do some intellectual work."

"Can we start with the Russian religion?"

"No, we will do math and writing first, as usual."

Two hours later, they took a break, and spent time playing with the pups. They had become noticeably stronger and more aggressive at play. "Now, back to history. This lesson will be about anti-Semitism in Russia," said Professor. "Do you know what this word means?"

"No."

"Semites are the people who originated in southwestern Asia, including Hebrews, Phoenicians, Aramaic, and Arabs. They all spoke Semitic languages. Nowadays, the word is used almost exclusively to refer to Jews."

"My mother said that she is not Jewish because she is not religious and that Judaism is a religion, not a nationality."

"Technically, she is correct. Judaism, just like Christianity, is a religion. People who practice the same religion could live in different countries. Remember the lesson about Russians choosing Orthodoxy over Roman Catholicism? If it were the other way around, we still would have been Russians, albeit with a different religion."

"I saw my mother's passport. It says: *Nationality: Jew.* If Judaism is a religion, why isn't she considered Russian then?"

"Are you sure you want to know the answer? You won't like it."

"Yes."

"We live in an anti-Semitic country. The Government wants to know who is a Jew, so they can make decisions based on this knowledge."

"What sort of decisions and why?"

"You are jumping ahead of yourself. By the end of this lesson you will understand more. Now, listen. Anti-Semitism came to Russia from Poland. In the fourteenth century, Poland was united under strong kings and was taken from a poor and barbaric country to enter the Western Christian Civilization. Much progress came with it; Poland became much wealthier and, naturally, attracted a lot of settlers from Germany. The Jews also came in large numbers, primarily to enjoy the success and the tolerance of the Polish State. Because of internal intrigues, Polish laws made it certain that trade and industry should be in the hands of foreigners, mostly Jews and Armenians. Jewish bailiffs were hired to manage big estates and became the only moneylenders and, in some areas, the only traders. At the same time period, Jews in Russia were not discriminated against. When, however, the Russian empire conquered large amounts of Polish territory, it acquired a large Jewish population along with them and thereby inherited the social problems associated with the prominence of the Jews in Poland. The Russian government tried to prevent Jews from settling outside of the old Polish borders, a policy which became known as "Pale of Settlement." In spite of this effort, anti-Semitism invaded Russia and has left tragic traces throughout Russian history. Any questions so far?"

"Yes. If Russia didn't take part of Poland in the first place, then anti-Semitism wouldn't have come to Russia?"

Professor paused and looked at Yule with a sideways glance. Yule knew this quizzical look; it meant that an unusual question was coming.

"You will turn eight in August, right?"

"Yes."

"Not bad for an eight-year old. It is a very logical question, but I have already explained to you in the past that a conqueror always inherits the problems of the conquered land. Unfortunately for the Jews, the Russian tsars treated them with stupid and brutal incomprehension, making them live in unlivable places and preventing them from getting the education that their talents deserved."

"But it is different now," interrupted Yule. "My mother is a doctor, my father is also a doctor, and my uncle is a professor of medicine in Leningrad."

"Well, after the Revolution, Jews started doing a little better. They are still, however, treated as a separate people. Since the 1930s Jews have been excluded from Soviet diplomatic services and other positions of prominence. Using the example that you have brought up about your mother, all Jews have their nationalities in their passports not as Soviet citizens but, rather, as Jews."

"Does that mean that I will have the same problem when I go back to Leningrad?"

"When are you going back?"

"My mother said that her contract will end in the spring of 1953, and that I will go live with my father in Leningrad, so I can get a good education."

"Tell her not to worry about your education. You are already at least five years ahead of children your age. As far as anti-Semitism, it will always be there. Let's check on the pups."

The wolf pups seemed to be growing by the day. Chook was noticeably larger than Cha; his paws were the size of Yule's hand. The bright orange fur on his face had dark gray spots throughout, the colors of adulthood already penetrating the signature orange of childhood. One ear was completely erect, whereas the other still had a soft tip that hung slightly forward. It gave Chook a goofy appearance, especially when his hind legs were carrying him sideways. "I will start them on solid food tomorrow," said Professor. "You have to collect the promised leftovers."

"I will do it today on my way home. So long."

Yule left Professor's *izba*, stepping out into the white world of the Siberian Tundra. After a moment's consideration, he decided to visit Semion's hut, where the hunter lived with his wife, Xenia, who also did her time in a neighboring female camp before being released and moving in with Semion. According to Yule's mother, she wasn't *officially* employed. Rather, she made a living by brewing and selling *samogon*, vodka-like hard liquor, mainly to the guards and hired personnel. There were two things that made it possible to survive Siberia—work and vodka. The work, no matter how hard it was, gave the prisoners some semblance of a purpose. Vodka, as the world's best and most natural cure for depression, kept them sane and helped them to forget their misery for at least a short while. Every moment of respite in

Siberia was priceless. Xenia's enterprise had prospered for years. The commander and the entire garrison knew about it. Not only did they know, but they patronized this business just as much as the hired labor.

Semion was home. He was a scrawny little man with a bald head and a completely white, long beard. He had a very close-set pair of small eyes. According to Yule's stepfather, Semion could shoot a squirrel in the eye from a substantial distance. He wasn't old, perhaps in his forties, but as the saying went, each year at the Gulag counts as two.

"Privet, doctor's boy," he said. "What brings you here?" He was clearly not in control of his speech; the words came out garbled and distorted. Yule saw this "condition" daily—being drunk was just a normal state of affairs. Semion took Yule by the hand and brought him to the table.

"Sit down, make yourself comfortable. You must be hungry. I have a treat for you," he said. Yule was taught to respect adults, though the rule did not clarify the state in which the adult must be to enjoy the respect. Yule, nevertheless, complied. The house was warm and cozy. A large, hot stove in the middle of the room was radiating pleasant warmth throughout the house. The table was set; a big pot was sitting on it, exuding a delicious aroma of some kind of stewed meat. A loaf of fresh bread was right next to it and, to crown it all off, a large bottle of some cloudy liquid stood in the middle. "We are ready to celebrate our first wedding anniversary," announced Semion. "Xenia will be back in a few minutes with some sweets, and a few guests are also coming."

"I can't stay too long. My mother will be worried if I walk home in the dark."

"There is at least one hour of daylight left. Besides, your mother doesn't get home before eight anyway. She treats a lot of *Zeks*."

Xenia, along with three other people, walked in laughing. Xenia was at least twice the size of Semion, nearly a foot taller, and a hundred pounds heavier. She had an impassible face that could stop a Trans-Siberian Express Train. As Yule's stepfather would say: a lid had found a pot (whatever *that* meant).

The rest of the company consisted of two off-duty guards and a woman who was apparently new to the camp. Xenia introduced her to Semion as a new telephone switchboard operator. Her name was Zeena. She was in her thirties, very pretty, and wore a crimson silk dress with large black maple leaves patterned onto it. Yule was introduced to her as the doctor's boy. The guards were already familiar to Yule. In fact, one of them took a shot at Yule last winter. Everyone sat down at the table while the cloudy liquid was evenly poured into small aluminum tumblers, including Yule's.

"What is it?" asked Yule suspiciously.

"Homemade miracle syrup, prepared just for this occasion by my wife," replied Semion proudly. "You will feel good from it, I promise."

Toasts were made to a happy marriage, to survival, to the safe return to the Main Land, and to many other things that Yule did not remember. Of course, the amnesia may be attributed to the fact that, after he had emptied hits tumbler, the room started to spin. He also felt slightly nauseous, so much so that he grew fearful of throwing up in the house. Yule got up and staggered out the door. No one noticed his departure. Twilight descended onto the camp, the air cold, dry, and refreshing. Yule felt much better psychologically, yet his legs appeared not to completely listen to his brain. Thus, he walked in a zigzag fashion, falling off the path, into the snow, getting up, and falling again. It took him about fifteen minutes to advance a few hundred feet. Then he saw Vladimir, who was standing in front of their house, looking in Yule's direction. After the subsequent fall and rise cycle, Yule felt the strong arms of his stepfather lifting him off the ground, putting him on his shoulder, and carrying him home safely.

"Where are you coming from?" asked Vladimir.

"Semion's."

"I will be right back," said Vladimir as he went out the door.

He returned in just five minutes, slightly out of breath. A few minutes later, Yule's mother burst into the room with an expression of horror on her face. Instead of attending to Yule (who was violently vomiting into a bucket), she started chastising Vladimir for knocking Semion out cold in his own house in front of the guards. "You must be out of your mind," she yelled, "or maybe you want to go back to being a *zek* but this time as a real criminal!"

"The bastard deserved it. You should attend to your child instead of yelling at me."

By that time, Yule had given up all of his stomach's contents and had fallen asleep. Zoya looked at him, checked his pulse, and walked away.

"He will be fine. His pulse is good, and his breathing is normal as well. He is a healthy boy and his body rejected the stuff Semion gave him. Now he needs to sleep it off. I am going back to the Ambulatory. Keep an eye on him."

Yule dreamt of flying again. It was different this time—he did not have to exert any effort to lift off or to gain altitude. Everything around him was spinning; the earth below was rotating slowly while his body was spinning like a bullet shot out of the barrel of a rifle, piercing through the thick clouds with ease. He kept going up, higher and higher, and when he finally decided to turn around and to return to the earth, he realized he couldn't do it. Instead, he continued his flight toward the sun. He felt the heat of the sun embracing his body. It was pleasant at first, a blissful departure from the freezing cold of Siberia. Gradually, however, the heat grew uncomfortably hot. Finally, the sensation of severe burning spread throughout his entire body. *I am destined to become a modern day Icarus*, he thought. The burning became unbearable as he spun ever closer to the sun. He felt his skin melting, the sensation of a rabid animal trying to crawl through his skin becoming ever more prominent. This was it; he was going to die. The sun was massive in front of him now, a colossus of burning and flickering orange. Yule finally gave in. He let out a mighty scream; the burning was too much to handle. He was about to crash into the sun. There was nothing but blinding light and more screaming.

Yule's eyes shot open. Both Vladimir and Zoya stood by his bed, their faces etched with concern. He must've been screaming. Sweat was trickling down Yule's entire body. A chunk of ice wrapped in a towel was resting on his forehead. "I had a dream that I was burning alive," said Yule.

"You are burning, because you have a high fever," said Zoya.

Yule looked out of his window. He could see a piece of the sky, an indication that it was morning already. Vladimir looked at Yule and said, "I feel as if it is a never-ending déjà-vu with you, Yule, all because of your poor judgment." Yule did not answer. He knew better. Sometimes he wondered what kind of a man Vladimir was. On the one hand, his stepfather was very hard on him, unforgiving, and occasionally abusive. On the other, Vladimir would come to his stepson's defense and protect him from harm. People are complex creatures.

Ten days went by. Yule was quarantined without the possibility of leaving his house, a house arrest of sort. He thought of Vladimir, proud of the fact that he knocked Semion out. Vladimir was once a decent amateur boxer (while in the navy) and occasionally taught Yule how to throw some meaningful punches.

Yule spent most of his quarantine days reading and playing war games with miniature figurines and military equipment, a birthday gift from his father delivered the previous summer.

Although there was a telephone in his house, he couldn't use it because the calls wouldn't go through the switchboard. Zoya had instructed the operators not to connect his calls. Yule missed Professor and the wolf pups.

Finally, the time came and the quarantine was lifted. The following morning, Yule stepped out of the house, breathing in the sweet air of freedom. The spring was prominently on display both in the air and in the surrounding environment. The morning, however, was still cold, about five degrees Fahrenheit. For a Siberian morning, that was considered moderately warm. During the day, the temperature would rise above the freezing mark and the pale skin of the people would, after being deprived of it for nine months, feel the warmth of the sun.

Professor opened the door even before Yule knocked. "Well, well, well," said Professor, "look who is here: the prodigal son."

"It wasn't my fault…"

"Don't strain yourself explaining. Semion was here and showed me his terrific shiner, courtesy of your stepfather."

"How are they?" asked Yule, pointing to the barn door.

"I have to keep them locked up because they are taking the house apart; they are much bigger and stronger and have a lot of energy."

The pups must've heard Yule's voice; they started whining with a very high pitch, occasionally interrupted by short barks. Professor opened the barn door and, almost immediately, Chook and Cha erupted out of it, falling over one another as they scrambled toward Yule. They had almost doubled in size during his quarantine period. Their features also altered. The pups now had longer legs, erected triangular ears, and much bushier tails. They still, however, had dark, penetrating blue eyes. Both of the pups crowded Yule, sniffing his boots with unmitigated excitement. Yule kneeled to pet them. The pups started sniffing his hair and sneezing.

"They know where you were and who you were with," said Professor. "When they are fully grown, they will be able to recognize thousands of different smells, even to smell your internal chemical processes, the hormones you exude, and even your fears. But the main question remains: what are we going to do with them? In a few months, they will weigh at least one hundred pounds each and will need a lot of food and exercise. Have you thought about it?"

"No."

"In that case, I will tell you what we will do. We will have to introduce them to the outside world as soon as possible. In about two weeks they will be completely weaned off of Chukcha's milk and will be eating solid food only. We will start taking them out in the dark so that others won't see them."

"Will they come back if we let them loose?"

"We will use a long rope in the beginning, to allow them some freedom. Now, let's do some work."

The lessons followed the usual framework; Russian literature was succeeded by chemistry. The last hour, however, was the *piece de résistance*—Russian history. Yule learned that, during medieval times, Russia consisted of "city-republics." The most prominent one was the city of Novgorod. In essence, Novgorod was an oligarchy of rich merchants ruled by the power of the prince and controlled by a popular assembly. The rich wore long red boots and loved to dress in crimson. The men had their beards carefully trimmed while the girls wore pigtails with ribbons. Women also wore headdresses tied under their chins. Yule also learned about one of Professor's "dangerous" postulates: despite all popular theories that Russian human nature requires a personal autocracy, the success of the city-republics proves these theories false. That was the quintessential Professor: full of theories, always analyzing, always thinking. One of his other theories was that the greatest truths are, most of the time, initially taken for blasphemies. His explanation for this phenomenon lied in the weaknesses of our mind and its inability to evaluate current events; mental inertia, adherence to established standards and generally-accepted opinions, and lack of foresight were the contributing factors.

Two more weeks had passed. The wolf pups' eye color had gradually shifted from blue to a captivating shade of golden-brown. Their facial expressions became noticeably more serious, no longer the goofy expressions that once characterized them. The unique "wolf gaze," as Yule called it, had become more evident as well. There is no other animal in the world that can look through you in the same manner as a wolf. Later in life, Yule had seen a semblance of this look in stray dogs that were forced to survive in the concrete jungles of the "civilized world." For the past several nights, Professor made a habit of taking the pups out for long walks. The pups were tethered to a very long rope, allowing them a certain measure of freedom in choosing their way and exploring the territory. As he had explained to Yule, this seemingly minor decision-making would potentially prove to be critical once the pups were released into the taiga.

Contrary to popular belief, the summer months in the Kolyma region could get rather warm and moist. Once the air and the ground warmed up, the moisture rushed in from the East Coast inland, bringing with it rains and occasional thunderstorms. Aside from the long anticipated warmth of the sun, the only other prominent feature of the summer was the great thaw, which allowed trucks with supplies to cross the mountain passes. For Yule, the most anticipated arrival was the first mail. Normally, he would get his birthday presents from his father and his uncle, Gregory, who both lived in Leningrad. Uncle Gregory was a *bookinist*, an antique book dealer; a birthday present from him meant at least two or three books. Yule was right in his assumption—three books were stacked in a large box next to other gifts he did not care about. The first book was "Little Lord Fauntleroy" by Frances Hodgson Burnett, an 1898 edition translated from English. It was a beautiful book, bound in green-gray stamp cloth and gilt-illustrated. The other two were WWII action books. The arrival of the books was very timely; Yule had run out of any printed material to read.

The August of 1951 became very memorable for Yule, who had just turned eight. He was introduced to the magic of an unfamiliar and mesmerizing art, something that metamorphosed into a life-long love affair. One day in August, a heavy thunderstorm with torrential downpours had blanketed and buffeted the camp. The roads and paths became absolutely impassable. Thus, Yule's mother had managed to send a message via a guard (whose post was closest to Professor's house) that Yule should spend the night at Professor's *izba* and under no circumstances should he attempt to walk home in the downpour. Happiness ensued; Yule was to spend an entire night with the man he admired so much.

A brief lesson was succeeded by playtime with the wolf pups and dinner, consisting of bear meat and boiled potatoes. Afterwards, Professor took Yule to the far corner of the room. The most notable landmark was a small table with some sort of box on top of it, covered under an old, dusty blanket. When the blanket came off, a rectangular platform with the word *Telefunken* on its front plate appeared. A half dozen elongated light bulbs were sticking out from it along with a few metal cylinders that resembled the bulbs. Some short wires surrounded the bulbs. The front of the object was dominated by a small wheel wrapped in coiled wire connected by a metal cable to a round knob. Professor flipped a switch; the filaments inside the bulbs lit up and a green luminous light (not unlike a cat's eye) filled the dark corner. Professor started slowly turning the knob, which in turn made the larger wheel rotate. The green eye became wider, then narrower, and then the room became filled with voices speaking foreign tongues.

"This is a short-wave radio," said Professor. "I have been waiting for the vacuum lamps since last autumn. Those glass envelopes are very fragile; the new ones are made of metal and can withstand the shipping and the heat. They are very hard to come by, but one of my former students was able to get them for me."

"What is this green eye for?"

"It is an electromagnet. It shows the precision of tuning to a radio frequency."

Professor continued to turn the knob, the green eye continuously flickering until it became as narrow as a needle. At that point, it stopped moving, and almost immediately, the room was filled with the voice of a man speaking English. After the brief introduction, a magnificently beautiful melody burst from the radio, a soaring sound of an instrument yet unknown to Yule; the enchanted melody somehow reminded him of his flying dreams, the rhythms of the drums and the base and then the piano, all playing their seemingly different tunes and yet, together, creating a marvelous and captivating mosaic, a euphony the likes of which Yule had never before experienced. Each instrument morphed into a complete harmony, a perfect concoction of pure bliss.

"What is it?"

"This is jazz, my boy. The man who is playing the clarinet is Artie Shaw. He is the leader of the band."

"I want to listen more."

"We will have an entire evening of jazz. Sit tight and listen."

After Artie Shaw came Glenn Miller with Tex Beneke, who was singing and playing his saxophone. They were succeeded by Gene Krupa, Lionel Hampton, and Wynonnie Harris with his "Good Morning Judge." The entire evening went by in one blazing minute; Yule couldn't get enough of this unbelievable music.

Professor had translated the announcements and, occasionally, the words of the songs.

"This broadcast is every day at the same time," said Professor, "but we won't get lucky every night with a perfect reception like we have now; the short-wave, high frequency signals are reflected from the ionosphere back to earth and then bounce up again and again over a long distance. That's why we are able to get this signal coming from Alaska."

"Is it really coming from Alaska?"

"Courtesy of the American Army radio station WXK in Kodiak. The announcer's name is Joe, and he plays jazz after the sunset."

"Why after the sunset?"

"Because the reflective properties of the ionosphere are much better without the interference of the sun."

"Unfortunately, I normally have to leave your house before the sunset."

"I will think of something so you can stay later."

The following day, Professor visited Yule's mother at her medical office. He asked Zoya's permission to start the daily lessons at ten A.M., citing the difficulties of getting up early in the morning. Permission was granted and duly recorded in his chart. Yule was ecstatic; he could now enjoy the mesmerizing music every evening.

The next day, during dinner, Vladimir brought up the subject of wolf sightings inside the Zona and the consequent disappearance of small domestic animals (including one of the commander's piglets). Yule's heart sunk into his stomach as his face turned a deep shade of red.

"Don't be afraid," said Vladimir. "Wolves don't attack people, especially in the summer."

Yule was glad that his reaction was attributed to a fear of wolves. Deep down inside, he knew that it was Chook wreaking havoc inside the camp. The following day, Yule and Professor examined the fenced area adjacent to the barn and found a sizable hole in the ground right under the fence. It was clear that the nightly raids were conducted out of this hole. The intelligent pups would go out, kill, eat, and return to being pets again, all in one night. They were, however, almost six months old. One could hardly call them pups at that point. Chook stood at least forty inches tall. Although Cha was slightly smaller, he still looked incredibly menacing. Professor and Yule glanced at each other and, without saying a word, understood perfectly well the implications of this silent conversation: the time had come to set the wolf pups free.

"You will have to do it tonight, when it gets dark," said Professor. "I can't get onto the other side anyway—they will shoot me."

"I will do it on my way home," whispered Yule, choking back tears. The pups were looking at him with a puzzled, almost human-like expression.

"They know," said Professor.

"How?"

"They can read us like an open book."

"Are they going to survive?"

"Based on the way they behave? A definite yes."

The station was playing Louis Armstrong's "Royal Garden Blues," followed by selections from Charlie Parker, Benny Goodman, and at the conclusion of the broadcast, "Moonlight Serenade." It was almost seven o'clock; dusk, broken up by the occasional dim lights of faraway houses, had descended onto the camp. Yule tethered the pups to two ropes and, without saying a single word, led them out of the door. They reached the spot where Yule usually climbed through the fence, the very same spot that was the genesis of his wolf adventure. It seemed only yesterday that Yule climbed through the small hole, attracted to the outer forest by some inexplicable curiosity. The hole was still there, about two feet off the ground. Yule climbed through it first and then encouraged the pups to do the same. They followed without hesitation. Professor had instructed Yule to take the pups at least a mile into the taiga before releasing them. Chook and Cha were seemingly enjoying the walk, utilizing the length of the rope to go left and right, sniff, and to mark the surrounding territory. It was a very good sign. Yule finally stopped about half an hour later. He slowly stooped down and proceeded to remove the ropes from the pups' necks. They stood in front of Yule, two magnificent and majestic animals on the cusp of wild freedom. The red fur had completely disappeared from their faces, replaced with the more characteristic charcoal gray; the fur turned a lighter gray toward the chest, as if awaiting permission to take off. Yule embraced both of the pups. There was no longer any need to kneel down; he had to lean only slightly forward and their cold, grainy noses were touching his lips. The tears were again streaming down his cheeks, both irrepressible and copious. Professor was right; the wolves somehow knew. As if by command, both of them turned around and walked away. That was it. In one transient moment, the wolves were gone forever from his life. Yule also turned around and started walking toward the camp, making a conscious effort not to look back. A few moments later, he could not resist the urge. Yule looked back, and the wolf pups were gone, perpetually vanished into the dark and woody wilderness.

The winds invading from the Arctic Circle had forced the inhabitants of the camp to take out their winter clothing. The merciful sunrays were still relatively warm but, nonetheless, failed to defend the camp from the harsh onslaught.

Yule's lessons continued along their conventional track. The history topics moved on to the Tatar-Mongolian invasion of Russia. He learned that, in addition to the invasion being the greatest disaster in the history of China and the Middle East, there was another side to the coin. Humanity, for example, has never been so near to the world state as under the Mongols. The great Khans ruled through an international civil service that had room for representatives of all nations. Furthermore, the organization of the Mongols was efficient; their rule was unimaginably ruthless to lawbreakers but also benevolent to the law-abiding. There was also another important lesson in Russian history that has permeated both time and geography: the rulers of the Golden Hordes (as the Mongols were called) soon discovered that prosperous subjects paid more taxes than burned cities. This axiom is believed to be true today as well.

Yule did not have any lessons the following month; Zoya insisted on a four-week recess from studies, to keep "the little brain from overheating," as she put it.

At the end of October, the snow had accumulated up to a few feet. In some parts of the camp, the snowdrifts had reached a height of about ten. Vladimir finally got his ammunition together, an arduous process which involved melting enough led to create both large and small caliber bullets, sufficient to hunt for bears and birds alike. Yule was equipped with his little sawed-off shotgun and ammunition of a smaller caliber designed only for small birds. Early the next morning, the two of them got dressed in four layers of clothes and donned their thick, felt boots with rubber soles. They carried the snow-steppers beyond the gates of the camp, putting them on only when they passed its demarcated perimeter. The snow-steppers oddly resembled tennis rackets with the handles facing backwards. Vladimir and Yule advanced very slowly and quietly, communicating only through hand signals. The deafening silence of the taiga was violated only by the occasional flapping of a wing or the distant howl of a wolf. There were also periodic drum-like sounds—the result of tree barks crackling due to the rapid drop in temperature. These sounds, however, were merely a part of the environment's harmony, both ubiquitous and characteristic. They were as much a part of the natural surroundings as the sights and the smells inherent to them. Thus, they were not alarming to the animals. The unnatural disruption of a human voice, on the other hand, would alert and frighten all inhabitants within a radius of a few miles. Thus, total silence was of paramount importance. About thirty minutes into the expedition, Yule and his stepfather reached the edge of a small ravine with sparse vegetation. The snow-covered *sopki* (low hills) stood in the distance. Vladimir abruptly halted and signaled Yule to stop. Approximately fifty yards down below, a wolf pack consisting of half a dozen species was crossing their path, heading toward the river. Yule looked at Vladimir, expecting some action on his part. Surprisingly, he did not see any lucid reaction, just a calm and re-assuring look on his face.

Wolves don't attack people, Yule remembered Vladimir saying, and it was true indeed. The large, jet-black pack leader merely looked at the two hunters, somewhat cautious about, yet seemingly indifferent to, their presence. The pack didn't even slow down to investigate the intrusion. A very light gust of wind suddenly blew from behind, bringing the human scent toward the passing wolf pack. One of the wolves separated from the rest, moved a few steps sideways, lifted his head, and started to sniff at the air. Yule studied the wolf and noticed a round black spot at the base of the tail.

"Chook?" whispered Yule.

The wolf made several more tentative steps in Yule's direction and stopped. There was no doubt about it; it was definitely Chook, larger than before, with darker fur and beautiful, amber-colored eyes staring straight at Yule. The rest of the pack had also stopped. Virtually all of the wolves were looking at the two of them, trying to discern the phenomenon that was taking place. Vladimir was also slightly perplexed with the unusual turn of events.

Chook was much larger; his face turned a light charcoal color with some remnants of orange spots on the forehead and much lighter gray fur under the chin. *He should be about seven months old now*, thought Yule, the approximate age to start hunting with the pack. Chook continued to stand there, looking at Yule with those piercing eyes but never approaching him. Occasionally, the wolf glanced at Vladimir. After a few seconds, Chook slightly wagged his tail, turned around, and rejoined the pack. His place in the pack was second to the last wolf, which looked remarkably like Cha. As the youngest members of the pack, they were outranked by the older wolves; they were, after all, still adolescents.

"What was that all about?" asked Vladimir.

"Just a wolf I know."

That was the full extent of their conversation; Vladimir was a man of few words, but Yule suspected that his stepfather knew about the wolf pup rescue all along.

Yule felt triumphant. The wolves survived, joined a pack and, despite all that, still remembered him. The triumph, however, was mixed with a feeling of melancholy. He missed the touch of their fur and the prickle of their whiskers. He missed their scent, which reminded him of the smell of boiled rice in his mother's kitchen. He also missed the way the wolf pups looked at him, right in the eyes; there was no challenge in that look, just pure and sincere love. Yule couldn't wait to tell Professor about his encounter with the pups. The next morning, he got up before his parents, got dressed, had a glass of milk with a slice of bread, and headed straight for the door. Right when he was about to walk through it, he heard Zoya say to him, "Do not rush, Ivan won't be teaching you today."

"Why?"

"He is not well. I have been visiting him every evening for the past two weeks. He has an advanced stage of pneumonia."

"Why doesn't anyone tell me anything? Why!"

Yule knew what pneumonia meant. He witnessed too many deaths as a result of it where the majority of the victims died of what was called *chakhotka*, an old-fashioned Russian word for the condition.

Although penicillin had been mass-produced in the US (especially at the end of WWII), it did not make its way all the way to the Gulag. Occasional single dosages were used primarily to treat the prison guards and their families.

"I am going to see him any way," said Yule. Zoya looked at him and realized that there was no way she would be able to stop her son. The stubbornness must have been painted visibly on his face.

"Just don't torture him with your questions. He is very weak," she said. "He is also very anemic; he has leukemia."

"Can't you cure him?"

"At least his pneumonia, if I had enough penicillin that is, but I have depleted all of my supplies, and the next shipment is not due until the spring. He also needs a blood transfusion, which is out of the question."

They looked at each other. Neither said a word; they both knew the inevitable outcome. It was just a matter of time.

Ivan Lensky was in bed. He looked unnaturally pale and had huge, dark blue and black shadows around his eyes. The book he was reading before Yule walked in was lying on his chest with the cover facing up: *Anton Pavlovich Chekhov, Short Stories.*

"*Kak dyela,* how are you doing?" Yule asked. It was a silly question and Yule knew it, but the awkwardness of the moment demanded something to be said. It was the best he could come up with.

"*Kak vidish*, just like you see."

"I see that you are reading Chekhov."

"Yes, he is my favorite. Very few writers know the Russian character as well as Chekhov."

"But there are millions of people in Russia; they can't have the same character."

"You are right and wrong at the same time. Individually, we are different from one another, but collectively, we have a common denominator. This common denominator has been developed over centuries of Russian history and has become a part of our genes. For instance, Chekhov calls the Russian peasant lazy, because during long and harsh winters there is nothing else to do but to drink, sleep, and drink again. But come spring, the same *muzhik* works like hell to provide for the next winter. You see, that is why…"

Professor did not finish the sentence; he covered his mouth with a towel and a long coughing spell shook his entire body for half a minute. After it was over, the towel was covered with red spots. Professor put his head on the pillow and looked at Yule apologetically.

"I will come back tomorrow," said Yule.

"No, no, stay with me. I don't know how long..." the words hung in the air. There was no need to continue the sentence.

"Would you like me to read for you?" Yule asked.

"I would love it. Here, this story is called *In a Strange Land.*" Yule started to read but soon stopped. Ivan Lensky had his eyes closed, but as soon as the reading stopped, he looked at Yule quizzically.

"You need rest," Yule said.

"I will get plenty of rest when I am gone. Resting in peace, so to speak. But, if you really have to go… I will see you tomorrow."

A flying dream again, it was more of a nightmare. The usual dark, amorphous danger was rapidly approaching, but this time, Yule had Professor holding onto him. Professor's body was very limp. Yule tried to fly away with him but could get only slightly off the ground. They fell into the brush, and almost instantly, the dark thick cloud enveloped them. Yule's mouth got filled with this dark matter; it tasted like cotton. He screamed, started to choke, and forced his fingers into his mouth to pry out the choking substance.

He woke up, alarmed and nervous. A corner of the sheet he slept under was in his mouth. He pulled it out and tried to catch his breath. He was probably screaming audibly because his stepfather approached his bed and asked if he had a bad dream.

"Yes, I did, about Professor."

"Your mother was called to his house around four in the morning."

"What happened?"

"I don't know. She is still there."

Yule jumped off the bed and looked at the clock. It was a quarter to six. He grabbed his clothes and began to feverishly put them on.

"Where do think you're going?"

"Professor's place."

"I don't think it's a good idea. Wait for your mother to come home."

One hour later, Zoya returned. She didn't have to say anything—Yule could read her face perfectly well. A male nurse carrying a large burlap bag walked in behind her. The nurse placed the bag next to Yule, looked at him apologetically, turned around, and left.

"This is for you, from Ivan. Things that he wanted you to have."

"How do you know?"

"He told me; he died in my arms."

Yule covered his face with both hands and started toward the door. He didn't want them to see his tears. He'd never cried before, at least not in front of his parents.

"Where are you going," asked Vladimir.

"I will be back in a minute."

Vladimir was saying something else, but Yule didn't hear it, nor did he care. He continued walking without realizing where he was going. Walking aimlessly, completely distraught by the loss of his only friend, he found himself by the Professor's *izba*. Two guards, out of their NKVD uniforms, walked out of the door carrying a bookcase and a table lamp.

"Why are you taking this?" Yule demanded.

"First of all, it is none of your business. Second, he doesn't need material things anymore," answered the ponderous guard whom Yule had seen at Semion's wedding party.

"Can you at least wait a little? Ivan's body is probably still warm."

"We've got permission from the commander, if you must know," said the other guard, seemingly embarrassed.

"Where is your human dignity?" yelled Yule. Almost immediately, he realized that he sounded just like his departed teacher. The thought made him feel warm inside, a brief moment of happiness in the darkest abyss. It was good to know that a little bit of Professor's character lived on inside him so that, as long as he lived, a part of Professor also lived on. Yule turned around and walked away, disregarding the stream of angry insults that followed his remark. He had seen people die before but never someone he was so close to. There was the void, the emptiness, the denial, and all kinds of other thoughts racing through his mind. Is it really so easy to die? One day you are here, talking, thinking, teaching, breathing... and the next day you are gone. Forever. Then he remembered his own brush with death during the snowstorm. Another thirty minutes, as Vladimir told him, and he would have been dead without knowing it. It *is* that easy to die. At this moment, Yule recalled Professor's words when he returned for his lessons following the near-tragic snowstorm: *I guess it wasn't your time.* Now Yule understood as the tears fell freely down his face.

After what seemed like hours, he went back home. Zoya had already left for work, while Vladimir was home working on his next oil portrait of Joseph Stalin. Yule opened the burlap bag and looked inside—mostly books. He started taking them out, one by one: Herodotus, Chekhov, Dostoyevsky, Kafka, Freud, Dante, Alexander Block. At the bottom of the bag, however, was the Telefunken radio. Tears covered Yule's eyes. He wiped them off with his hand and looked out the window. Masha the pig was walking inside the fenced yard, enjoying the warmth of the late morning sun. Her litter was gone; some piglets went to the commander, some were sold. Yule pulled his eyes away from the window and looked at his stepfather. Vladimir got up, walked over to Yule, and hugged his stepson. Yule was utterly shocked, rendered speechless by the uncanny display of emotion; it was very unusual, to say the least. Nothing like it had ever happened before. The display of emotion was so against the usual asperity displayed by Vladimir over the years that Yule lost his ability to speak for a moment. Neither one said a word. After a few awkward moments, Vladimir returned to his easel. Adults, one moment they whip you with a belt, and the next thing you know, they hug you as if they sincerely care about your pain.

"Who is going to teach me now?" Yule asked, finally breaking the awkward silence.

"Your mother has someone in mind. She just has to go through some formality to free him up and move him to Ivan's house."

"Who is he?"

"A former professor of psychiatry at the Leningrad First Medical Institute."

"What's he in for?"

"I don't know. He is relatively new to the camp."

Yule spent the next hour trying to set up the Telefunken. The speaker it came with was a converted, old radio with large black parchment paper shaped like a bullhorn. Yule hung it above his bed and placed the radio on a nightstand. It was too early for the Voice of America; besides, during the day, the reception wasn't good enough to listen to anything. Meanwhile, Yule busied himself with the cornucopia of books. It was initially hard to decide which one to start from, but having just learned that his future mentor was a psychiatrist, Yule chose Sigmund Freud's *The Interpretation of Dreams*. He was, furthermore, curious in interpreting his recurrent "flying dreams." He found the needed paragraph and started reading: "dreams in which one flies with a feeling of ease or falls in terror, I know nothing from my own experience." So far, not very encouraging. Yule continued looking for more relevant information and found the following: "the exciting games of childhood are repeated in dreams of flying, falling, reeling and the like." Nothing even close, though it was possible that Grandpa Sam, who had adored Yule and spent most of his time playing all kinds of games with him, had something to do with it. Yule was too young to remember. Disappointed in Freud, Yule put the book aside. The book was published in 1900 and was translated into Russian in 1904. It was possible that later research would shed more light on the subject, but it was the only book available in Russian on the subject because, during the 1920s, psychoanalysis had fallen from grace and was dismissed altogether as a bourgeois practice. Soon thereafter, it was declared dangerous and, finally, illegal.

Doctor David Borisovich Stein was a tall and slender man with piercing blue eyes and dark hair. Judging by his last name, he was an Ashkenazi Jew of German extraction. He looked, however, like a Spanish nobleman from one of Velasquez's paintings with his elongated aristocratic face defined by high cheekbones and a prominent, well-shaped nose. He was of the same genetic make-up as Yule's father. Dr. Stein was most likely of a family relocated from Germany, forced to escape from random anti-Semitism and, thereby, settling in Eastern Europe in the late fifteenth century. He appeared to be in his forties, though Yule wasn't very good at determining the age of adults. It felt odd to be in Ivan Lensky's house, merely two weeks after his death, with a complete stranger occupying his place. The house was the same inside, sans the furniture taken by the two security guards. The same bed and the same four chairs still remained.

"Since tutoring you will be my only job, I will take it very seriously," said Dr. Stein. "Besides, I owe that much to your mother. Before we begin, I need to know what level of knowledge you are at. I have prepared a test for you on four basic subjects: mathematics, language, history, and literature. All four have been divided into several sections. For instance, history has three sections: Russian, European, and the Ancient World. The rest of the subjects are divided similarly. Are you ready?"

"Yes, I am," answered Yule. "Should I address you as Dr. Stein, or as David Borisovich?"

"Whatever you prefer; I have not been called 'Doctor' since I got to Kolyma."

"My stepfather told me that you are a psychiatrist."

"A psychopathologist, to be exact. Do you know the difference?"

"I do."

Dr. Stein looked at Yule with apparent curiosity. "What's the difference, then?"

"It is about people who are not like everybody else."

Dr. Stein raised his eyebrows and, quite unexpectedly, burst into a fit of laughter. He laughed rather hard yet, surprisingly enough, there was nothing insulting in his laughter. It was rather contagious, though. Yule could not help smiling. He looked at Dr. Stein, anticipating some kind of an explanation.

"I am sorry. I'm laughing at my former students. Every single one of them would've given me a five-minute answer filled with sophisticated terminology. You, on the other hand, just nailed it. I wish my students hadn't lost the ability that only a child's mind can offer. I often think of Freud's famous quotation, referring to a distressing contrast between the radiant intelligence of a child and the feeble mentality of an average adult."

"Are you saying, Dr. Stein, that I am right?"

"That's exactly what I am saying. Being considered normal is to conform to the rules of the microcosm you live in. When you move to a different world, get ready to behave differently."

"Do you know about Freud's interpretations of dreams?" Yule asked.

"Of course I do; it is my job to know," said Dr Stein, smiling. "What is it you see in your dreams?"

The test was quickly forgotten. It looked as if both of them enjoyed the subject. Dr. Stein was deprived of professional discourse for a number of years and now, despite the fact that it wasn't his usual milieu, fell in love with it all over again. His amazement with the little boy grew by the minute. Yule described his recurrent dream with all of its variations. He also expressed his disappointment with Freud's interpretation of the dreams; that particular part elicited a smile from Dr. Stein, who immediately made a note in his notebook. When Yule finished his descriptions, Dr. Stein remained silent for a few seconds, clearly contemplating the information and formulating an answer within his mind. After the brief pause, he advanced his interpretation. Dr. Stein believed that Yule was, in essence, escaping from some danger, represented by an amorphous matter, by flying away from it. That was a much more plausible and sophisticated explanation than Sigmund Freud's "childhood games" theory. Yule took a liking to this new teacher almost instantly. He had a feeling that they would get along just fine. His mind, however, kept gravitating toward Ivan Lensky. The new impressions and the anticipation of being exposed to different viewpoints, however, made the pain of the loss slightly duller.

Yule finally took the test and answered all of the questions without any difficulties. In fact, most of the material had previously been covered with Professor last year. Yule, however, decided not to say anything; he wanted to cover some of the material for a second time, especially material pertaining to history and literature. Most notably, he was excited by the prospect of learning about some of the more subjective materials from a different vantage point, specifically the interpretation of Dr. Stein. Yule had a lot of questions for his new teacher but decided to give him more time to get used to his new situation and to prepare himself for the inevitable barrage of questions.

"When you come tomorrow, I will have the lesson plans ready based on the results of the examination," said Dr. Stein. "I will walk with you a little. I haven't had this privilege for a few years," he added. "By the way, I will most likely see you tonight, at the House of Culture. Are you coming with your parents?"

"I do not know anything about tonight. Why do we need to go there?"

"Oh, maybe I wasn't supposed to tell you, but it's too late now. A theatre from Magadan is going to perform *Romeo and Juliet*. They are touring the Kolyma region and performing in most of the camps."

"Are they any good?"

"You will be pleasantly surprised to see that the artistic quality of this theatrical production is comparable to the best theaters in Moscow."

"Really?"

"Yes, *really*, my sarcastic friend. You, most likely, are not aware that the forced migration of many artists to Siberia resulted in a Renaissance of sort, especially in Magadan. You will see top-quality acting tonight. If you choose to come, that is."

They said *poka,* so long, to each other and went their separate ways. Dr. Stein's mind kept returning to Yule's references to Freud. It was a rather painful subject for Dr. Stein to begin with, but an eight-year-old child was a most unusual source of reference, quite strange, as a matter of fact. As a medical student, Dr. Stein had done a lot of research on the subject of psychoanalysis. At the time, Stalin and Trotsky had praised psychoanalysis. There were even nursery school curricula developed based on psychoanalytic principles. As it frequently happened in the Soviet Union, however, at the end of the 1920s, psychoanalysis had been condemned as a bourgeois practice and was declared dangerous. Simply put, the USSR had lost its interest in Freud. Luckily, David Borisovich Stein had already become a doctor; otherwise, his research would've been disavowed. Dr. Stein was a very optimistic man who believed that good must always prevail in the end, and that some day he would return to teaching in Leningrad. He had only seven months left of his sentence. Now, freed from hard labor and charged with an exceptionally bright pupil, he thought that his life had taken a turn for the better. He was wrong.

"Do you like your new teacher?" asked Zoya at the dinner table.

"I do."

"He was a prominent psychopathologist in Leningrad. When he was a student, he worked at Professor Ivan Petrovich Pavlov's laboratory, looking after the dogs at first. Later he participated in the 'Innate vs. Conditional Reflexes' study. He became a professor of psychopathology and a consultant for the Leningrad Psychiatric Prison. That was the beginning of his problems."

"The problems that brought him here?"

"Exactly, but maybe you should ask him yourself. I would feel more comfortable if it came from him. One thing I can tell you, though, is that he is one of the best scientists today, and you are lucky to have a teacher of his caliber."

Later in the evening came the big event: the theatrical performance of William Shakespeare's *Romeo and Juliet*. The House of Culture was full of prisoners, off-duty guards, and in the first row, the ponderous commander in his NKVD uniform accompanied by the voluptuous Zeena, resplendent in her crimson dress. Yule's parents, along with other non-prisoners of some significance, were also present for the pageantry. Yule spotted Dr. Stein in the third row and, after asking his mother for permission, joined him in the adjacent seat. As the lights dimmed and conversations ceased, the heavy red velvet curtain with the ubiquitous hammer and sickle embroideries on it slowly rose up. To most of the spectators, especially to those who had spent many years in the isolation of the Gulag, the scene was surreal. The stage set was obviously done by professionals; the silhouettes of a Medieval Italian city, the narrow streets, the piazza, the magnificent buildings were all very impressive. The stage was a window to a new world, the realistic microcosm of a distant environment and culture. This sudden transformation to the city of Verona, Italy, the ancient feud, the sword fights, the language and, of course, the love story, were pure magic. The acting was very good. Dr. Stein kept glancing at Yule throughout the play, as if to say *I told you so*. The spirit in the camp was visibly high for the next several days. Ah, the magic of the arts.

The following day, Dr. Stein and Yule went over the results of the test and the future lesson plans were finalized. At the end of the day, Yule, following Zoya's advice, asked Dr. Stein about the events that had brought him to the Kolyma Forced Labor Camp. His answer was short, and his account, in essence, was very similar to Professor's story. In fact, the only substantial difference was the setting; Dr. Stein's story had taken place in Leningrad rather than Moscow. The Psychiatric Prison Dr. Stein worked in was notorious for "treating" notable dissidents. Psychiatric imprisonment was a common method of isolation used to deal with human rights activists—one can't, after all, be normal and critical of the official policies at the same time. These people needed to be cured. The diagnoses ranged from "socially dangerous" to a "sluggish schizophrenic." On one particular occasion, Dr. Stein had expressed his doubt that a patient belonged in a psychiatric ward at all. He was immediately reported by one of the numerous snitches to the prison authorities; the rest painfully reminded Yule of Professor's arrest: interrogations, solitary confinement, sentencing, and the train ride in a cramped cattle car to the Gulag was all a near mirror-image of Ivan Lensky's journey into captivity. Dr. Stein was "lucky"—he was given only three years of forced labor to teach him a lesson and, as the presiding judge put it, "to clear [his] head of ideas to doubt the authorities."

1952 brought some troubling news to the camp. The aging and paranoid Joseph Stalin was seriously troubled by the deaths of several Communist Party leaders. Since the deaths had come in a quick succession, Stalin suspected a conspiracy and stated that, "The old doctors must be replaced by the new ones." That was good enough for Stalin's aids to start the process known as the *Doctors' Plot*. It just so happened that the majority of prominent medical doctors in the USSR were Jewish. Thus, by default, the case became the *Jewish Doctors' Plot*. "Doveriay no proveriay," trust but verify, Stalin's saying had become the motto of the new wave of prosecution. Yule's mother, who was two months pregnant and whose contract with the Gulag was about to expire, became very concerned that she wouldn't be able to work as a physician upon returning to Leningrad. Dr. Stein, who was about to be released, had the same fear. His case was even more egregious because of the conviction.

One day in April, Yule arrived at Dr. Stein's house for their usual lessons. As soon as he stepped through the door of the familiar *izba*, he noticed something amiss from the usual décor. A throw rug was placed on the floor, right next to Dr. Stein's bed. It was made of an extravagant animal fur, about five feet long. The color of the fur, however, seemed very familiar: it was charcoal gray sprinkled with orange specks throughout. Yule looked closer and immediately noticed a black round spot at the base of the fur, around the tail area. It looked liked Chook's fur, but the spot was much smaller. The familiarity was immediately obvious. "Where did this come from?" Yule asked, trying to sound calm.

"I traded it with Semion for three packets of Chinese black chai."

"It is very pretty," said Yule, whose heart was pounding. "Did he say when this wolf was killed?"

"He said two years ago, about this time of year."

Everything made perfect sense now, the mystery clarified and solved. The bizarre disappearance of the pack and the two newborn wolves left to die in its wake had just been explained, all by a seemingly insignificant furnishing. This little weasel, this perfidious bastard Semion was the one who had made Chook and Cha orphans. An unquenchable sense of rage griped Yule. Semion was the one who had endangered the lives of two precious wolf cubs, the cold-blooded murderer who slaughtered a mother whose only concern was the welfare of her newborns. To Yule, it was no better than slaughtering a human being. Semion surely must have known that the wolf was a mother, yet the knowledge did not stop him from performing the senseless act. And for what? A rug? A petty furnishing to be thrown onto the floor and stepped on without remorse? Semion would pay for this, a price equivalent to his crime. Yule was so angry and distracted that the lesson was ruined. Dr. Stein, perplexed by Yule's strange and seemingly unprompted behavior, had no choice but to send him home.

Yule, normally rapt and attentive during his lessons, relished the opportunity to go home and plan his revenge. One question dominated all thoughts: how was he to punish Semion? Should he be confronted directly? No, it would have to be a serious punishment, one with long-lasting consequences. It would have to be significant, something beyond a few bruises or scars. Perhaps the destruction of his guns? Some other valuable belongings? Why something specific? Yes, that was it—his house. Yule wouldn't take *just* the guns or *just* some meager personal belongings. No, he would take the whole damn thing. The plan began to hatch immediately after its conception. By the time Yule returned to his house, he knew exactly what he had to do.

In order to kill some time, he tried to read. Instead, he found himself staring at the same paragraph for several minutes without comprehending it. He put the book aside and pulled out a box with war toys. Although Yule was still distracted by the thoughts of vengeance, he was more successful at reenacting the battle of Kursk than at attempting to read. As always, he became seriously involved in following the military account of the battle, positioning the tanks and the infantry as close to reality as possible. It was almost like a game of chess. Yule often liked to assume command of the losing side, which in this specific case were the Germans. His task was to outsmart Marshall Zhukov, the man in charge of the Soviet Army during the battle. One of the main reasons for the annihilation of the best German Tiger and King Tiger tanks during the battle was their insufficient side armor, easily penetrated by the Russian anti-tank artillery. Time almost always flew quickly whenever he attempted to solve this problem. Yule looked at the clock on the kitchen wall and, sure enough, it was already five o'clock.

It was a rainy day. Had it been a few degrees colder, the rain would have definitely turned into snow, something not unusual for early April. It was a great day for a covert operation. Yule did not expect his mother home until eight, and Vladimir was most likely drinking with his buddies, other "free settlers" throughout the camp. Yule had at least three hours to implement his plan. He pulled out a black sweater and a pair of black sweatpants and put them on. His hair, however, would prove problematic. It was honey-blond with natural highlights, easily prone to reflect any light. The hair would have to be covered. After a few minutes of searching around the house and not finding anything suitable, Yule decided to use Zoya's dark gray babushka. He covered his forehead first and tied the ends behind his neck. When he looked in the mirror, he decided that he looked like a pirate. It was time to act. No better opportunity would present itself. Yule took Vladimir's screwdriver and stuck it under his shirt. He then located Zoya's lighter and put it into his pocket. He was about to take a flashlight but changed his mind when he realized that it would be an unnecessary liability; he had excellent vision in the dark, probably the result of a combination of several factors (such as living in the dark most of the year and an abundance of vitamin A, given to him by his mother).

The trip to the one-story brick building where *Kommendatura* (central command) was located took just a few minutes. Most of the floodlights were not on yet; it was too early. The only visible lights were the ones filtering through the dirty windows of the compound; they couldn't penetrate the grime that accumulated over many years. In fact, the very faint lights could not even reach the ground below. Unnoticed, Yule circled around the *Kommendatura* and emerged in its rear, where he found a storage shack containing supplies of ammonal. The front door had a large padlock on it, to secure the dangerous explosives from the prisoners or from innocent, curious bystanders. Discouraged, Yule went around the back and noticed a small *fortochka* (ventilation window) about six feet above the ground. It had no glass or any kind of frame inside of it. Yule looked around and spotted a tree stump, normally used as a wood-chopping block for the large, wood burning stove within the building. The stump was about two feet in diameter and very heavy. Yule couldn't lift it. Thus, he was forced to drag it to the side of the shack and to stand it upright. When the stump was upright against the shack and directly below the *fortochka*, he climbed on top of it and looked inside. Wooden crates were stacked up along the walls in all four corners of the shack. With an effort that taxed his strength, Yule pulled himself up and squeezed his shoulders through the tiny opening. He leaned all the way inside, folded his body at the waist, rested the palms of his hands on a crate below, and pulled his entire body through until he was able to stand on his feet. Once fully inside the shack, Yule jumped down onto the floor. It took a few seconds for his eyes to adjust to the relative darkness. As the world returned to focus, he walked around, looking for an open crate. He found one in the far corner of the room. The sign nailed onto it read *Ammonal*. Below that was an ominous *Opasno—Vzryvchatka* (Danger —Explosives). Yule reached inside and brought out a stick of ammonal with a Bickford's fuse, about a foot in length. Satisfied, he put the stick in the pocket of his sweatpants, climbed out the same way he got in, moved the stump back to its original place, and started quietly toward Semion's house. As the rain turned into a slow drizzle, the temperature dropped noticeably. Yule was afraid that if the rain turned to snow, his footprints would be easily detectable. He hurried on, refusing to give in to second guessing thoughts. He set out for vengeance, and vengeance was the only thing he would have. In fifteen minutes, he reached his destination. The house was dark and quiet. Semion was probably hunting while his wife, as far as Yule knew, got a job as a switchboard operator and often worked night shifts. Yule approached the house from the back. He carefully placed the end of the stick of ammonal on the ground, so its entire length leaned against the wall of the house. Without any doubts or second thoughts, he pulled out the lighter, shielded the wick from the rain with his free hand, and lit the fuse. As soon as the hissing sound of the burning fuse became steady, Yule took off as far as his legs would carry him. He knew that he had about thirty seconds to get away before the impending explosion. He counted as he ran and, as soon as he approached the count of thirty, stopped and hid behind the nearest tree, looking intently at the house. Nothing. Another ten seconds passed, which felt more like ten minutes in the heat of anticipation. Nothing. The world seemed eerily silent. Did the fuse fail? Yule decided to go back to the house and check the fuse. He stepped out from behind his cover and took a step toward the house. As his foot touched the ground, a blindingly bright cloud appeared behind the house, followed by a thunderous sound that shattered the surrounding silence. A plume of smoke rose above the trees, and the crackling sound of burning wood immediately followed. A few seconds later, the second explosion shook the air. The third followed almost immediately after, each explosion as loud and as violent as the one before. In an odd way, the scene looked like the First of May fireworks display. The substantial arsenal of Semion-the-Hunter went up in smoke together with his house. The air became filled with the smell of gunpowder mixed with smoke. It was the sweet smell of revenge; a gun took away the life that Chook and Cha were supposed to have, so it was ironically fitting that Semion's stockpile of guns, ammunition, and gunpowder took away everything that he had as well. The wooden house was completely engulfed in flames and, in just a few quick minutes, turned into a pile of smoldering rubble. It wasn't easy to take his eyes off the spectacularly scintillating fire, but Yule made an effort to turn around and to start his trip home.

Thankfully, Vladimir and Zoya were still out. Yule wasted no time. He immediately took off his wet clothes and hung them to dry in the corner of the mudroom, away from the entrance. He put on his usual clothes and returned to his reenactment of the Battle of Kursk as if nothing was amiss. The German army had only five hundred tanks left out of their original two thousand. The cuckoo clock in the kitchen sounded seven times. Vladimir came home at around seven fifteen. "Have you heard the explosion?" he asked. "Semion's house is completely destroyed."

"How?"

"Apparently, he kept a lot of ammunition, bullets, loose gunpowder, and so on at home. The whole thing exploded and burned the house to the ground."

"Serves him right."

Vladimir just looked at his stepson but, as usual, didn't say anything.

Zoya soon came home as well, also excited by the news of the explosion. It appeared that no one felt sorry for Semion; he wasn't well liked at the camp. It made Yule feel as if he performed a public service of sort. Vladimir was slightly drunk, not to the point of unruliness, but enough to immediately fall asleep. It was a rare occasion for Yule and his mother to be alone, to be able to have dinner together and to talk.

"You probably know by now that I am pregnant," Zoya said. "You will have a brother or a sister around July. My contract is going to end in May, and we will go home." She looked at Yule and added, "You will go home to your father; Vladimir and I will go to stay with my Aunt Sophia in the Ukrainian city of Stanislawow, next to Poland. Aunt Sophia has a large enough apartment for the two of us and the baby."

"Why can't we all go to Leningrad?"

"You already know the answer to that question. The situation with the so-called 'Jewish Doctors' Plot' is so dire that most Jewish doctors in the big cities are out of work. That includes your father. At least I have a chance to practice medicine in a smaller town, away from politics."

"I don't want to go to Leningrad without you. I don't even remember my father."

"Your father loves you, and it wasn't his fault that I took you away from him."

"It doesn't make any difference who is at fault, Mom. I still want to be with you."

Zoya sighed in resignation and said, "I didn't even notice how you grew up so fast or how you became so logical and so knowledgeable. Dr. Stein told me that he is afraid to argue with you for fear of losing an argument." She paused. "Let me think about it."

This time his flying dream started in the middle of a battlefield. He was steering a Soviet T-34 surrounded by German King Tiger tanks. There were Luftwaffe airplanes roaring overhead, spraying his tank with anti-tank machine gun bullets. The armor of the T-34 tank was thick enough to protect him and his crew from the metallic rain pounding against the side. Dr. Stein was the gunner while Professor manned the main gun up in the turret. Yule was attempting to maneuver his tank to face the exposed side of the closest King Tiger. Professor fired the main gun as the T-34 shook from the unfathomably powerful recoil; the King Tiger's turret was completely destroyed. Another German tank was fast approaching from the left, with its main gun aimed at the T-34's tracks. Yule quickly put his tank in reverse; he pulled the left steering stick all the way back and pushed the right one completely forward, effectively spinning his tank around so that the two tanks faced each other. Suddenly, the hatch on top of the King Tiger turret flew open and Semion, garbed in a German uniform, appeared through it. He was holding a stick of ammonal with its fuse burning, a deathly and knowledgeable smile on his face. Before Yule could react to this unusual threat, Semion hurled the stick right into the T-34 driver's hatch. The stick landed directly behind Yule's plywood seat and rolled all the way to the back of the tank, where it exploded in a blinding light.

The interior of the tank caught fire almost immediately. Almost simultaneously with the explosion, Professor fired his main gun and took the turret off the King Tiger, with Semion still leaning out of it. Yule rolled out through the driver's hatch and Dr. Stein followed. He grabbed Dr. Stein by his wide leather belt and both of them started rising into the smoke-filled air. The T-34 below was completely engulfed in flames; Professor didn't make it. This time around, Yule did not have to make any extra efforts; the flight was easy. He kept climbing higher and higher, until he was able to see his house. He flew toward the camp. They hovered for a while above the camp, observing all of the activities: the prisoners were getting ready for their daily trip to the goldmine, the guards were standing around, and the horses were finishing their morning feed, eating out of their hanging burlap bags. From high above, the figures were small and, on the snowy background, the entire scene resembled something out of Peter Brueghel's paintings. It was not unlike observing the activities of an ant colony, the world below insignificant yet brimming with activity. They landed safely next to Dr. Stein's house and proceeded to their respective homes.

He woke up; it was only five in the morning and still dark outside. Yule turned his head to the side and looked at his dream catcher hanging directly above his bed. It was a beautifully made round frame encased in mink fur, about six inches in diameter with long feathers hanging from it. Inside the frame, there was an elaborate pattern resembling a spider web. That was a gift from Innu, the only *Chukcha* (Eskimo) who worked at the prison camp. Innu lived about ten miles to the north, making his daily trips by skiing in the winter and riding his tiny pony during the summer. He lived alone and was charged by the Prison Camp Administration to be responsible for the firewood supply. He was of an undetermined age; his face was so beat up by the weather that he could have been anywhere between thirty and seventy years of age. He was short, stocky, and deceptively strong. Yule liked him very much. The man was quiet and dignified. His Russian was very limited; he spoke some throaty dialect, most likely a remnant of the ancient Mongolian invasion of the region. The dialect was prevalent in the basins of the Indigirka and Kolyma Rivers. Nevertheless, Yule and Innu understood each other very well. After Yule shared his flying dreams with him, Innu made a special dream catcher that could allegedly trap a bad dream before it got to Yule but let a good dream through. Innu believed that all objects have spirits, some good and some bad. *Koryaks*, who are closely related to *Chukchi*, also shared this belief. Yule kept staring at the dream catcher, trying to figure out whether the dream he just had was bad or good. He came to the conclusion that it was a good dream, turned onto his side, and fell asleep once again.

The June of 1952 was unusually warm—the temperature had reached eighty degrees Fahrenheit. The top layer of the permafrost had melted and turned into an impassable, sticky mud. Yule was wearing prison-issued, knee-high rubber boots as he headed toward Dr. Stein's hut. While passing the place where Semion's house once stood, he noticed a lot of activities: Semion, Innu, and several off duty guards were pouring liquid cement into a shallow square hole in the ground. Semion was apparently rebuilding his house, using the unusually warm weather to lay the foundation. Yule waved to Innu from the distance and passed them by without saying a word.

Dr. Stein was seated at his plywood desk, surrounded by stacks of all kinds of files and loose papers. "Good morning, my learned friend," he greeted Yule. "I've heard that you are leaving us at the end of the month."

"Yes, we are all going to Stanislawow, a small town next to the border with Poland. My grand aunt lives there. What are your plans?"

"Courtesy of your mother, I am going to take her place in August, after my term ends." Dr. Stein paused and added, "She is a saint."

"How long are you going to stay here?"

"I am going to sign a two year contract. Hopefully, things will change in Leningrad during the two years, and ultimately, I will be able to go back to practicing psychiatry. Meanwhile, let's get to chemistry; we missed a lot of lessons."

"Speaking of chemistry, Dr. Stein, my father got a job as a chemist, rather than a doctor, because nobody would employ him."

"I know, it's pretty bad in Moscow and Leningrad. That's why I am going to stay here for a while. Hopefully sanity will come back to Russia some day." Dr. Stein looked at Yule and added, "This is our last lesson, but I will see you at your house tomorrow. A few friends are also coming to say good-bye."

"Can we skip chemistry today and have a different subject?"

"Yes, of course, but why?"

"There is something Professor once said that bothers me. He is gone now, and I need to clarify one thing he said. I am sure you can do it."

"Let's have it."

"Professor had mentioned several times that Anton Chekhov used to call the Russian peasant *glupiy* (stupid). At the same time, he was hailed as an altruist and the defender of the simple folk.

"There is no contradiction, just the recognition of the limitations on the part of the Russian peasant. Russian writers traditionally expressed the conscience of their nation. Don't forget, the social responsibilities of Russian writers were not without danger."

"What kind of danger?"

"Being punished for a conflict with the authorities is not a new phenomenon. You have studied the history of Russia and surely know that throughout the last century, most of the great Russian writers ended up in serious trouble: Tolstoy was excommunicated by the Church, Dostoyevsky ended up in Siberia, and all that took place even before the revolution. Now, in the more recent years after 1917, Blok was prosecuted, Gumilev was shot, and Esenin committed suicide."

"It looks like nothing has changed since."

"But we still hope that the time will come…" Dr. Stein went silent for a moment and then continued, "when we could join the civilized world."

They spent another hour discussing the subject of human "mental laziness," as Dr. Stein characterized it. According to him, it is the instinctive reaction of the mind to protect the nervous system from mental stress. Complacency and adherence to the popular opinion of the majority was explained as a protective reaction as well, protection against an "overload," resulting in habitual and automatic actions. Dr. Stein ended the discussion with a passionate statement, one that held a very personal connotation.

"Imitating each other blindly and following superficial judgment develops a societal conformist mentality and destroys individuality as well as identity," he said and stopped abruptly.

Yule sensed the awkward tension in Dr. Stein's pause. A change of subject was in order. "I am sorry, but I have to go," said Yule. "It's time for my fighting lesson."

"What fighting lessons?"

"Shamir teaches me hand-to-hand combat. There is also a former Spetsnaz man, Vitaliy Prishchemikhin. He is also a great fighter."

"Shamir Mamboev, the Brigadier?"

"That's right, the *Bugor* (mogul). He is an incredible street fighter and a former SAMBO practitioner from Vasiliy Oschepkov's training camp."

"Who's Oschepkov?"

"He is the inventor of SAMBO and the official instructor of the Special Military Division."

"I saw Shamir ordering ZEKs around, and was wondering how he managed that—he looks so short and skinny, after all."

"Yes, he is small, but I wouldn't recommend tangling with him in a dark alley; he knows how to kill with just one blow."

"Go ahead. Get your lessons, killer."

They parted laughing.

The next day, Zoya started cooking at noon. There was a supply delivery truck that had brought some much-needed medical equipment to the camp a few days earlier. Apparently, Zoya had ordered some additional items. By five o'clock, the dining room table featured a bottle of *Sovyetskoye Shampanskoye* (Soviet Champagne), a glass jar of red caviar, and a bottle of real vodka with *Moskovskaya* written across the label. This was most definitely not the poisonous stuff Semion had once given Yule to drink. All of it must've cost a fortune, but how many times in a lifetime can one leave the Gulag? Zoya also cooked perogies with potato and meat. The *piece de resistance* was Zoya's patented Napoleon cake with her homemade custard, Yule's favorite dish by far. Dr. Stein showed up at seven, dressed in a smart, linen, gray suit and a blue shirt. He looked very handsome. Upon walking into the house, Dr. Stein solemnly handed Zoya a stunning bouquet of field flowers. In Yule's eyes, the action made him a true gentleman. About ten minutes later, the commander showed up with Zeena. Yule never saw the commander out of uniform; had he not been so fat, he would've been a good-looking man. He had big brown eyes, a well-shaped nose, and a prominent chin. Unfortunately, the rest of his body was difficult to define, other then the fact that he was *big*. Zeena was as pretty as always and looked especially delightful in her red silk dress and high-heeled shoes. The last person to show up was a male nurse—the one Yule had met on the day Professor died. His name was Yuri and he looked very young, perhaps twenty-years-old. Yuri worked very closely with Zoya, a true humanitarian who was always very loyal to her. On one occasion, he had walked ten miles in mercilessly brutal negative-fifty-degree weather across the tundra to the next *pryisk* (goldmine), simply to fetch medicine for a seriously injured prisoner.

"*Dobro pokzalovat k stolu*, welcome to the table," said Zoya. Yule was seated next to his mother; Vladimir was on the other side of her. The commander and Zeena were placed across from them, while Dr. Stein and Yuri flanked the table. The cork was popped, champagne was poured, and the commander immediately took over, pronouncing a very long (in the Russian tradition) toast, the quintessence of which was that the administration was going to lose one of the best physicians that worked in the system. After everyone took a sip of champagne, the commander looked at Dr. Stein and added, in a callous manner, his hopes that the replacement was going to be as good as the original. Dr. Stein, well-versed in the politics of the Gulag, knew better than to respond, and so the party continued. There were, of course, many more toasts; champagne and vodka began to flow like the Kolyma River itself. The mood improved greatly, especially after Zoya cranked up an old gramophone and the voice of Lydia Shulzhenko filled the room. The Commander was dancing with Zoya, Vladimir with Zeena. Yule, however, was listening to the conversation between Dr. Stein and Yuri. Dr. Stein was naturally curious about Yuri, especially about his seemingly uncanny youth. It turned out, however, that Yuri was twenty-nine-years-old and had nearly ten years of experience as a nurse, five of which were in an operating room back in the small Ukrainian town of Proskurov. The other ten were given to the Gulag. When Dr. Stein inquired after Yuri's motivation to move to the Kolyma region, Yuri responded that he wanted to earn enough money to buy a house and get married. In turn, Dr. Stein gave a brief account of how he got to Kolyma. Yuri listened politely, but he already knew the full story from Zoya. Commander joined them, wiping beads of sweat off of his forehead. The copious quantity of alcohol had apparently uninhibited him and, without his usual uniform and major's chevrons, he became just another human being festering in Siberia. He had no family and, his wife refused to join him after he had been assigned to the post of commander. She eventually divorced him and re-married. At the end of the story, Yule felt sorry for the commander. If one lesson was to be learned, it was that people are not always what they seem to be.

One day before the fast approaching departure, Zoya was asked to visit a neighboring pryisk, Yagodnoye, where the local medical team needed her consultation. Yagodnoye was a much larger village. It had a school, a theatre, and even some semblance of a three-story apartment building for the NKVD officers and their families. Yule hadn't seen another child since his arrival at the Gulag. Where he was the only child at his camp, Yagodnoye, being a much larger settlement, had more children. It was an unusual and unsettling experience for him. The first thing that Yule realized was his inability to relate to other children at all. He just couldn't find a subject to talk to them about. The most remarkable encounter he had was with a young woman by the name of Natalia. She played the accordion and told Yule that she was from Moscow. Her father was executed by the order of Stalin when she was very little. She was probably eleven or twelve years older than Yule, her head full of black, thick hair; she looked more Middle Eastern than Russian. Natalia seemed very kind and, on the whole, they had a nice chat. On the way back to their pryisk, Zoya asked if Yule knew with whom he was talking with earlier.

"Her name is Natalia," answered Yule.

"Natalia," said Zoya, "is the daughter of Stalin's executioner, Ezhov, who was responsible for murdering thousands of innocent people."

"Didn't you just say that Stalin had him executed? I am confused."

"There is no confusion. Supposedly, Stalin did not know about the atrocities committed by Ezhov. When he learned the truth, Ezhov was immediately dismissed and later shot."

"She is still nice," said Yule, keeping quiet the rest of the way.

The day of departure had finally come. Every non–prisoner living in the pryisk of Shturmovoy showed up to say good-bye to Yule's mother. Apparently, Vladimir had not made a lot of friends; only several people came to see him off. An old, beat-up truck had been loaded with the Kiselev family's belongings, and after prolonged waiving, air kisses, and promises to write, they departed and took the "Road of Bones" toward Magadan. This time around, it took only one day to get there. The next step was to cross the Sea of Japan, which separates Magadan from Port Nakhodka, near Vladivostok. Then, they were to take a small commuter plane to Yakutsk to a larger airport that could accommodate an Ilyushin passenger plane for their flight to Moscow.

The flight to Moscow was uneventful and very long, nearly twelve hours to be exact. Vladimir and Zoya conversed for most of the flight, discussing what to buy with the money they had saved. Yule was reading and could catch only small bits of the conversation, words such as house, vacation, kilim, etc., but Yule's mind was occupied with his own future encounters with other children his age. He was both happy and anxious, trying to mentally prepare himself for this new, unknown world. Dr. Stein had spent a good chunk of the last several lessons on coaching Yule how he should behave. He told Yule not to correct anyone, not to argue, and to mostly listen rather than talk. He repeated many times that if Yule were to demonstrate his academic superiority, he would be immediately ostracized and left without any new friends. "During the classes, answer only the questions asked by your teacher, no more than required. Do the tests the same way, no more and no less than needed to get a high grade. Do not show off—no one likes it. After several months, you will be able to tell who is who, and then decide with whom to share your friendship." That was Dr. Stein's very last pearl of wisdom. That particular lesson ended with Alexander Pushkin's verse:

> Accept the flattery and slander
>
> With indifference,
>
> And never argue
>
> With a fool.

The plane landed at Sheremetyevo at five o'clock in the morning. There was a huge line at the taxi stand. Moscow was waking up to face another day of uncertainty and fear; who would be the next victim, another casualty at the hands of one of the hundreds of thousands of willing informants, some looking for favor with the state and others just vengeful neighbors who would like to settle a score? On the surface, however, the city looked very presentable: the streets were being swept and sprayed by trucks equipped with big sweeping arms and powerful water jets. Yule had no memory of ever being in a big city; he was only three years old then and did not remember anything of import. Tall buildings flanked them in every direction and, in the streets and sidewalks below, automobiles and people weaved through the urban canyons like synchronized ants navigating their colonies. The city, on the surface, was like a well-oiled and constantly moving machine containing an inherent rhythm, an almost lifelike quality and character. All of it made Yule, unaccustomed to this ubiquitous clamor, slightly dizzy.

"Can we go to the Red Square to see the Lenin Mausoleum and the changing of the guards?" asked Yule.

Zoya and Vladimir looked at each other. "We should at least drop the luggage off at the railroad station; it is on the way to the Red Square," said Vladimir. Vladimir took the suitcases to check them in at the station while Zoya and Yule waited in the car. The taxi driver was an old man garbed in a worn and faded military uniform without any insignia. He was chain-smoking the entire time, coughing and wheezing between puffs. His breath contained a hint of masked alcohol odor from the night before. Zoya looked at him disapprovingly and said, "It sounds very bad."

"What are you, a doctor, *grazhdanka* (citizen)?" said the driver sarcastically.

"Yes, I am. As a matter of fact, I am a pulmonologist and can tell you that your lungs are basically shot, and if you don't get immediate help, you are going…" she paused. "You are going…" She couldn't bring herself to say it, and paused again.

"Are you trying to say that I am going to die?" The driver came to her rescue. "I know that, and I don't care. I made it so far, which is a miracle on its own, provided the shit I've been through."

"The war?"

"The war is one of many things. There are the wounds. Oh, and the extermination of my entire family by the Fascists, the lousy treatment I got when I returned home from the war, and now…" He spat through the window without finishing the sentence.

"Your entire family?" repeated Zoya in absolute disbelief.

"My wife, my sister with her husband, two of my children, and my nephew, we lived in the village of Yershovo, not far from Moscow, where we stopped the German advance. They locked dozens of captured Russian soldiers together with the civilian residents in the local church, stuffed the church with explosives, and blew it up."

Yule studied the old man and thought: *We left Kolyma thousands of miles behind us, but apparently the suffering was not endemic to the Gulag; here is a man, in the Soviet capital, itself, as miserable as a Zek back in the pryisk.* It's often difficult to determine or gauge which is worse: physical depravity or internal torment. This man, however, was subjected to both. He became so tormented that life itself had become nothing more than a burden.

Vladimir returned to the taxi, looking seemingly relieved that the huge and weighty suitcases had been left elsewhere. "Red Square," he said to the driver as he sat down in the front passenger seat, closing the door with an audible metallic *thump*. The car slowly moved and joined the weak stream of Volga, Pobeda, and Mosksvich cars and small open-bed trucks navigating the streets of Moscow. The driver went silent, continuously smoking his non-filtered cigarettes; the silence was occasionally interrupted by his very loud coughing. Vladimir glanced at the driver and muttered something that sounded like: *that's what happens to people who smoke*. He was clearly referring to the fact that Zoya also smoked.

Despite the early hours, the Red Square was full of visitors. The line to see the embalmed body of Lenin stretched way beyond the boundaries of the square. "We don't have that much time," said Zoya. "Besides, I won't be able to be on my feet for so long; you two seem to keep forgetting that I am eight months pregnant."

"Let's just see the changing of the guard," said Yule. They all agreed and moved toward the Mausoleum, a black granite structure with a sign above the entrance that boldly read *Lenin*. As soon as the huge Kremlin clock started to chime, three guards emerged from around the corner. They were moving in a precise, slow-motion goose-step, holding rifles with bayonets attached to them. Two of the guards replaced the outgoing ones that flanked both sides of the entrance. The new guards took their respective positions with the final stroke of the clock. They would remain motionless for one hour, until the next changing of the guard. It was an impressive sight, though the goose-step march reminded Yule of a German army parade he had once seen in a newsreel.

The train ride to Stanislawow was much more comfortable than Yule's previous one to Kolyma. They had a sleeping compartment all to themselves. Yule got the upper foldable cot and was able to see the changing scenery and landscapes through the window while in bed. Everything here was so different compared to the frozen expanses of Siberia. Trees with luscious leaves, tall grass, a cornucopia of flowers, wheat fields, cows, people walking across the fields without being guarded by riflemen... all of it was overwhelming, almost alien to Yule. It was as if he had taken the first steps into some strange new world, far removed from all that he had ever known. It would take some time to get used to. Some of the landscapes reminded Yule of an old Russian painting by Ivan Shishkin: *Morning in a Pine Forest*. The rhythmic and hypnotic sound of the wheels hitting the gaps between the sections of the rails had quickly put Yule to sleep.

Yule opened his eyes. A giant field stretched before him, brimming with endless rows of German soldiers marching in goose-step toward a small house where Yule, Zoya, and Vladimir were apparently hiding. There was an eerie silence in the air, violently penetrated by the thunderous sound of a thousand boots simultaneously hitting the earth. The only escape was to fly, but there were three of them and Yule didn't know whether he could carry the burden of two more people. He had to make a choice. First, however, they had to get out of the house. They climbed out through the back window and, shielded from view by the house, started their frantic run. Zoya couldn't run fast enough. The advancing German army was getting closer and closer, the thunder of their march becoming more and more audible behind them. The front row of the German army was already so close to them that Yule could smell some kind of strange herb in their breaths. He grabbed Zoya by the arm and leapt up into the air in order to facilitate the takeoff. He was only about fifteen feet above the ground when the Germans caught up with them. The soldiers in the front row raised their bayoneted rifles and started poking the deadly blades toward Yule and Zoya. Yule strained himself, tightening every muscle in his body in his attempt to go higher.

He woke up abruptly. It was early morning already. A waiter had brought them three cups of tea on a stainless steel tray. The aroma of Chinese chai filled the compartment. Zoya and Vladimir were sitting by the window, fully dressed and looking at a map of Ukraine spread out in front of them. They looked puzzled; the map must have been printed before 1940 because it displayed pre-war borders, showing Stanislawow as a Polish town. Yule looked down at the map and said, "We grabbed Eastern Poland at the same time that Hitler occupied the rest of the country. Now it's Western Ukraine." He paused and added, "You need an updated map."

Vladimir and Zoya looked up at him but didn't say anything. The waiter, who was obviously one of the Poles who came with the territory taken over by the Soviets, looked at Yule with seeming appreciation and muttered something in Polish. It sounded something like *psiakrew* (dog's blood). Whatever it meant, it didn't sound very complimentary or pleasing. After the waiter left, Vladimir looked at Yule again and this time said, "Watch what you say before strangers; you can bring all kinds of trouble on our heads. Don't you think we have had enough misery already?"

"I'll be careful," responded Yule.

Both of his mentors had warned him numerous times about the potential perils of being outspoken. Yule made a promise to himself to be more careful in the future. He also decided to get a Polish-Russian dictionary as soon as possible.

STANISLAWOW

The town was called Stanislawow because it was named after the father of Polish nobleman Andrzej Potocki, Stanislaw Potocki, around the 1660s. At that time, the area was used primarily for hunting. During his frequent strolls, Yule discovered that Stanislawow was a beautiful city, even more so in reality than in a description he had once read in a history book. The view of the Carpathian Mountains was absolutely breathtaking. From virtually any place in the city, one could see the highest peak, Gerlachovsky, towering over the surrounding Carpathians, not unlike Atlas himself standing sentinel over the Earth. The Carpathian Mountain range begins in Slovakia and extends along the Czech-Slovak border to Poland, running along the Polish border all the way to the Danube River.

The architecture of the city was unmistakably Franco-Italian. The first architect, a man from Avignon by the name of Francisco Corasini, was hired by Andrzej Potocki himself. Corasini had designed the Potocki Palace, a magnificent castle that replaced the old wooden fortress built to protect the city from Tatar invasions. As Yule wandered the streets of the city, reading the names and memorial plaques on the walls, the history lessons given to him by Professor became real in a way both vivid and more meaningful now that the words were partnered with the living imagery of history. Back in the frozen labor camp of the Gulag, all beautiful things seemed surreal, entities that were purely scholastic and remotely unattainable. Now, as if by some strange sorcery, all the theories had materialized to become a living, breathing history. Everything was so tangible, places and deeds and other images were no longer confined to the limits of imagination. Here was a plaque describing the attack by Turkish forces in 1672. The heroic defense of the city by its people had prevented the Turks from capturing and pillaging the city the way they had devastated the neighboring town of Kamenetz–Podolsk. Yule remembered the lesson about the role that Jews and Armenians had played in the Polish Renaissance of the eighteenth and nineteenth centuries. Stanislawow was once the center of Armenian culture in Poland. Yule saw evidence of that when he walked into the beautiful Cathedral of the Holy Intercession on Virmenska Street. Exploring further, he found out that the magnificent blue structure used to be an Armenian Church. The Jews were also allowed to build a Synagogue at one of the town squares.

The street led him to Sheptitsky Square, where he faced a baroque-style building with a main façade cupola and two much taller towers flanking both sides of the façade. The towers reminded Yule of the local Hutsul wooden architecture. The sign above the massive front door read *Cathedral of Holy Resurrection*. Yule recalled that around the early 1770s, Poland had been divided and Stanislawow became a part of the Austro-Hungarian Empire. It remained as such up until 1918, when the Empire collapsed. The city changed hands several times among the Western Ukrainian National Republic and Poland. Finally, during the September of 1939, the city was invaded and annexed by the Soviets, only to be invaded by the Nazis in 1941. All of these perturbations had left their marks on the city walls, monuments, various structures, and most importantly, on the memories of its inhabitants, their children, and grandchildren. The most unfortunate events had taken place in the mid 1940s, when the Soviets forced most of the Poles to leave the city and to settle throughout the so-called "Recovered Territories." No wonder the waiter on the Moscow-Stanislawow train had become so upset when Yule mentioned the old Polish border. According to a Polish-Russian dictionary that Yule had picked up in a city library a day earlier, *psiakrew* literally meant "dog's blood." Not a very flattering description of the Soviets. On the other hand, Yule thought, the Germans were much worse. In this very city there were about twenty-six thousand Jews before 1941. By 1945, however, only fifteen hundred had survived the *aktion*, mass extermination and mass starvation. He painfully came to the realization that he no longer had the unlimited resources of Professor's knowledge and his ability to analyze historic events. Yule would have liked to ask him many questions. How was it possible that the people who had given the world Beethoven, Goethe, Marx, Freud and many other outstanding minds, the nation which still had some of the oldest institutions of humanity, that people of discipline and rational thinking could get involved in burning other human beings alive, burying them alive, and purposely starving to death millions of people? Do nations have characters, just like single individuals? Or perhaps, are the single individuals responsible for shaping the characters of nations and their peoples? Do these characters combine good and evil so that the same person or the same nation could act so differently under different circumstances? Yule had gotten so engrossed in these thoughts that he hadn't noticed that he was in the middle of the street, gesticulating and talking aloud. Reality arrived in the shape of a small truck, which screeched to a stop about a foot from Yule's leg. A huge man, wearing a machine-oil stained tank top and equally stained pants, jumped out of the truck.

"Czy maly czlowiek completnie stracil swoj umysl?"

"I am sorry, I was just thinking and …"

"Czy mowisz po Polsku?"

Yule could not respond.

"I almost killed you." The driver switched to accented Russian, realizing that Yule didn't speak Polish. "Where are you going?"

"Home."

"Which street? I will take you home before you get run over."

"Plaza Mickiewicza, next to Moniuszko Theatre."

"That is smack in the center of town. How did you get there?"

"My mother got it. She is a doctor."

They drove along Halicka Street, around the *Rynek,* the City Market. Yule pointed to a nice-looking, five-story house.

"We live on the second floor, but the entrance is from the courtyard because our apartment has been divided to make a private entrance for us."

"The second floor? But there is only one person who lives on the second floor: Sophia Lewicka."

"She is my grandaunt. She has the two front rooms, and we have one large room and a small one for me."

"Now I know who your mother is. Your Aunt Sophia and I go back many years; I worked for her husband, Max. This building used to be his, but it was taken over by the Russians who left his family just the second floor. He was the owner of the largest pharmacy in town and employed fifteen people, including me. I am, or should I say, I *was*, a pharmacist too and look at me now, fixing cars. But again, people have to survive and feed the families." He sighed deeply as his huge chest rose and fell. "What is your name?"

"Yule."

"*Bardzo przyjemnie*, pleasure to meet you. My name is Marek."

On the tenth of July, Zoya gave birth to a baby boy who she named Vladimir Jr. When he would grow up, people would address him as Vladimir Vladimirovich. With his swift arrival, Yule's life had taken an unusual turn. He had become, almost overnight, a babysitter, a nursery school teacher, and a night attendant. Zoya couldn't feed little Vova, apparently, because her milk was missing some key ingredients, so they found a surrogate who had just given birth and could feed little Vova together with her own baby. Yule's responsibility was to take his half-brother to this woman four times a day and feed him out of a bottle in between, if necessary. Zoya found a job very quickly; there had been a shortage of doctors in the region. She started working just a few weeks after she gave birth. Vladimir had no such luck; his skills were not needed in this new and unfamiliar world.

In early August, an unexpected letter arrived from Leningrad. The letter heralded the arrival of Yule's father, Efim, who was to travel to Stanislawow for a brief visit in August. It stated that Efim would be in Moscow for a meeting at the Ministry of the Chemical Industry and then would take a train directly to Stanislawow. It looked, at least from the letter, like Yule's father had made significant progress in his new, non-medical career. Ordinary people don't, after all, just *go* to a ministry of anything in Moscow for a friendly meeting. Yule didn't really care one way or another. He didn't remember his father at all.

Efim arrived in mid-August. He was tall and elegant, his characteristics dominated by his dark-hair and deep blue eyes. He looked, as a matter of fact, remarkably like Dr. Stein. The resemblance granted Yule some semblance of ease and familiarity toward the stranger who was his father. Yule liked that Efim didn't kiss him or pick him up in a dramatic show of affection. Rather, he simply placed his elegant hand, with its long, aristocratic fingers, on his shoulder and said, "Hello, son."

"Hello," said Yule. He couldn't bring himself to say "father," at least not yet. And how could he? The man was, of course, his father in the most literal and biological sense. That was all relatively superficial, though. Yule had not seen his father since he was very little, and thus the man was a near stranger to him, a man only tied to him by blood rather than temperament or affinity. Efim brought with him a large Pullman suitcase, which primarily contained books for Yule as well as some gifts for Zoya. He stayed in a local hotel, just around the corner, on one of the streets leading to the *Rynek*. Surprisingly, and quite unexpectedly, Efim was very warm toward Zoya. Despite the fact that it was Zoya who had left his father quite abruptly, Yule didn't sense any animosity on his part. It had, after all, been seven years since it happened. Efim had a new wife and a stepson of Yule's age who came with the second wife.

Conversation between Yule and Efim primarily centered on Yule's inevitable return to Leningrad, a topic that was often frequented whenever the two spent time together. Yule promised to come back in a few years. At the moment, however, Zoya required his help to look after the younger brother. Vladimir was no help at all. Unemployed and miserable, he resorted to drinking heavily and getting involved in a few fights with the locals. Vladimir had been arrested a few times and, finally, left altogether. Rumor had it that he had returned to his first wife who lived in Kiev.

School had begun on the first of September, the traditional date of commencement for a school year in the Soviet Union. Yule was, according to his age alone, assigned to the fourth grade. Despite Zoya's argument that her son was ahead of his grade age by at least five years, the school principal insisted that Yule had to prove his worth. If Zoya's insistence did indeed appear to be the case, Yule would be examined in three months in order to determine his appropriate grade level.

The first class was Ukrainian Literature, succeeded immediately by Ukrainian Language. These subjects were both new and fascinating, and anything that was new and fascinating almost always interested Yule. History, math, and Russian, on the other hand, were at a most basic level and thus proved very boring. There was also a Spanish language class, taught probably to honor the Spanish Civil War in which the Soviet Army, disguised as volunteers, participated. The Soviets fought on the losing side (General Francisco Franco had triumphed over the Soviet-sanctioned Republicans), but the legend and the romanticism of that period would linger on for generations to come.

During school hours, Yule kept to himself. He had no interest in playing what he viewed as infantile games, nor did he have an interest in mauling over salacious rumors that the Physical

Education teacher had been seen making love to the teacher of Russian Literature after-hours in the courtyard. As Dr. Stein had suggested, Yule stayed away from the children. He was, however, courteous, choosing mostly to observe and to listen. The other children didn't really know what to make of Yule. Other than developing some degree of respect for his encyclopedic knowledge on most subjects, they couldn't figure him out and thus relegated themselves to being cautiously curious. Yule spent most of his off-school hours with his little brother, occasionally accompanied by his new friend Marek. The two had struck up a friendship and Marek Krasinski, who had discovered a great partner in political discourse, became a frequent visitor to the Kiselevs's apartment. Aunt Sophia also enjoyed Marek's frequent visitations in the evening and quite often spent her evenings with the two politicos.

Marek Krasinski was a descendent of Adam Stanislaw Krasinski, a bishop of the neighboring city of Kamieniec in eighteenth-century Poland. Adam Krasinski was most widely known for his promotion of religious tolerance and his adamant support of the Kosciusko Uprising. Marek spoke of his ancestor with pride and, of course, considered himself to be the living perpetuation of the torch of religious tolerance in the twentieth-century. And indeed he was. According to Yule's grandaunt, Marek hid her within his house throughout the German occupation of Stanislawow and actually saved her life during the *aktion*. Sophia's husband Max, however, wasn't so lucky. He was rounded up with the rest of the Jews who were working during the day, taken to the outskirts of town where they were made to dig their own graves, only to be methodically shot one by one. There was no love lost for the Soviets either, explained Marek. After the USSR had permanently annexed Eastern Poland, it once again became Western Ukraine. The Polish culture, its language, and its religion had been under assault ever since. Most of the Poles (those who had survived the first wave of the resettlement) were forced to leave the now Soviet territory. Marek was different. His roots, going back to the eighteenth century, and his pride did not allow him to flee.

"Someone must carry on the traditions and stand up for our culture," he explained.

"Just don't stick your neck out *that* far," Aunt Sophia used to say. "You must remember that the Russians are no longer allies of Poland—they are her occupiers."

"I know what to expect from these people, Sophia. You and I have survived the worst."

"That's true, Marek, but remember how friable you and your movement are."

"What do you mean by my movement, Sophia?"

"Didn't you tell me recently that the majority of remaining Poles don't want Russian Orthodoxy to replace their loyalty to Rome, and that you and your friends will continue to maintain your religion regardless?"

"It is hardly a movement. We just want to worship the way we used to. Instead, we have just been thrown back to the time of Kiev. The nescience with which the Russians are trying to turn back history is maddening."

Exchanges of this nature were held on a regular basis, and Yule loved them dearly.

1953 brought many ominous signs that heralded the probable genesis of a new wave of terror. Jews were arrested throughout the vast expanses of the USSR on ridiculous and wide-ranging charges. In January, *Pravda*, the official Communist Party newspaper, announced that a group of Jewish doctors had been arrested for plotting to kill some prominent members of the government. The painful memories of the 1930s suggested that there would be other victims besides the Jews, that virtually no one would be safe from the inexorable onslaught of accusation and terror. Fate, however, had very different plans. On March 2, 1953, it was announced that Stalin had had a stroke. He never regained consciousness, and three days later, his death was announced to a shocked world. Yule was genuinely surprised to see people openly crying, hugging, and consoling each other in the wake of Stalin's demise. His mind couldn't even *reconcile* the horror, the torture, and the deaths that Stalin had inflicted on his own people. How could people shed tears for this monster, especially a monster cold and dead in his grave? Was it a case of mass madness or perhaps some kind of twisted Stockholm syndrome?

Marek couldn't conceal his unequivocal joy, though he had no idea of what Stalin's death actually meant for him and the rest of the Poles who lived in the annexed territory. It was, more likely than not, a symbolic joy, a superficial happiness. Stalin was, after all, the very embodiment of evil for many, the face of terror and merciless oppression. Everyone, however, agreed on one thing: it couldn't get any worse after Stalin's timely death.

After the mass-hysteria of mourning had subsided, a collective sigh of relief could be heard from Warszawa to Magadan. Those Russians and Poles whose relatives had been sentenced to hard labor in the Gulag as *politicheskie* (political prisoners) grew hopeful of their release. The releases had indeed begun as early as June. Unfortunately, the real criminals, the murderers and thieves of the USSR, were the ones that were released first. In the August of 1953, thousands of hardcore murderers, robbers, and rapists had returned to towns and villages throughout the Soviet Union. Stanislawow had received its quota of the released thieves and burglars. Finally, at the beginning of 1954, a group of Polish political prisoners were released, some of them native Stanislawowians. Marek was understandably excited with the expectation of seeing some of his old friends return.

"I don't even know whether they are aware that their hometown is in a different country now," said Marek one evening when he had joined Aunt Sophia, Yule, and Vladimir Jr. (routinely called Vova, a diminutive from Vladimir) for dinner. They all looked at Yule for some clarification. He was very proud of the fact that he, even as an eleven-year-old child, was the de facto authority on the Gulag and the Siberian region.

"They know," said Yule. "They know absolutely everything, even before we do."

"How is that possible?" asked Aunt Sophia. "They get no newspapers and are not allowed to have a radio."

Yule looked at her with an air of superiority and said, "There is a network within each pryisk as well as networks among pryisks throughout the Kolyma Region. The guards, and especially the officers who have access to up to the minute information from Moscow, disseminate it immediately to the subordinates who, in turn, bring the news to the Zeks."

Marek looked at him doubtfully. "So they already know something that we have yet to learn?"

"Here is an example for you, Marek," said Yule. "My teacher, Dr. Stein, wrote me a letter right after Stalin died. He described what would happen in the aftermath of the death, and his information about the release of the criminals was one hundred percent correct."

"Is he a clairvoyant?"

"He is one of the most intelligent people on earth," Yule paused and added, "and, in addition to that, he is a psychopathologist who can predict the twists of the sick mind. So yes, he is a clairvoyant."

Everyone in the room laughed. "How do you know him?" asked Sophia.

"He was one of my teachers back in the pryisk."

"No wonder you grew up to be a wunderkind," remarked Marek, rolling his eyes.

Everyone laughed again. Little Vova was sitting on Yule's lap, following the flow of the conversation by moving his eyes from face to face as if watching a heated tennis match. He was almost two years old but had not yet developed a full, sentence-based speech pattern. Rather, he communicated with single words and had a problem with pronouncing the "R" sound, which is notably the most difficult sound in the Russian language. The vibrations of the tongue that are necessary to form the sound are complex and difficult to master. Thus, as a rule, "R" is the last sound developed and mastered by a Russian child. Despite being Vova's brother, Yule had developed at a much different rate. By the age of two, he spoke full sentences and, in fact, had routinely corrected his grandfather Sam. This was while he still lived in Leningrad, before his mother had whisked him away to Kolyma.

"Every child develops at a different speed," Zoya used to say. "Just give him time." She had been a wise woman in most aspects of life (especially in matters concerning others), but never in matters concerning her own affairs. As far as Vova's speech was concerned, Yule grew progressively worried. He couldn't just sit idly by and hope for the best. Thus, he started to read medical literature on the subject. There hadn't been much. He found the most relevant information in the local library, under the heading *Logopedia,* which literary means *to teach the word* (from the Latin *logos* and *pedia*). Most of the literature viewed speech as a combination of many muscular movements and, as the result of this singular point of view, speech defects were treated by overcoming the motor difficulties of articulation. Respiratory correction techniques were also recommended as part of the treatment. Although this approach was very limited and did not take into consideration the complexity of speech and its connection with human mental development, it guided Yule to undertake steps in correcting Vova's speech. Taking the muscular movement deficiency as the reason for Vova's inability to pronounce a vibrating "R," Yule took a pencil and tried to crank up little Vova's tongue using a circular motion. After dozens of attempts, Vova's tongue could produce two to three vibrations at a time. It was not enough to constitute a full-fledged "R," but it was a success nonetheless. The subsequent daily sessions had produced the desired result. In about two weeks, little Vova was imitating every passing motorcycle and every truck. There was no other sound in the apartment for the following two weeks except for a vibrating *r-r-r-r*.

The letter from Dr. Stein also stated that he was planning to return to Leningrad closer to the end of the year. Yule immediately commenced a preliminary campaign of persuading his mother to let him move to Leningrad. He argued that he was not learning anything new at school and that he was very tired of speaking Ukrainian, which was made mandatory in the schools.

"What do you mean, you are not learning anything?" said Zoya. "You speak and read both Polish and Ukrainian, and in addition, you have conquered the art of correcting speech. You taught your little brother to pronounce the letter "R" and to speak in full sentences. I don't understand you."

"I did it on my own, Mom. What I need is someone like Professor or Dr. Stein, someone to look up to and to learn from."

"They don't make them like that anymore. Most people of their caliber are still in Siberia, mostly dead. Only a few are still alive."

"I don't even have anyone to talk to here, except for Marek."

"Are you trying to insult me by implying that there is nothing to talk about with your own mother?"

"No, but you are never home, and when you are home, you spend all of your time with your new man."

"I think you are just being jealous. After all, Konstantin treats me much better than any man before."

"If he is sober, of course."

Zoya looked at him with apparent surprise. "What do you mean?"

"I saw him the other day when I was walking home from school. He couldn't even walk straight."

"He has a limp because of the combat wound he received at the end of the war."

"I can tell the difference between limping and being drunk."

"I am sure that you are mistaken."

"Mom, why are you always drawn to handsome losers? You are a great doctor and a beautiful woman. I think you deserve someone who is, at the very least, equal to you."

Zoya gave her son a long stare, hugged him, held his head on her chest for a few seconds, and let him go without saying a word. As Yule was walking out of the door she said, "Let me think about it." Almost immediately, she qualified her statement, saying, "You're moving to Leningrad."

It was finally Sunday, a day of no school and no homework for Yule. He was still living off of his Siberian schooling and thus spent most of his free time reading and listening to American Jazz on his new short wave radio. The voice of Willis Conover, along with the music he brought every night to Yule's apartment, were Yule's links to the departed Professor and the wolf pups, remnants of a very different time and place that, at times, seemed almost too surreal to have ever been true. Yule frequently thought of them and, occasionally, had seen them in his flying dreams. The dreams, not unlike his life, had changed drastically. No longer was he escaping from an unknown danger. Now, the dreams were defined more by a nostalgic revisiting of his childhood, of the serenity of the Tundra and, most of all, his four-legged, furry friends with their silky vibrissa gently brushing against his face. Sometimes, Yule was able to think so hard and fine-tune his imagination of Chook and Cha so vividly, that they would appear in his dreams with remarkable clarity. He had to, of course, fly all the way to the pryisk, but he had become so skilled in his night flying that it now took him only a few minutes to cross over the entire span of the Asian continent. Some mornings, he would wake up still feeling the prickly touch of the pups' hairs on his skin. Yule also missed being alone, to have the ability to disappear from the civilized world and to immerse himself in utter tranquility at nothing more than a whim's request. Now, however, he was eternally surrounded by people. The urban life offered no recluse or escape. People, moreover, could become very annoying, especially when he wanted nothing more than to be left alone. They spoke too much, most of the time uttering self-explanatory, mundane, and redundant things, things that were well understood without the added complexity of words and repetitions. He missed the silence, perhaps as much as he missed the pups and his mentor.

Yule reached the building where Marek lived. The building was visibly old. The top layer of stucco had crumbled, revealing the brickwork inside. The Ionic columns, however, were still intact and looked very stately. There was a small, elaborate balcony on the second floor. Two small, alabaster griffons were glaring down at Yule from the top of the balustrade, guardians and watchmen of the old, dilapidated building. Yule lifted the bronze door-knocker and released it once.

"*Kto tam jest*, who is that?" He heard Marek's voice coming from upstairs.

"Yule."

"*Wejdz na gore, drzwi sa otwarte*, come up, it's open."

Yule struggled for a moment with the enormously tall and heavy door. Once he opened it, he walked up to the second floor, where Marek was sitting at a large table full of glass jars, retorts, and Petri dishes.

"*Co nowego*, what's new?" asked Marek.

"*Nie duzo*, not much."

"*Jak radzi sobie maly*, how is the little one?"

"*Wszystko jest dobrze,* everything is fine."

Marek switched to Russian. "Your Polish is becoming more fluent."

"I read a lot. There are some authors that I could only get in Polish."

"Such as..."

"Freud, Kafka, Pasternak," Yule paused and looked at Marek.

"I see, I see."

"My passive Polish is pretty good—I can read anything now. It's my speaking that needs more work."

"I think you are progressing very nicely. How is your mother? I haven't seen her lately."

"She has a new man in her life by the name of Konstantin. I already saw him drunk once on the street. That's all she needs, one drunkard replaced by another."

"Don't be so harsh, Yule. It's not easy for a woman to be alone." Marek looked at Yule with obvious disapproval. "Describe this Konstantin to me, please."

"He is tall and slim, has dark, long hair combed backwards, and—oh, he has a limp."

"Konstantin Murawsky," said Marek without hesitation. "He is a watchmaker and recently lost his job at the Patek shop because of his drinking."

"Just as I said," Yule whispered, as if to himself. "That's all she needs, another bum."

"I heard you," said Marek.

Yule immediately changed the subject. "What is all that on your table? It looks like a chemistry laboratory."

"I am making medications for the local pharmacy as an additional income. They don't have a position for me, but from time to time they give me work. Nothing heavy, just some innocuous concoctions: tinctures, syrups, emulsions, suspensions, and vitamins."

"What do you mean by *heavy?*"

"Narcotics, sedatives, pain killers, and the like."

"How would you classify morphine?"

"It's a very potent painkiller. Why do you need to know?" Marek looked at Yule suspiciously.

"I found a syringe and a box of ampoules with morphine in our apartment."

"Did you ask your mother? Maybe she uses it when she makes house calls."

"No, I didn't, but I am very worried. She also drinks more than she used to back at the pryisk. I think it's that bum Konstantin. They drink together."

All that Marek could do was shake his head in sheer amazement. Here was this boy, a child by numerical standards, who was charged with affairs that most adults never had to deal with. The boy fought for his mother, took care of his little brother, had lived in a Gulag, witnessed the death of his beloved mentor, and was thrust into the world of adults and politics at an uncannily early stage of life, experiencing very little interaction with other children his age.

"Just don't do anything to him," said Marek. "You can inadvertently harm your mother."

"I will be careful," responded Yule. It was unclear what he meant by that, though. Marek decided to let it go.

They said their good-byes at the door. Marek stood on the front steps, observing Yule crossing the street. *What a personality*, he thought to himself. *Good looking, too*. Yule was about five feet nine inches tall, had narrow hips, long legs and a well developed chest. *I should get him involved in athletics,* thought Marek. *Maybe wrestling or boxing. It might take his mental and physical energy away from vengeance and channel it toward something productive—might.*

Marek Krasinski was a decorated Greco-Roman wrestler in his youth. He was about six feet tall and, though he had put on some extra weight recently, was an extremely powerful man, weighing close to three hundred pounds. It was truly amazing to watch how deftly he manipulated tiny pills and friable ampoules with his huge hands.

The following week heralded another devastating event into Yule's life. A recently released political prisoner had come home from the Magadan region. He was an old friend of Marek Krasinski and, having no family members who survived the war, spent much of his free time with Marek. During one of his visits to Marek's house, Yule acquainted himself with this man. His name was Cieslaw, and he had done his time in a pryisk not far from Magadan. They immediately established that Cieslaw knew of Yule's mother and her replacement, Dr. Stein. The devastating news was that Dr. Stein, while waiting for a plane in Nakhodka Bay, was murdered by a group of recently released criminals who were terrorizing the locals and preying on the newly released politicals. Apparently, his warm coat had attracted their attention. When he was found, his coat and his watch were both missing. Yule was inconsolable: first Professor and now Dr. Stein, perhaps two of the closest figures he ever had to a father, his mentors and dear friends. Both were gone. Dr. Stein was so deeply excited about the prospect of restarting his life, of continuing his research in the field that he loved dearly. Those dreams were severed as easily as they came, ripped apart by the merciless forces of the world.

Yule had fallen into the deepest state of depression for the following several weeks, refusing to eat or to leave the apartment. Marek visited him on an almost daily basis, bringing books in Polish and old photographs of his family. He had told Yule that his family was completely wiped out, his parents by the Russians in 1939 and his wife by the Germans in 1941. He encouraged Yule to be strong, even in loss.

"You have your entire life ahead of you," he said. "You are so talented and knowledgeable, and you are still a boy. I can only imagine the wonderful things you will accomplish. Snap out of your malaise; your little brother and Zoya need you."

Perhaps it was Marek's little pep talk, or maybe it was the passage of time doing what it does best, healing wounds. Regardless of the reason, Yule gradually emerged from the abyss of his depression. It wasn't a sudden snap. The process was slow, but obvious nevertheless.

A few weeks later, Yule had joined Marek at the local gym. It was located in the basement of a local *Kosciol*, Polish Catholic Church. The gym was fairly large, dominated by the two boxing rings in the center. One corner of the facility had been designated for weightlifting. Two boys in their early teens were pounding away at each other in the middle of the ring. They were wearing huge boxing gloves that looked larger than their heads.

"Why such huge gloves?" asked Yule.

"They are oversized, thirty-six-ounce training gloves. It's hard to inflict serious damage if you have them on."

"Can you box?"

"Not really. I am a wrestler." Marek looked at Yule. "I see that boxing doesn't appeal to you."

"You are right. I'd rather work with the weights."

"I wouldn't recommend it. You are too young and weightlifting could slow down your growth. Try wrestling."

"Too many rules. Rules are useless in a street-fight."

"You sound as if you have some knowledge of hand-to-hand fighting."

"I do. I took lessons from someone who was trained by Vasiliy Oschepkov."

"*The* Vasiliy Oschepkov? The inventor of SAMBO?"

"The one and only. It was a tragedy that he was executed in the Gulag. I'll tell you more later."

Visibly exhausted, the boys in the ring had finished pounding at each other. Sweat was pouring down their faces. In the unusual quiet of the moment, Yule could hear a faint sound drifting from upstairs. At first it sounded like a conversation, then it became louder and Yule could make out some Latin words spoken by a man with a very pleasant, soothing voice. The words were repeated by a chorus. Yule had no trouble understanding the words and, for just a split second, had an image of Professor teaching him Latin. A fleeting sensation of internal warmth came and left. The main line of the prayer was repeated again.

Ave Maria, gratia plena, Dominus tecum. Benedict a tu in mulieribus, et Benedictus fructus ventris tui, Iesus.

Hail Mary, full of grace, the Lord is with thee. Blessed art thou amongst women, and blessed is the fruit of thy womb, Jesus.

It was beautiful and mesmerizing. Yule wanted to hear it again.

"Can we go upstairs to see it?" asked Yule.

"This is not your religion. I am sure you know that."

"I have no religion. I am free from any beliefs. Nevertheless, I like what I just heard."

"Then you are not hopeless after all, my feisty friend. Everyone needs something or someone to believe in."

"As far as something, I believe in the power of science. I believe in myself."

"That is the arrogance of youth talking. I hope that you will never go through what we went through, when the only hope left for you is God..."

"I've seen enough to realize that no god, if indeed one existed, would've allowed for such horrors to take place."

"Read the Bible," said Marek. "The answer is in there."

They proceeded to walk up two flights of steps, up to the main floor where a small side door lead them into a very large, open space. Yule had never been inside a church before. His first impression was that he was standing within a beautiful, elaborate railroad station. The ceiling was so high that it threatened the careless observer with a loss of balance. Yule had to stop looking up in order to preserve his waning equilibrium, though it was markedly difficult to cast his eyes away from the grandeur. At about two hundred feet in height, the ceiling terminated with a dome decorated with ornate stained-glass windows that cast a resplendent mixture of subdued, warm colors onto the inside of the church. The side door, through which they had just entered, was very close to the main entrance and on the left hand side of the entrance stood a wooden platform with a large basin on top of it.

"Is this a bathroom?" asked Yule.

Marek couldn't suppress a wide smile. "Even you don't know everything. It's a baptistery. The baptism is performed by pouring water onto the head of the individual. That's what the basin is for."

"I know that, initially, Russians had been baptized in a river."

"The general idea is the same—water."

Yule stood near the front entrance, observing the vast nave full of wooden pews that stretched all the way to the carved wooden altar at the fore of the church. The three front rows of the pews were occupied by parishioners. They were all looking at a man who stood on the elevated chancel in front of the altar, facing them with folded hands and a solemn countenance. The soothing, pleasant voice that Yule heard earlier belonged to him.

Sancta Maria, Mater Dei, ora pro nobis peccatoribus, nunc et in hora mortis nostrae. Amen.

Holy Mary, Mother of God, pray for us sinners, now and at the hour of our death. Amen.

The parishioners repeated the verse in a strange monotone, half whispering and half singing. There were several more prayers that preceded the conclusion of the service. Marek and the priest apparently knew each other because, as soon as the priest walked off the chancel, he headed toward Marek, a warm smile painted across his face. As he approached them, Yule realized that the man wasn't young at all, most probably about Marek's age. He was slim and had an ascetic look to him. The look was augmented by his long, black cassock; his head, without the presence of a hat, was exposed.

"Good to see you, Marek," said the priest. "You've been neglecting your soul for a while, I see."

"You are right, Ivan," said Marek, an embarrassed, almost guilty look on his face. As if to change the subject, he turned to Yule and said, "This is our Bishop, Ivan Sleziuk. And that is my friend Yule."

"Bishop?" asked Yule in disbelief. "But I thought..." He did not finish the sentence.

"I normally don't preach," said Ivan Sleziuk, almost in answer to Yule's apparent confusion. "But we don't have our priest anymore. He has been transferred to Stryi, not far from here. But that's not the worst of it. The terrible news is that our church will be converted into an art museum."

"When did you find out?" asked Marek, a pang of disbelief infiltrating his voice.

"Last Friday. I was summoned to a meeting with the Communist Party Committee of the city. They had informed me of the decision. We have until the end of the month to move out." He paused abruptly. "Not that there is much to move anyway," he muttered bitterly. "Most of the paintings and the sculptures have been stolen, first by the Russians and then, whatever was left of them, by the Germans. We will have to relocate the pews to the Chapel and will perform the services there for the time being."

"Did they give any reason or justification for this?"

"Yes, they did give a *reason*: not enough Roman Catholics to justify such a large church. There are not so many Poles left in Stanislawow, and though some Ukrainians are Roman Catholic, the majority are Eastern Orthodox."

The Bishop studied Yule. "Is this the future of the Catholic Church, then?" he asked jokingly.

"I'm working on it," replied Marek, and the three of them shared a laugh. Yule definitely liked the Bishop, who appeared to be a man that exuded both intelligence and warmth—and he had a sense of humor.

As Yule and Marek were walking away from the church, Yule stopped suddenly and turned around to observe the massive structure from a distance. Despite its size and grandeur, the church looked very harmonious and well balanced. Influenced by the school of Classicism, the building was flanked by two small towers, one on each corner. The walls were painted a bright, almost pastel yellow with a white trim throughout. On the left side, practically adjacent to the church, stood the comparatively minuscule chapel that the bishop had mentioned earlier. It looked remarkably like a small version of the church.

"By the way," said Yule, "you addressed the bishop as Ivan. Do you know each other well?"

"Of course we do; he *is* family, after all. I was married to his sister." Marek looked critically at Yule, as if assessing the level of trust between the two of them. Clearly satisfied, he added, "Ivan spent nearly ten years in a labor camp at Vorkuta, not very far from where you were, in fact. He is one of those friends of mine recently released from the Gulag."

"What did he do to deserve ten years?"

"It's what he didn't do. He refused to cooperate with the Soviets."

"And they have allowed him to be a bishop again?"

"*They*, as you call them, have no power or jurisdiction in the Church of God. Ivan was ordained to the priesthood by Bishop Khomyshyn in 1945, and he will stay a bishop until he dies or until the Church decides otherwise."

Both walked the rest of the way in silence, digesting the news.

Marek broke the silence as they approached his home. "Come back to the church tomorrow, at around six. I will introduce you to the wrestling coach."

"Is this a particular type of wrestling?"

"Greco-Roman."

"I'll see you tomorrow, then." They parted, going their respective ways.

Yule glanced at his watch. It was time for his daily rendezvous with Willis Conover's "Jazz Hour." The reception of *Voice of America* was crystal clear because the retransmitted signal was coming from Salonika, relatively close to the Western Ukraine. Over the last few years, Yule's knowledge of jazz had improved exponentially, while his love for the art and his enjoinment of it had grown accordingly. The Modern Jazz Quartet had completely mesmerized him with its divine, almost otherworldly compositions. The sound of the vibraphone would linger in his head all day long. Sometimes, he found himself humming some of the more familiar tunes, almost unconsciously. Although the broadcast was regularly jammed, Yule had found a way to tune slightly off-station, avoiding the jamming frequency while still getting the music.

Aside from the *Voice of America*, Yule also frequented another radio broadcast, one transmitted from Warszawa. He had named it the *Window to the World.* The government-controlled press of the USSR would never inform the Soviet citizens of any world or political event that didn't portray socialism in a positive light. Some significant events were, as a consequence, completely ignored. It was the Polish broadcast from Warszawa in the June of 1956 that brought the news of the violent uprising by Polish workers in Poznan. The uprising was brutally put down by the government, but surprisingly enough, the newly appointed First Secretary of the United Workers' Party, Wladislaw Gomulka, had managed to negotiate several significant concessions from the Soviets. The most important ones involved the reduction of Soviet military presence in Poland as well as more favorable trade conditions. Once again, there was some semblance of hope for the country that had been bullied by its powerful neighbor throughout its pained existence.

29 October, 1956. Yule woke up in the middle of the night from a plangent roar coming from the outside. The entire building was vibrating, the windowpanes shaking and rattling fervently, on the verge of shattering or falling out of their frames. He jumped out of his bed and looked out the window. Tanks. Angry behemoths of metal as far as the eye could see. An endless procession of heavy T-35 tanks, medium T-34s, light SU-76s, along with a countless number of armored transporters laden with infantry. They were heading west, figured Yule, toward Poland. Although the road did split right before the Carpathians, the northern spur would take them to a relatively narrow piece of land, where Ukraine shared a mutual border with Hungary. *Is this another dream?* Yule went to the kitchen and tuned his short-wave radio to Warszawa. A news broadcast was in progress. A woman was, in a dispassionate, professional voice, telling the world that the "Thirty-eighth Soviet Army, stationed in Stanislawow, headquartered in Lviv, consisting of Seventieth Guard Hlukhiv Motor Rifle Division accompanied by Eighth Guard Tank Army under the command of General of the Army Pavlo Batov... en route to Hungarian border..." It was unclear whether the USSR was actually going to invade Hungary or merely show off the unfathomable might of the Soviet Army to stop the spread of the uprising in the streets of Budapest. There was absolutely nothing in the Soviet press or on the radio about the uprising, which was apparently a week old already. The serpentine trail of tanks continued to roll through the town until dawn. On November fourth, a thousand Soviet tanks entered Budapest and brutally suppressed the uprising that eventually became known as the "Hungarian Revolution." The Hungarians were inspired by the success of their Polish brothers just four months earlier, but the outcome was quite different. Thousands of Hungarians were slaughtered and hundreds of thousands, fearing for their lives, had to escape to Austria.

As the 1956-57 school year was drawing to an end, Yule's conviction to join his father in Leningrad was becoming stronger. Konstantin Murawsky, the perpetually drunken war veteran, had moved in with Zoya. He still drank a good deal, though not to the level of incoherence or debauchery. One evil, however, was merely replaced (or more like supplanted) by another. Yule had suspected, for quite some time, that his mother was using morphine, a habit she had probably developed back in the Gulag. Now, however, the morphine was paired with the alcohol that Konstantin had introduced into Zoya's life. So it was not that Yule was looking forward to join his father, his new wife, and her child from her first marriage; he just wanted to flee from the ever-depressing and worsening situation.

On the fifteenth of June, 1957, Yule boarded the train for Kiev where he would eventually switch to a Leningrad-bound train the following morning. The departure from Stanislawow was relatively painless. Only Zoya, along with little Vova and Marek, had accompanied him. Aunt Sophia did not feel well and had to stay home. The good-byes were brief. Little Vova couldn't grasp the significance of the event whereas Zoya was seriously crossed because of Yule's attitude toward Konstantin. Only Marek was visibly upset. He took Yule's head into his huge hands, kissed him on the forehead, turned around, and walked away, not a single word uttered. Yule thought that he saw Marek's hand going up, as if to wipe away tears, but he wasn't certain.

FAMILIARLY NEW

Efim and his new wife stood on the platform, both of them looking at the train as it pulled into the covered section of *Vitebski Vokzal*, the Vitebski Railway Station. The train pulled into a train shed, which was on the second floor of the station. Yule spotted his father from afar. The woman next to him was relatively tall and slim with a head full of thick, dark hair and a pleasant face. As soon as Yule stepped down onto the platform, Efim gave him a hug, planted a kiss on the cheek, and said, "Finally." The woman approached Yule and, looking inquisitively into his eyes, introduced herself as Dina.

"Would you like to walk? We live within a thirty-minute walking distance from here, or we could take the metro. Your choice," said Efim.

"I'd rather walk," answered Yule. "I always prefer walking. I want to look at some of the architecture, if that's fine with you."

Efim and Dina merely exchanged looks, shrugged subtly, and proceeded to depart from the station. Efim took Yule's cumbersome suitcase from his hands and walked out through the massive gate. The station looked abnormally distinguished with its huge arched window and lavish architectural embellishments. The style of it looked remarkably like Art Nouveau, or a watered down version of it at the very least. Nevertheless, it was obvious that a large portion of the décor had been removed from the facade. The building also had a pseudo-Renaissance cupola and a square clock tower that loomed above it. Yule couldn't believe, at least from the exterior, that it was a mere train station.

"I understand your curiosity," said Efim, "but I suggest taking the metro; it's new and beautiful. There is nothing like our metro in the entire world."

"That sounds like a slogan put out by the Politburo," answered Yule. "*Everything we make is the best in the world.* I've learned that since I was two years old."

Efim's immediate response was to stare at Yule, a strange concoction of amazement and frustration painted across his face.

"Perhaps, in this case, it happens to be true," he finally said. "In general, however, you should refrain from statements of this nature in public. We will discuss it at home. The Metro station is right there." Efim pointed toward a pavilion next to the rail station. A large statue of Alexander Pushkin stood next to the metro station, one arm outstretched over the pavement below and the other pressed firmly against his chest. Efim was not exaggerating; the Pushkinskaya Metro Station looked very impressive indeed, both inside and out. It had taken them several minutes to descend to the train platform via the escalator. The platform itself was *at least* one hundred fifty feet underground, and Yule had to swallow his saliva a few times in order to restore his sense of hearing. The semi-arched, ornate ceiling of the station looked as if belonged in a church or in a palace. The pure marble floor was incrusted with elaborate ornaments of numerous different shapes, sizes, and colors. Everything down in this subterranean wonderland was surreal, almost out of place. Yule could do nothing but look at his father and ask, "Why?" That was all he had said, one simple word, but Efim immediately understood what his son had meant. He was already getting used to Yule's straight-to-the point remarks and poignant inquiries.

"You see, the station, in addition to being an underground railroad hub, is also a fallout shelter, designed to protect people in case of a nuclear attack."

The train pulled up to the station, the pneumatic mechanisms hissing as the doors slid open. The car, like the station itself, was also brand-new, lustrous amid the ubiquitous grandeur. The ride was quick, two stops. They arrived at *Ploshchad Vosstania,* the Square of the Uprising. Remarkably enough, the station was even deeper than the first one, penetrating at least one hundred seventy feet underground. The style, although similar to the previous station, exhibited some differences. The arched ceiling, rather than resting atop the squire columns, sloped all the way down to the marble floor, forming an almost uninterrupted, perfect semicircle. As far as the décor went, the station was richly appointed with a plethora of statues, busts, and panoramic frescos. The exterior of the structure was a round pavilion dominated by ornate Corinthian columns and titanic arched doors. The walk from the station to the building where his father lived took approximately fifteen minutes. They walked down Vosstania Street, only to turn left onto Baskov Pereulok and to number fourteen. That was the address where Yule had spent the first few years of his life until Zoya had whisked him away all the way to Magadan. Yule had no memory of Leningrad, just a few random images, like pieces of an incoherent puzzle.

"Where is Grandma?" inquired Yule.

"She's not well. Heart problems," replied Efim. "She hardly leaves her room anymore."

Yule vividly remembered an old, daguerreotype portrait of his grandparents in their twenties. Grandma Shifra was tall with luscious dark hair, beautiful big eyes, and high, prominent cheekbones. It was hard to picture her otherwise, but Yule had already learned, sometimes painfully, that no one can escape the ravages of time, not even the most beautiful and powerful people. Time did not discriminate.

The apartment itself was on the second floor; Efim said that it was considered a high *belle-étagère*. The entrance to the apartment was located at the end of a large courtyard, used primarily for storing firewood for the wood-burning fireplaces and water heaters. The courtyard served a secondary purpose as a playground for the young residents. Although they lived in building fourteen, Baskov Pereulok, the entrance was ironically through the courtyard of building twelve. Since the apartments had been partitioned into smaller units, the former service entrances from the courtyard had become the only way to enter the back units, such as theirs.

The apartment was spacious enough with its high ceiling and large, arched windows. Although the entrance into the actual apartment was through the kitchen, an L-shaped corridor led to a very large, airy room accented by a stunning fireplace and an ornately decorated ceiling. Adjacent to this huge room was a sizable bedroom, partitioned by a huge burl-wood armoire to provide a private space for Grandma's bed. The furniture was eclectic, but each piece was an antique. The walls, covered with a vast array of oil paintings, further augmented the antiquarian decor of the apartment. One of them was set in a massive gilded frame, at least eight feet wide and six feet tall; it hung on a semicircular wall facing the windows. The painting itself depicted a famous battle at the Black Sea, waged between the Russian and the Turkish fleets. The artist's signature read *Ayvazovski*, a famous Russian marinist. The walls, visible between the paintings, were wallpapered with a light green-and-gold motif. The opulence of the interior was something unexpected, sharply contrasted with the dilapidated exterior of the building and rusty rails on the staircase.

As if sensing his son's bewilderment, Efim said, "Your grandpa Sam was an antique dealer. When the New Economic Policy had ended, and they had expropriated private capital for the second time, the contents of the store had been moved here. Most of the pieces are original, including the eighteenth-century paintings and same period furniture."

It was interesting, Yule found, that his father used *they*, just like Bishop Sleziuk did when he was explaining why his church was slated for closure. It reminded Yule of Kafka's *The Trial*, with its untouchable court and invisible law. The *they* was something tangible yet invisible, ubiquitous yet veiled.

"Why does the apartment have such an abnormal layout, with the entrance through the kitchen and a long, curved wall in the big room?" asked Yule.

"This apartment has been carved out of the entire floor that used to belong to our family. Before it happened, we were using the main entrance off the street. The courtyard backdoor entrance was reserved for domestics." Efim fell silent for a moment. "*They* told us that we had too many square meters per person and took three quarters of our apartment away. I used to ride my tricycle in the long hallway behind this wall."

Yule, sensing that his father was becoming emotional, decided to change the subject. "Where is my stepbrother?"

Dina, who was invisibly quiet thus far (probably assessing the newcomer), finally contributed an explanation of Alex's absence. "He is at a summer camp and will return in two days."

The following morning, after Efim and Dina had left for work, Yule retraced yesterday's trip from the Ploshchad Vosstania Metro to the apartment. The morning of this last day of August was pleasantly sunny and cool. The sun, rearing its golden head after a long night's slumber, had just showed up above the rooftops, illuminating the opposite side of Nevsky and bathing it in a warm, welcoming glow. Despite the shabby facades in desperate need of a paint job, the buildings looked oddly impressive.

After about a minute's walk down the Prospect, a magnificent Neo-Baroque palace materialized across the street. Four mighty Atlantes were holding up four formidable Corinthian columns in the center, while two more flanked each side of the sprawled beauty. The windows were very tall, crowned with elaborate semi-arches. The plaque on the cornerstone read *Bartolomeo Rastrelli, Architect.*

Still under the impression of the awe-inspiring palace, Yule found it exceedingly difficult to switch his gaze toward yet another palace, one designed in a Neo-Classical style, called Anichkov. It was apparently named after the Anichkov Bridge, which was located immediately next to it. Yule counted twenty-two columns, each with simple Ionic capitals. Eight of the central columns were grouped in pairs, whereas the remaining ones were spread apart from each other, eight in front of each wing of the building. The Anichkov Bridge was a masterpiece in itself, mainly due to its four sculptures of the Horse Tamers, created by Peter Klodt von Urgensburg. As Yule crossed the bridge, he noticed that the pedestal under the sculpture on the left was severely damaged. The plaque next to it said that the damage was the result of the bombardment by the Germans during the Nine-hundred-day Siege. The four bronze horses were utterly magnificent, each denoting a sense of wild power and grand proportions. The tamers themselves looked like young Greek gods. Pedestrians were passing by, traveling over the beautiful bridge. Not one of them looked or even *glanced* at the statues. *Can one become desensitized to beauty*, thought Yule? Apparently, the answer was yes. It had been said that one could get used to great ugliness as much as great beauty. Granted, it was said about people, but Yule discovered the adage to be even truer when in the context of one's surroundings.

Nevsky Prospect had not impressed Yule as being particularly sinister or having a tangible, negative energy, as Googol had suggested. Granted, decimated by starvation and many battles during the recently-ended Second World War, the population of Leningrad was at about a quarter of its prewar number. There weren't many pedestrians, and only a few cars graced the road. Although Stalin had been dead for many years, the feeling of being watched had never quite gone away. Every person who hadn't been engaged in some kind of employment or working activity would have been met with the utmost suspicion. The passersby wore busy, haggard looks on their faces, their eyes flitting neurotically toward the eyes of approaching fellow citizens in an attempt to distinguish friend from foe. A group of three men stood on the corner of Nevsky, next to an Art Nouveau building with a giant, stained-glass, arched window on its façade. The sign on the granite edifice read *gastronom*, a grocery store. All three, gloriously red-faced and loud, had their hair combed back with water. They were either already drunk or in the process of collecting funds to share a bottle of vodka, the new version of the famous *Russian Troika*. They were the protected species, the sacred cows of the Soviet Union. The drunks had always received a lot of respect in Russia, and the punishment for being drunk in public was a night in *vytrezvitel*, a sobering place usually attached to a militia station. An epidemic of drunkenness and, as a consequence, disorderly conduct had been plaguing the city; thus, a special unit of the militia had been created just to deal with the problem. After a drunk had been picked up and transported to *vytrezvitel,* he would receive a cold shower, a hospital-esque robe, and an opportunity to sleep it off in a bed with clean linens for twenty-four hours. That was the full extent of the punishment, a comfortable stay at the Hotel *Vytrezvitel.* Most recipients of this service naturally made multiple trips to the sobering facility, which as a consequence, had begun to resemble a morning social club.

Yule realized that he was hungry, so he scanned the street for a café or any other kind of eatery. Across the street from Duma, he located a small café called *Sever*, The North, located in yet another classical building. A long line of people was streaming from the inside of the semi-basement space, extending all the way down along Nevsky and almost to the next intersection. Yule approached the last person on the line, an older woman with deep, dark circles under her eyes, and asked, "Excuse me, madam, what is this line for?" The woman, clearly dumbfounded, looked at him as if she'd seen a ghost.

"Did you address me as *madam*, young man?"

"Yes, I did. What's wrong with that? You do look like a madam to me."

"No, no, there is nothing wrong. It's just that I haven't heard it the last twenty years."

"If I offended you, my sincere apologies. I couldn't force myself to address you as *grazhdanka*."

The woman's eyes widened even more. "How old are you, young man?" she asked.

"Fourteen."

The woman remained silent, observing Yule with a critical eye. After a moment's pause, she said, "You must be from Moscow."

"What makes you think that I am from Moscow?"

"Your diction and pronunciation of some words bespeak the Moscow School, and before you say anything, you should know that I am a Professor of the Russian Language at the Gerzen Pedagogical Institute."

"You mentioned a Moscow School. Is there a *Leningrad* School?"

She looked at him hesitantly, as if assessing the degree of trust she could exercise. "We call it the *Petersburg* School, the same name that it has borne since its conception in the eighteenth-century, after the Russian Language Reform."

"I've never lived in Moscow, but my first teacher was a Muscovite."

"Well then, *that* should explain your lucidly Moscow School speech pattern," she exclaimed, proud of her accurate assessment.

The line, meanwhile, was moving slowly, sucked into the building by the tantalizing scent of fresh-baked pastries. The two of them soon found themselves inside a pastry shop, located right underneath the Café *Sever*. The display was absolutely mouthwatering: Napoleon Pastries, Kiev Cakes, and sugar cones filled with custard or chocolate cream. Yule must have audibly swallowed his saliva, for the two young girls in front of him had turned their heads around and giggled. Yule's ears turned red as he averted his gaze.

"You must be hungry," said the old woman, smiling.

"Not really, it's just—it all looks so delicious."

"I'll tell you what," she said. "We will go to my apartment, which is just around the corner, and we'll have some tea with pastries. I'd like to talk with you a little more, if you don't mind. It's just that you fascinate me. It is already unusual for a fourteen year old to have old-world manners, and even more unusual for one to have the linguistic skills of a college professor."

"Thank you, madam, but I don't even know your name. Mine is Yule."

"I am Irina Alexandrovna," she said, offering Yule her small hand. She had an unexpectedly firm grip.

It was finally their turn to order and to pay. Yule attempted to give Irina Alexandrovna three rubles for the pastries he had chosen, but she refused to take the money. It was hard to tell how old she was; the dark circles under her eyes belied her age and made her appear aged. Her skin, however, was very smooth, almost aglow. As a matter of fact, Yule had noticed that many women in Leningrad had beautiful skin, most likely because of the very moist air coming from the rivers and canals, the Finnish Bay, and also the frequent rains. Londoners were also famous for their good complexions, which most likely resulted from the constant rainfall that London was so famous for. The only difference was that, unlike London with its temperate climate via the Gulf Stream, Leningrad was not subjected to the warmth of Kura Siva, while the winter temperatures could plunge below zero.

It was indeed a very short walk to Irina Alexandrovna's apartment. The six-storied building with the massive double-door entrance was the second off Nevsky Prospect. The stairs leading up to the apartment were wide and grand with their elaborate cast-iron railings. The grandeur, however, was somewhat neutralized by the strong smell of urine permeating throughout the staircase. Irina Alexandrovna looked at Yule apologetically.

"Leningrad is full of crapulous and debauched people who are used to urinating outdoors all their lives, satisfying their need to piss whenever and *wherever* it arises. Of course, there are the native ones who have long since turned to alcohol, who half the time don't even know where they are," she remarked, unlocking another massive, dark-wood door which led to her apartment.

The apartment resembled that of the Fine family, only a smaller version of it. Old-world furniture, paintings on yellow-and-gold wallpapered walls, and a round Chippendale table in the middle of the room with four tapestry-upholstered chairs all gave the apartment an air of elaborate and meticulous grandeur. Irina Alexandrovna pulled two white and dark-blue cobalt cups with saucers out of a beautiful mahogany china closet. The teapot, also a part of the white-and-blue set, looked magnificent as well. The set was handmade with the utmost artfulness; the slight asymmetry of the pattern only added to the charm of the pieces themselves. Yule must have been visibly impressed by this aesthetic display, for Irina Alexandrovna was discernibly proud. It was a feast for the eye and the palate alike.

They spent at least two hours exchanging their life stories. Irina Alexandrovna had lost her entire family, her husband, and her two sons in the war. She no longer had any relatives left; her students were her family now. She was born in Leningrad and lived in the city her entire life. She told Yule that she loved the city, even offering him a walking tour before the commencement of the college year. Yule, in turn, told her his story, mainly focusing on the two teachers who had shaped his conscience and had given him his remarkable wealth of knowledge.

"How is your mother now?" she asked.

"Not so well. Her new man drinks and, I suspect, abuses her as well."

"I think you shouldn't have left her."

"There's nothing I could've done! Every time I criticized her or said something negative, she defended the brute!" exclaimed Yule, impatience creeping into his voice.

Irina Alexandrovna just looked at Yule, then remarked that he was too young and naïve to understand the complexity of the relationship between a man and a woman. "You may be smart, Yule, but you are not yet well versed in the paradoxes and complexities of life. Only age can bring wisdom that books and mentors alone cannot instill. Don't judge your mother harshly. It looks as if life wasn't easy for her either."

Amazingly enough, Irina Alexandrovna had just repeated, almost word for word, what Marek had said back in Stanislawow. Yule thought of Marek and immediately realized that he missed him. Marek was probably the only friend he had. Yule always thought that Zoya, his own mother, was his best friend. She *was* his best friend, until her addiction had changed the equation. The surreptitious creature that called himself Konstantin was the new variable. It was getting late, and the time of departure was drawing near. "Come visit me again sometime," said Irina Alexandrovna. "My students frequent my apartment all the time." They said their good-byes to each other. Yule promised to return for the city tour as soon as he could. He stepped out of the apartment complex and took another look at the clock tower. It was still too early to go home, not even two o'clock in the afternoon, so he decided to continue his walk on Nevsky.

The sign above the next bridge directly ahead of him read *Canal Griboyedova*. He looked to the right and saw a church overlooking the right side of the canal. It looked as if the church was sitting atop of the canal and that the street somehow weaved around it. The onion cupolas had apparently lost their gold-plated glory some time ago; they were almost black, sparsely spangled with remnants of dull gold and broken pieces of blue ceramic. The church looked unmistakably medieval Russian and reminded Yule of St. Basil's Cathedral that he saw back in Moscow during his brief visit on the way to Stanislawow. The church looked somewhat out of place amidst the predominantly Baroque and Neoclassical architecture that was ubiquitous in the area. Despite the obvious state of disrepair and the visible damage to its exterior, it still looked impressive. Yule walked over to the main entrance, his curiosity again getting the better of him. The bronze plaque, darkened by years of neglect, read *Church of the Resurrection of Jesus Christ.* The massive door handles were chained together, bound by a huge, rusty padlock that left no doubt that the door had not been used in years. Yule walked around to the side door, hoping to catch a glimpse of the interior. Suddenly, he was accosted by a burly man who, despite the warm weather, wore a fur hat. "What do you need?" the man barked, looking at Yule with suspicion.

"I just want to see the inside of this beautiful church."

The man looked at Yule as if he had just fallen off of the moon. "There is no *church* inside. It's a warehouse for the opera theater. Besides, everything has been stolen from the inside after the Revolution."

"It's a shame," said Yule as he walked away, leaving the man wondering whether he had meant the ransacking of the church or the Revolution itself.

Alex, Yule's new stepbrother, had arrived from his summer camp the very next day. He was, in sum, big, hairy, and had his mother's eyes. The thought that those eyes somewhat resembled the pensive eyes of a chewing cow forced Yule to conceal his mirth, lest he somehow upset his stepbrother. After a brief exchange of niceties, Yule, to his utmost disappointment, realized that Alex hardly read any books and shared virtually no interests with him. As a matter of fact, it appeared as if Alex had *no* interests to begin with. Alex had most likely sensed Yule's disappointment and, as a consequence, had distanced himself from Yule, a reticence that would last for years to come. The dislike, although mutual, had never manifested itself into a conflict. "Civilized neutrality" was perhaps the best description of their relationship.

There was only one day left until the beginning of the school year. Yule's father had taken his sealed transcript to school No. 194 on Nekrasov Street, in order to ensure that Yule would be admitted into the school. His father, however, came back rather hastily and noticeably irate.

"*Why* didn't you tell me that all your papers list you as Kiselev? Needless to say, that is *not* your name. Now I have to prove to the school administrators that you are my son," he said, anger prevalent in his voice.

Yule could not understand the irrational frustration. "It's very easy to do. Just show them my birth certificate and your passport."

"I know what to do," Yule's father grumbled back. "It's the embarrassment I'm talking about."

Incredulous, Yule could not think of a response to his father's damaged hubris. Instead, he merely shrugged his shoulders and left the apartment, an action that he knew would further augment his father's anger. The relationship with his father was, for some reason, turning sour. Whether it was linked with the return of his second son, or merely an impatience with Yule's matter-of-fact, independent disposition, Yule could not accurately diagnose the source of the growing aloofness between himself and his father. Regardless of the cause, it made Yule yearn for someone to talk to. He recalled days dominated by long conversations with Marek, with his mentors, even with his mother. Perhaps this yearning was what drove him toward Nevsky. In twenty minutes he found himself standing next to Irina Alexandrovna's building.

She opened the door right in the same instant that Yule raised his fist to knock.

"I saw you walking into the building," she explained. "My desk faces the window overlooking *Malaya Konyushenaya* Street. Please, come in and make yourself comfortable."

She stepped aside, letting him through, and locked the heavy door by throwing a substantial deadbolt lock into the reinforced doorframe. The heavy contraption looked almost identical to the one on Yule's apartment door. His grandfather, who had stayed in the apartment during the Siege, had the door reinforced with sheet metal and an elaborate locking mechanism. Grandpa Sam had died when Yule was in Siberia. He was only fifty-two years old when he passed away, but he had survived nine hundred days of the Siege. Not only did he survive, but he had also helped hundreds of people make it through the starvation and the bitter cold by sharing his food and firewood. He was a wealthy man when the war started but, upon its end, had very little left after depleting his assets on systematically saving the people of Leningrad.

"Would you like a sugar cone pastry? I have a chocolate one left," Irina Alexandrovna asked.

"No, thank you. I don't want to ruin my appetite. We are going to have a family dinner tonight," responded Yule. "Can we instead have that little tour of the city that you promised?"

"Yes, of course! What are you particularly interested in?"

"Well, I like the churches… the variety of their architectural styles fascinates me."

"Good choice, and we don't even have to go very far. There's a Roman Catholic Church between my street and *Bolshaya Konyushenaya*."

And so, they walked around the block in search of the church. As soon as they made a turn, there was a setback and an open space between two buildings that Yule must've missed in his prior exploration of the area. Within this open courtyard stood a simplified copy of the Polish Church in Stanislawow, one without the side towers. Everything else, however, was identical, from the yellow and white coloring to the central dome and huge arches supported by Corinthian columns.

"This is the Church of Saint Catherine of Alexandria," said Irina Alexandrovna. "The last Polish king, Stanislaw August Poniatowski, is buried here."

They walked closer to the main entrance. The sign above the massive wooden door read: Domus Mea Domus Orationis, *My House Shall Be Called a House of Prayer.*

"The structure almost looks unfinished without the corner towers, a little unbalanced even," remarked Yule.

"You, young man, have a very good sense of style—quite unusual for a fifteen-year-old, but you are right. The project was done by three different architects who succeeded each other and made all kinds of changes and alterations. Pietro Trezini had started the project by choosing this particular spot, Vallen-Delamot had realized most of it, and Antonio Rinaldi had finished its simplified version, the one without the towers."

"Are there any more interesting churches around this area?" asked Yule.

"Of course. There's actually an Armenian one nearby. Would you like to see it?"

"I would love to."

After only a very short walk, a similar setback revealed a smaller version of the Armenian Church that Yule had seen back in Stanislawow. The church, predominantly white and sky-blue, was topped with a stunning and vibrant green dome. A blue portico, supported by four round columns that towered above the main entrance, had a remarkably lifelike bas-relief depicting Catholicos Grigor baptizing Tsar Trdat, who had made Armenia a Catholic nation.

"Why do you like Churches so much?" asked Irina Alexandrovna. "As far as I recall, you have been brought up as an atheist."

"I don't believe in God, if that is what you are asking. My interest in Churches is not really spiritual; it's more aesthetic in nature. Professor also once told me that you can learn much about the history of the world and the various forms of the arts that emerged from religions by just observing them. That, and I'm also fascinated by church architecture and design."

"I see. Well in that case, we will continue our tour, but not today. I'm expecting some visitors rather soon. Incidentally, do you have a telephone in your apartment?"

They exchanged their numbers and said their good-byes.

REGIONAL 194

The first of September had finally arrived, thus heralding the commencement of a new school year. Yule took a seat at one of the desks in the last row. Each desk was built to accommodate two students. Yule's neighbor already sat at the desk, a student who had a mane of red hair, a freckled face, and big brown and intelligent eyes. His name, Yule later discovered, was Genna and, as a matter of sheer coincidence, he lived on the same exact street that Yule occupied. Genna, at his ripe age of fourteen, was already a grandmaster in chess, no petty accomplishment for a person so young. The mutual liking was evident from the beginning. Yule took a sweeping glance at the other students present in the classroom, quickly realizing that there were no more than twenty students in his entire grade. The birth rate, Yule later found, was uncannily low during the war years, especially in Leningrad during the siege.

Once the physics teacher, Betty Nikolayevna (who was also their grade advisor), had walked into the room, the ambient chatter quickly died down. She was a relatively small Mediterranean-looking woman, most likely somewhere in her late thirties. She set her books down on her desk with a barely audible thump and immediately looked toward the back of the room, seemingly directly at Yule.

"We have a new pupil," she said, not unkindly. "His name is Yule Fine and he grew up in Siberia." Almost immediately, all heads turned to the back of the room. Much to his chagrin, the entire class was looking right at him. "Do you have any questions for Yule?" continued Betty Nikolayevna.

"I have a question," said a boy with a bony face, deep-set, minuscule eyes, and a military-style crewcut. "What kind of name is *Yule*?"

"It's short for Yulee."

A mischievous-looking boy sitting immediately next to the one with the bony face then proceeded to raise his hand, seemingly emboldened by his comrade's bravery.

"Boris has a question," said Betty Nikolayevna.

"Is it really so cold in Siberia that when you spit it gets frozen before it hits the ground or when you piss the urine freezes and becomes a rainbow?"

Yule paused before he answered, simply staring at Boris in dumbfounded amazement. "Yes, it's that cold. It's also very dangerous for people with small brains, because the empty space in their heads becomes frozen and is known to explode."

There was the briefest of silences, then an explosion of mirth and laughter that penetrated it. Boris started to laugh too, only to realize that the rest of the class was looking directly at him. Then his laughter left just as quickly as it came, replaced by a look that resembled some strange mixture of embarrassment and fury. It appeared, after all, that Yule had hit the bulls-eye. The boy obviously had a reputation. He continued to stare at Yule and proceeded to run his hand sideways across his neck, as if he was cutting his throat. Betty Nikolayevna quickly intervened, ending the rather unorthodox introduction and moving on to the next item on the list, specifically, inquiring into how everyone had spent their summer recess.

"Watch out," whispered Genna. "That one is from a family of criminals; his father is in prison."

A short break was announced after the first forty-five minutes of the lecture, during which most of the boys left for the bathroom in order to smoke cigarettes. Although Yule didn't smoke, he accompanied Genna. Boris, of course, was already there, angrily pacing between the stalls. He accosted Yule as soon as he walked in. Yule sized up the brute and realized that they were roughly the same height. Boris, however, was much heavier.

"Who do you think you are, disgracing me in front of the class like that?" he demanded angrily.

"Is that a rhetorical question?" asked Yule.

"*What*?" Boris's face turned a whole new shade of red; the word "rhetorical" was obviously unfamiliar to him. To avoid any further humiliation, Boris took a wild, savage swing, the destination of his fist indubitably marked toward Yule's head. Boris, however, was slow. Yule followed the trajectory of the oncoming fist and stepped aside at the very last moment. The fist flew by and the inertia carried the attacker's body past Yule who spun around and faced his assailant's backside. Now behind the confounded Boris, Yule put his foot behind the ogre's knee and pressed his calves down, forcing Boris to kneel down on the cold, dirty bathroom floor. The scene was almost comical, with the attacker on his knees, unable to move or to get up.

"I don't want to hurt you," said Yule calmly.

Boris mumbled something unintelligibly, and Yule finally released him, his eyes unwaveringly fixated onto his attacker the whole time. When Boris finally stood up, he faced Yule, further angered by his calm demeanor. Boris's face presented quite the contrast, burning and full of hatred, anger, and humiliation. The silence was almost deafening, the only audible sound coming from an autumn fly that was buzzing by the grimy bathroom window. After a few seconds, Boris turned around and walked away, ending the brief confrontation.

"It's not over for you, at least not yet," said Genna, pointing at the assailant with his eyes. "They are two years older than you, and both of them play ice hockey for the adult city team."

"Am I supposed to be impressed?"

"No, but you shouldn't let your hubris get the better of you in this case. They're both very strong boys, regardless of what happened in that bathroom. Even the teachers are afraid of them. I'd be more worried about Boris's buddy though. His name is Yuri Scheglov and he is dangerous."

Yule dismissed the forebodings of his friend with a faint smile. "The strength of character is more important, at least more important than a reputation."

"Not if you get hacked with a hockey stick over your head." He paused, then quickly added, "From behind."

They looked at each other and could not restrain a quick outburst of laughter.

"Do you play chess?" asked Genna.

"A little."

Genna reached into his briefcase and produced from it a travel-sized chess set. The figures had little pegs on the bottom for insertion into the holes in the middle of the checkered squares. It had taken Genna a grand total of fifteen minutes to destroy Yule's defenses and to announce check-mate.

"That wasn't too bad," praised Genna, responding to Yule's dismayed countenance. "It usually takes me no more than five minutes with the other classmates."

"Is it true that you are a grandmaster?"

"No, not yet at least. I need to first win a few more national tournaments."

The clattering of the bell filled the classroom, finally announcing the conclusion of the first school day. Yule and Genna walked home together.

"See! You're already somewhat of a celebrity in the school," said Genna, smiling.

"And why is that?"

As if in response to his question, two rather pretty girls from the senior grade passed them by. One of the girls pointed at Yule and whispered something in her companion's ear, which elicited a giggle from both. Yule could not conceal his slight blush.

"*That's* why," said Genna, pointing at the girls. "Boris and Yuri are known bullies, perhaps the most dangerous in this school, and you singlehandedly humiliated one of them."

Yule's building was closer to the school and there they said their good-byes. "What are you doing tonight?" asked Genna. "Come to my place, I'll be home all night. Apartment three on the first floor."

"*Poka,* see you soon."

September days were very short in Leningrad, so short that by six p.m., the world was enveloped in complete and utter darkness. At around seven p.m., after the family dinner had concluded, Yule headed out to visit Genna. In order to get to the street, he had to first go through two courtyards interconnected by monumental arches that ran the lengths of the buildings and formed quasi-tunnels that housed all sorts of containers filled to their brims with rubbish and construction debris. Other than the subdued lights permeating out of the grimy apartment windows at both ends of those passages, there was no lighting whatsoever. As soon as Yule made his first few steps into the first of the arches, two shadows had seemingly detached and materialized from the wall ahead, moving toward him at a ponderous pace. *Here we go*, thought Yule, instinctively glancing back for a possible retreat route. Alas, it was too late for any thoughts of escape; two more silhouettes materialized at the entrance behind him. A quick scan revealed a small space between two dumpsters that both protruded from the wall, creating something that resembled a three-sided box with space enough for one person. Yule stepped into the space and turned around to face his assailants, a strategic move that would shield him from any sucker punches, with the two dumpsters protecting his flanks. Although he couldn't exactly see the faces, two of the four silhouettes looked particularly familiar. The other two were tall and lanky, most likely hockey players as well. Yule couldn't help but remember the prophetic words of Genna back at the school.

The first punch was aimed squarely at Yule's face. It was an easy, hesitant one that Yule managed to dodge by bending his knees and ducking slightly. There was a dull thump above Yule's head, right where the fist met the solid brick wall. The ensuing scream could put a wounded wildebeest to shame. The air became filled with the sweet, sophisticated music of foul language, which eventually amounted to a discourse about the despicable things that would be done to Yule's mother and his non-existent sister.

"Get out of your hiding and fight like a man," screamed one of the lanky ones.

"Real men fight one on one," responded Yule, "but you are obviously not one of them."

"Get out of your hole, then. I'll fight you one on one," said the lanky one.

Yule, rather foolishly, stepped out of his little niche. The attacker, who was about five inches taller than Yule, had assumed a boxing stance and started bouncing side to side, all pomp and no substance with his petty fighter's dance. A faint sliver of light from the nearest window reflected off a shiny object in his mouth. *A boxer with a golden tooth*, thought Yule as he traced the progress of the bouncing simpleton with his eyes. He faked a quick jab with his left hand and, while the "boxer" reacted by raising his hands in defense, kicked him in the groin with his right foot. The heavyweight champion of the gutters doubled over in pain, which was naturally followed by a colorful cacophony of even more descriptions of the despicable acts to be done to Yule's mother that rang through the darkness. Next, however, came a sucker punch from behind. An already familiar wild swing caught Yule's mouth. His lips swelled up almost instantaneously as blood filled his mouth. He spat it out, turned around and, with disgust and fiery anger painted across his face, yelled, "You fight like a filthy vermin!" But he only saw the back of his assailant, who was bolting toward the street, most likely content with his dirty deed. Yule's upper lip was split in the middle, and the corner of one of his front teeth was chipped. A brass knuckle had clearly been used in the assault. Yule's first intention was to turn around and go home, but when he thought of the expression on his stepmother's face, as well as the inevitable drama and endless questions that would ensue, his decision was to stick with the original plan and to see Genna.

That plan, however, was quickly disrupted. As soon as Yule had turned the corner into the next courtyard of building twelve, he bumped into a woman who was apparently dumping some construction debris into one of the dumpsters. She was in her thirties, with light brown hair tied into a neat bun. She had kind, tired eyes.

"*Ostorozhno*," careful, she said. "There are nails in these planks." Then she looked at Yule's face and gasped. "My God, you are bleeding! Who did this to you? The boys who just ran out of here?"

Yule nodded in silence.

"Come with me," she said as she put her hand on his back, guiding him into the building's entrance. She lived on the fifth floor in an apartment that was subdivided for three families who shared one bathroom and one kitchen. She opened the door into her room, which was surprisingly spacious, and told Yule to take a seat on the couch. A little boy with blond hair and blue eyes was playing with some toys, apparently the woman's son as the resemblance was obvious. He showed no interest in the visitor, only briefly glancing at Yule before returning to his toys. The woman came back with a small bowl of hot water and a towel. She dipped the corner of the towel into the water and wiped some of the blood off of Yule's face and neck. The sensation of the hot towel on the lips was very soothing.

"Do you live in the buildings?" she asked.

"Yes, in the fourteenth."

"Which apartment?" she asked. "I haven't seen you around here before."

"Seventeen."

"Really. And what's your name?"

"Yule."

"*My God!*" she exclaimed again. "You must be Zoya's boy!"

Now it was Yule's turn to be surprised. "You knew my mother?"

"Of course I knew your mother. Everyone did. She was beautiful and outgoing and had a lot of friends. I remember the ensuing scandal that day when she practically kidnapped you from your apartment. Your grandma, Shifra, who loved you very much, wouldn't let you go, so your mother was compelled to take you away." There was a silence in the room, interrupted occasionally by the blond boy, who was imitating the sound of a car engine shifting gears.

"How is Zoya? I haven't heard anything about her in ages."

"She's fine. She's a doctor in Stanislawow, a small town in the Western Ukraine."

"Well then, the next time that you're in touch with her, tell her that Maria Ivanovna Putina says hello."

The boy had finally pulled himself away from his toys and looked at Yule, sizing him up for a few seconds in silence.

"Do you know how to fight?" the little boy asked.

"A little."

"I want to learn how to fight," the boy said.

"What's your name?" asked Yule.

"Vladimir."

"I have a brother whose name is also Vladimir, but I call him Vova. Is that what the boys call you?"

"No. The boys call me Putka."

"Why?"

"Because my name is Putin."

"He picks fights in the courtyard all the time," interjected Maria Ivanovna, "and always gets into some sort of trouble. He's only turning six this November, but most of the kids on our street are older and stronger."

"Well, he is right, then. He needs to learn how to defend himself."

Maria considered the proposition for a moment. "Fine. But please don't speak of this to his father, or all of us will be in big trouble. He doesn't want our son to be a fighter. Speaking of him, he should be coming back any minute now. Would you like to stay and have a meal with us? Vladimir also knew your mother pretty well."

"No, thank you very much, but I promised a friend that I would visit him. I'm already late as it is. But again, thank you so much for everything that you've done."

Genna resided in a four-story apartment building that, without a doubt, used to be some family's wealthy residence before the Revolution. There were elaborate balconies on the upper floors, supported by all kinds of mythological characters and creatures. Granite Doric semi-columns flanked the entrance. The building was now used as a place for communal living, where the strict rule of "one room per family" applied. A bathroom and a kitchen on each floor were shared by the tenants. The telephone in the hallway was also communal property. The door leading into the first floor apartment had five doorbells attached to it, one for each family.

Genna opened the door as Yule rang one of the bells. "Looking good," he said, studying Yule's battered face. "Didn't I warn you that these guys are mendacious bastards? Go and wash the blood off of your face." He pointed to the bathroom at the end of the long, narrow hallway.

There was an old, dilapidated mirror in the bathroom, yellow with grime and age. Yule looked into it and was surprised at what he saw staring back at him. His lips were split down the middle and were twice their normal size. The chipped tooth sent a shot of pain into his head whenever it interacted with the cold air. Yule was forced to keep his mouth closed, breathing through his nose in order to mitigate the pain that resulted from his abnormally sensitive tooth.

"There were four of them," said Yule. "Yuri and Boris were among them, though they probably think I don't know that. The other two were tall and lanky guys, one of them with a golden tooth."

Genna gave him a strange look and said, "You just took on almost the entire junior hockey team of the Army Sports Club. Looks like they won."

"Wait just a few more hours. The casualties will be better seen in the morning," responded Yule. "Can we have a game of chess? It hurts to talk."

It was the third of September. The first class of the day was French, taught by the beautiful Sophia Arnoldovna. The pupils, out of common courtesy and respect, had to stand up whenever a teacher walked into the classroom. They did so without hesitation when she walked in. She was in her mid-thirties, wore high heels, a knee-length skirt, and had her hair in a thick, braided tail that reached down almost all the way to her slender waist. The boys collectively held their breaths. Her first name implied a foreign origin, perhaps even French. That only added to her allure.

"Bonjour, asseyez-vous, s'il vous plait," said she in her melodic voice. "Beinvenue a la huitieme annee."

"What happened to you, Yuri?" asked Sophia Arnoldovna, pointing at Yuri Scheglov's arm, encased in a hard-shell cast from shoulder to the fingertips.

"I fell on the ice and broke my arm while playing hockey," responded Yuri. The tips of his ears, however, betrayed the lie as they turned red. The humiliation was too much for him to handle, as somehow everyone already knew of last night's ambush. The sight of the huge, hard-shell cast provided further evidence of the confrontation, thereby fueling even more speculation and excitement.

"Is that your handy-work?" asked Genna, looking at Yule.

"No, he did it to himself," said Yule. It was, after all, half-true. Genna, however, took it as a hilarious joke and rolled under his desk in laughter.

"What's going on over there?" asked the teacher.

"Genna is crying because he is devastated by the terrible news," said Yule, pointing at Yuri Scheglov's broken arm. The class laughed again, even louder this time. Boris and Yuri looked at each other. The humiliation was impossible to bear for them. In an instant, Boris jumped off of his seat and covered the distance between himself and Yule in one giant leap. Startled by Boris's audacity, Yule had virtually no time to stand up. Instead, from his sitting position, he lunged his head forward, ramming Boris hard in the stomach while he was still airborne. The blow completely knocked the wind out of Boris, who fell backwards, unable to breathe. Yule simply stood up and returned to his seat, calmly looking at Boris who was still gasping for air. Genna emerged from under the desk.

"Now you see what I mean," said Yule. "They really *do* do it to themselves." Boris finally started to breathe again and stood up, slightly disoriented.

Sophia Arnoldovna, shocked at first, took control over the situation. "Both of you—*out*," she said firmly. Boris, it seemed, was glad be excused from the classroom. Yule, on the other hand, was disappointed with the injustice of it all. He realized, however, that she was reacting to the end result, not to its cause. Boris had already walked out first and disappeared around the corner into a dimly lit corridor. Yule went outside to take a walk around the block. He had about thirty minutes to kill.

When Yule returned to the classroom, there was a message from the principle on his desk demanding that he go to her office immediately. The principal's office was on the first floor. Yuri and Boris were already there, sitting on a wooden bench along the wall. It was quite obvious that they were already accustomed to and familiar with the upcoming procedure. The school principle was a classic, almost textbook dried up spinster. She was tall and wore her gray hair in a neat, tight bun. Her name was Zinaida Vasilyevna, also lovingly referred to as *Vobla,* Dried Salty Fish.

"Sit down," she said firmly, looking at Yule's cut lips and pointing at the bench. Yule had no choice but to sit next to Boris, who instinctively moved away to allow Yule more space than he actually needed.

"What happened to your lips?" she continued. It was a crucial moment for all three of them, because participation in a fight would most probably result in an expulsion from school. That would, in turn, automatically exclude Yuri and Boris from the hockey team. Yule was pretty sure that they would deny everything had he told the truth.

"I fell off my bike," said Yule.

"A fateful chain of events indeed," said Vobla sarcastically and with a crooked smile. It was obvious that she wasn't buying the story. "One fell on ice, another one fell off his bike, and yet the third slipped and fell in the classroom," she continued. Yule's assumption was confirmed on the spot—they did indeed deny everything.

"All of you are free to go," she said. "But I'll be watching you."

In the corridor, the two hockey players stopped and turned toward Yule.

"Come on, you surely cannot be that stupid to have at it here," said Yule, throwing his head toward the principal's office. "Let's take this outside."

"No, no, no," whispered Yuri, glancing neurotically at the principal's door. "We just want to thank you, for not squealing on us."

"I don't squeal on anyone," answered Yule as he walked out the front door. He didn't feel like returning back to the classroom. One thing, however, he knew for sure—nobody would ever again dare touch him within or outside of the school, at least within the Dzherjinsky Region, which encompassed about thirty city blocks.

It was the fifteenth of September when the letter from Marek had arrived. It was written in Polish, most likely because Marek wanted to keep its contents confidential.

Moj braciszek, wszyscy tesknimy za toba, zwlaszcza Vova, My little brother, everyone misses you, especially Vova.

That was how the letter commenced. The rest, however, was rather disturbing. Konstantin was drinking often and, while drunk, became very abusive. Vova now lived with his grand-aunt Sophia. Marek apparently had a mild heart attack but was feeling fine now. In sum, the letter was asking Yule to return to Stanislawow as soon as possible, even if just for a short visit. Unfortunately, neither Marek nor Zoya had a telephone, so as a consequence, their exchanges were limited to writing. Yule sat at the dining room table, pen and paper on hand, and began his letter: *Dorogoy Marek*, he started to write in Russian, thought for a second, and switched to Polish. He knew that his friend would be ecstatic to receive a letter written in the native language he was so proud of.

Moj drogi Marek, I wish I were there to take care of things. Yule had to explain that he had virtually no means of his own to travel nor could he work, because he was only fourteen. The next visit to Stanislawow would be in summer, and then he could stay there for two months.

The school year dragged on for what seemed like an eternity. Yule was merely an average student. He didn't study at all, just showed up for the finals and did them, regardless of the subject or the teacher. For the most part, Yule depended on the wealth of knowledge given to him by his Gulag professors. He didn't make any close friends either, with the sole exception of Genna. He did, however, enjoy the respect of his peers, which was enough for Yule, as he never really sought anyone's close company at the school in the first place. He had found most of his classmates puerile, ignorant, or both. Perhaps it was just arrogance or condescension on Yule's part, but the more probable explanation for his seemingly unsociable behavior was the fact that he practically grew up with intellectuals and never had a childhood in the first place.

12 June. The train carrying Yule finally departed from the Vitebski Station. Its ultimate destination was Kiev, and from there, Yule would board another train that would head to Stanislawow. Equipped with an excellent book, Yule hadn't even noticed how he made the substantial trip to Kiev. The book was about one of Yule's heroes, specifically about Tadeusz Kosciuszko, who was born in Poland. Now, however, his birthplace lies in the little village of Merezsowszczyzna, located in Belarus. Perhaps the most fascinating thing about reading the book was the realization that history does indeed continue to repeat itself. Millions of people had lost their birthplaces and found themselves belonging to a different country virtually overnight, to a culture almost alien to them. Marek was a perfect modern example of it, along with several million other Poles.

At two o'clock in the afternoon, the train had pulled into the Stanislawow Railroad Station. Yule immediately spotted his little brother, who was accompanied by Aunt Sophia. There was, however, no sign of his mother or of Marek. Both surely knew of his arrival so their absence was rather disconcerting. Yule quickly observed that little Vova had grown a few inches since last he saw him. He also had a short haircut and, to Yule's amusement, looked somewhat like Putka, with whom Yule had been recently acquainted. They were, after all, of the same age, born just three months apart. Vova spotted Yule just as his foot made contact with the concrete platform. With a start, his little brother broke away from his aunt and started running toward Yule as fast as his little legs could carry him. Vova was screaming with excitement as he leapt into the air, nearly knocking Yule off of his feet upon impact. Yule caught his little brother by the armpits and, much to little Vova's delight, threw the little body up into the air, caught him again, and eased him down onto the platform. Tears of happiness and excitement, mixed with discharge from his running nose, covered most of his face. Neither of them paid any attention to it. They were just happy to be together again.

After the brief explosion of joy, Aunt Sophia gave Yule a kiss on his cheek and pulled away in an unusually abrupt manner. Yule looked her in the face and noticed that she was hiding her normally vivacious and risible eyes from him. He realized that something was definitely amiss.

"Where is mama?" asked Yule as they were walking toward the exit, fearful of the response.

"She is not feeling well."

"What about Marek?"

Aunt Sophia looked at Yule, her eyes teary. "He is in the hospital—another heart attack, this time a very serious one."

Yule went silent, his mind wondering and confused. Was this some sort of a bad kismet that plagued him at every corner of his life, or was it merely a part of life that everyone was subjected to at one point or another? Was it his fate or was it just humanity? The more he thought about it, the more convinced he became that he carried the burden of a disproportional share of the collective misery that was bestowed onto humanity.

Yule knew what was wrong as soon as he set foot into the apartment. Zoya had her left arm in a sling. She looked pale and tired. She also gained weight and, in general, looked quite like a different person from the beautiful, lively, and vivacious person that she had once been. Konstantin was sitting at his desk, wearing a round watchmaker's magnifying glass in one eye. He threw a quick glance at Yule and said, "*Privet,*" as if they had just seen each other yesterday.

"What happened to you?" asked Yule, ignoring Konstantin's remark and pointing at the arm in a sling.

"I fell on the stairs."

"Are you sure that's what happened?" said Yule, all the while looking at Konstantin, who seemed to pay absolutely no attention to the visitor.

"What do you mean?" asked Zoya in a very low, nervous voice, her eyes quickly peering toward Konstantin before retreating again.

"What I mean is that there are persistent rumors that both you and little Vova are being abused by Konstantin."

Zoya's face turned even paler than before. The telltale sign was fear, clearly visible in her eyes. Yule didn't need any more proof that the rumors were true, as the truth was lucidly conveyed through his mother's neurotic demeanor, through the manner in which her eyes flitted and her voice trembled. The two closest people in his life were being abused both physically and psychologically by this pathetic vermin, whose only positive quality was his looks.

"Konstantin," said Yule. "If you lay your filthy hands on my mother again, I will kill you." Sophia, sensing the mounting tension in the room, took little Vova by the hand and escorted him away. Konstantin slowly lifted his head, meticulously removed the watchmaker's tool out of his eye socket, and calmly rose from his chair, all in one continuous motion that conveyed some petty air of annoyance at the undesirable distraction. Obviously irritated, he finally stood up and looked at Yule squarely in the eyes. He said, "It looks like you and your mother are made of the same dough. Too smart for your own good and obscenely arrogant, looking down on anyone who is not of your intellectual *caliber*. And as far as you are concerned, when did you actually stop wetting your pants, boy? Or maybe you still do? Now watch me prove to you that you are nothing but an insolent little rodent, and that you can *do* nothing." He crossed the room, approached the now terrified Zoya and, while facing Yule, slowly put his right arm outwards, as if in a position that implied an impending face slap. Whether he actually meant to do it or whether it was merely an act of stupid grandstanding in front of the teenager, Yule would never find out. Uncontrollable rage had gripped his entire body, a rage he had never sensed in his entire life. This drunken fool, this impudent pile of filth and human debris, instead of being appreciative of having a beautiful and worldly woman in his life, threatened to strike her in front of her own *son*.

The Gulag "fight-to-survive" instinct kicked in almost automatically. Yule had to take down a larger opponent multiple times throughout his training. Now, however, the maneuver had to be performed in a real-life encounter. Perhaps different circumstances would fluster Yule, but this was different. He was driven by an acute sense of vengeance, by a determination that transcended even his very instincts. Before Konstantin brought his outstretched arm back, Yule launched his entire body forward, aiming his right shoulder squarely into Konstantin's crotch. He grabbed the parasite's legs and elevated him into the air, simultaneously driving his body a few steps backward and, finally, slamming it down onto the hardwood floor. Konstantin's head hit the floor with a dull thump, and his body went limp. Yule didn't notice. He started raining a flurry of punches down onto

Konstantin's loathed, handsome face, determined to beat it into a bloody and hideous pulp.

Zoya's screams slowly penetrated into Yule's mind as his instincts started to regress and his surroundings started to flood back. "Stop! Stop, stop, *stop*! You're killing him!" she shrieked, her voice feverishly shrill and weak.

Yule finally got up and looked down with grim satisfaction onto Konstantin's blooded, battered face. Then he turned to look at his mother, who continued screaming all the while.

"You—you *killed* him! Who asked you to protect me! I don't need your help, I..."

Yule never heard the rest of his mother's tirade. He found himself running down the stairs and into the street. He kept running, devastated not by what he did to Konstantin but, rather, by his mother's reaction and her harsh words. It seemed, at that lonely moment, as if there was no place for him anywhere in the world, as if he didn't belong or fit in no matter where he went. Even his own mother had apparently abandoned him, the only person who was always there throughout his entire life, once his source of solace and comfort.

After what must have been a few minutes of running, his heart started to pound rapidly within his chest, ready to jump out like an animal escaping from the confines of its cage. He switched to a fast trot and then a slow stroll, finally halting and coming to a complete standstill. He didn't know how much time had elapsed or where he was. There were, Yule observed, no buildings around, just trees and the distant silhouette of a mountain in the horizon. The Carpathians. Poland, Yule realized, lied just over that mountain. That realization somehow helped Yule's mind to slowly return to rationality. His suitcase was still packed. He hadn't had the time to settle down since his arrival at Stanislawow, and that now became fortuitous. Yule had to leave. Staying at his mother's place was out of the question. He hadn't decided yet on his course of action, but one thing remained certain; Yule had to visit Marek at the hospital before his departure.

The Regional Hospital was just a few blocks away from Zoya's apartment. Yule turned around and started walking toward the city. It had taken him about half-an-hour to return to the center of town. The two-storied hospital lobby was guarded by a woman of massive proportions. She had to have been six feet in height and probably weighed about three hundred pounds. The guard wore a dark gray uniform, faded substantially from its original black. A blue-and-yellow chevron was displayed on its left sleeve. Had it not been for a conspicuous mustache and even more prominent sideburns, her face would have even passed for pretty. She was, however, taking her position very seriously.

"What is the purpose of your visit?" she demanded, looking down at Yule with her big, serious brown eyes. "Visitors are allowed only from 16.00 to 20.00 hours."

"I have just arrived from Leningrad and must return to there later tonight, but before I go, I need to see my friend. He's a patient at this hospital. Actually, he is more than a friend a to me, more like an older brother."

"Name," she uttered.

"Marek."

"Marek Krasinski?" she asked, her eyes turning eerily dreamy.

"Yes, that's him," said Yule, sensing that a window of opportunity had just opened up.

"I will let you through," she said. "Please tell Marek that Maria made an exception for him."

It was clear that Maria had some candid feelings for Marek, and that she was using this opportunity to earn Marek's benevolence. Yule doubted, however, the reciprocity on Marek's part, but it didn't matter.

Marek was on the second floor at the end of a long corridor. He was sharing his room with two more patients. Marek looked pale and thin, at least judging by his face, and had dark, dreary shadows under his eyes.

"Finally," he said. "Where have you been? I've been expecting you all morning!"

There were no chairs in the room, so Yule had to perch himself at Marek's feet, on the edge of his bed.

"I had a few things to take care of," answered Yule.

"Like beating the living crap out of Konstantin?"

"How do you know?"

"Everyone in town knows already knows about it. He was brought here by an ambulance, still unconscious."

"Is he okay now?"

"Well, if you call a broken jaw, a broken nose, and a severe concussion okay, then he is perfectly splendid. Now, tell me what happened."

Yule described in detail the events that transpired in the morning. Marek listened carefully without saying a word.

When Yule finished, Marek hesitated and said, "I didn't want to tell you, but it has been going on ever since you left."

Yule just looked out into the distance, his face unreadable and eerily calm.

"I will not go back, Marek. I *cannot* go back. Nor will I return to Leningrad. I don't want them to know… you understand."

"Of course I do, but where will you go then?"

When Yule did not answer, Marek proceeded and said, "You can stay at my place. It's empty now."

"Thank you, Marek. I just need a few days to decide what to do, then I'll be out of your way."

"Please, Yule. You can stay with me. In fact, you can live with me as long as you want, even if and when I return from this confounded hospital. You know I love you like my little brother, right?"

Yule could not answer. Choked by emotion, he simply squeezed Marek's hand.

"Easy, you," said Marek. "You have the grip of a blacksmith."

They both laughed. The two other men, to whom Marek and Yule were oblivious to for virtually the entire time, were following the exchange with the utmost interest. One of them, the younger one with a bandage around his head, pointed at the half-opened door that led into the corridor and said to Yule, "Your mother just passed by."

"How do you know it was my mother?"

"Everyone in town knows your mother. She always makes house calls, and she has respect for people, she talks to the simple people and never looks down on them. She's a good person, Yule, and I'm glad that you worked that little leech over."

There were apparently no secrets in this town. The older man, who seemingly had no discernible reason for being in the hospital said, "If you want a job for a few months, I can help. I'm going to be discharged tomorrow. Come to the office at Five Rynek Square tomorrow afternoon and ask for Vitaliy."

"What kind of work is it?"

"A real man's work. Something that's not for a sissy or for the weak of heart."

Marek gave Yule a set of keys to his apartment and explained which was which.

"Thank you, again," said Yule. "Oh! By the way, Maria let me through. She wants you to know that she has made an exception."

"Oh joy. I'll make sure that she gets a medal for that," said Marek. All four of them had a good laugh.

"I'll see you tomorrow," said Yule as he left, cautiously peering down the corridor and trying to sneak out without seeing his mother.

15 June. The office at Five Rynek Square was a dingy little room, hardly large enough to be called an office. The room seemed even smaller than it actually was due to the fact that a massive metal desk and two equally massive metal chairs dominated virtually the entire office space. The posters, covering most of the walls, showed muscular coal miners with chiseled features, all pointing at Yule. They were accompanied with signs that boldly read: *Donetsk Coal Basin Needs You* and *The Country Needs Coal.* It seemed that the motherland always needed something from you. Back in Siberia, Yule recalled, it was metal. Now the demand seemed to be for coal.

Vitaliy was sitting at the desk, telephone receiver in hand and talking loudly and angrily. "I *told* you, I was in the hospital! You don't expect me to work out of a hospital room, do you?"

He waved to Yule and pointed at one of the chairs. Vitaliy wore a pinstriped suit with the stripes so wide and so contrasted in color that he looked something like an American rodeo clown. He hung up the phone with a loud thud then proceeded to walk around his desk to vigorously shake Yule's hand. Vitaliy, Yule observed, was limping, which was the only indication of any reason that warranted a hospital stay. He caught Yule's look and explained, "A coal mine accident. Sometimes, the pain is so bad that I have to be admitted into a hospital." He looked at Yule and added, "I hope I didn't scare you because, as you probably have already guessed, I am going to offer you a job at a coal mine. Although from what I saw yesterday, you don't seem to be a timid lad."

"There is no coal around here, as far as I know," said Yule.

"Quite right, quite right; we are talking cities like Stalino, Makeyevka, Gorlovka, the area known as Donbas... areas where the young and the strong are needed."

"I know," said Yule, inclining his head toward one of the posters. "The Country Needs Coal."

Sensing sarcasm, Vitaliy asked, "Are you even interested, or am I just wasting my time here?"

"I'm interested... just tell me how it works."

"It's simple. You will sign a contract for a year or two, the length is up to you. I, in turn, will give you three hundred rubles of start up money and a train ticket. That's all. You can leave tomorrow, if you want."

"I do want to leave tomorrow, but I can't stay out there for more than three months. School starts in September."

"If you break your contract, you will have to return the start up money."

"And then?"

"And then you are free to leave. Don't say any of this to them ahead of time."

There was a knock on the door.

"It's open," yelled Vitaliy.

A young man, likely in his teens, walked into the room. He was short, skinny, blond, and blue eyed. The youth wore a dingy brown suite that was, quite comically, a few sizes too large for him, along with a dirty formerly blue shirt lacking its two uppermost buttons.

"Come in, Kolya, sit down, sit down," welcomed him Vitaliy eagerly. "I am glad that you have changed your mind. Look! Now you have a fellow traveler, and it looks like both of you are headed to Gorlovka tomorrow."

Yule and the newcomer acknowledged each other with a nod. Meanwhile, Vitaliy, with the skill of some conjurer, produced two typewritten pieces of paper and laid them on his desk. He slid both along the metal desk toward Yule and Kolya. The contract was simple—one year of labor in a coal mine, three hundred rubles of start up money, a one-way train ticket to Gorlovka, and a free room in a dormitory. The boys signed their respective contracts and looked at Vitaliy, anticipating the start up funds and further instructions. They received only the latter. "I will meet you two tomorrow morning, at 6:30, at the railroad station by the ticket window. You will get the tickets and the money, and I will see you off." He shook their hands yet again and walked them out. And just like that, the deal was done.

Kolya was silent, looking down at his feet as they were crossing the Rynek Square. The place was bustling with activities. Peasants from the surrounding areas had spread their fresh produce and homemade dishes onto their carts. Wooden barrels filled the air with scents of pickles and sauerkraut. Some vendors had foreign-made clothing for sale, mainly from Poland, that hung on makeshift racks. The two left the market and entered Halicka Street. "Where are you going?" asked Yule, if not only to break the long and awkward silence.

"I—I don't know yet," answered Kolya in a small, quivering voice. Yule began to suspect that Kolya was simply shy.

"What do you mean *you don't know*. Don't you live somewhere?"

"I—I do… I did… it doesn't matter."

"You don't have to tell me anything," said Yule. "I have a place to stay for tonight. You can stay with me, if you wish."

Although Yule was at least three years younger than Kolya, he felt like a paladin solving someone else's quandaries.

"Thank you," muttered Kolya quietly but not insincerely.

"We have to stop at my aunt's for a minute to pick up my suitcase. The place is right here, next to the theater," Yule pointed at the building. "Wait for me here, I'll be right down."

Aunt Sophia was in tears. She was sitting at the dining room table, feeding Vova and wiping her watery eyes with a kitchen towel. Vova immediately jumped off of her lap and galloped to Yule who, as was now the custom, picked him up and threw him into the air.

"A detective came in yesterday, looking for you," she said, sighing deeply. She added, "He's still in the intensive care ward, you know."

"I don't care if he dies," responded Yule. "How is Mom?"

"She's in the hospital, staying with him."

"Scum like him usually survive," said Yule. "It's always the good ones that perish."

His aunt didn't say anything, only sighed again.

"Anyway, I have to go," he said while he pulled his valise from the same corner where he left it the day before. "I'll see you soon. *Poka*, Vova."

Kolya was sitting atop the stoop of the adjacent building. He was looking at Yule while crossing the street, seemingly without any acknowledgement or recognition. He was, it appeared, in his own little world, wherever that world was.

"Are you somnambulating?" joked Yule, trying to draw his attention.

"Samna-what?" Yule's jest only seemed to have an adverse effect on Kolya.

"Never mind. Let's go. I also have to stop at the hospital to see a friend one last time."

Maria was on duty again. She wore the same oddly-looking black uniform with the strange insignia on the sleeve. Only now, however, did Yule realize that the trident didn't belong to King Poseidon, but rather to Simon Petlyura. It was, in essence, the symbol of *Samostiyna Ukraina,* of the Independent Ukraine. Petlyura was the leader of the movement who started the fight for independence against the Russians in the 1920s. The fight didn't last too long. The Russians notoriously had no patience for disobedience or insubordination.

It was, Yule knew, still too early to be let through the hospital doors. Thus, in order to gain entrance, he had to resort to an outright lie.

"Good morning, Maria," he said in a cheerful tone of voice. "I forgot to tell you that Marek sends his regards. He appreciated that you let me in yesterday and asked if you could do it again today."

"Really," said Maria incredulously, not sure of whether she should believe Yule or not.

"Yes, he did say that," Yule continued. Maria studied him suspiciously, trying to detect any signs of irony or deceit. It was time to go into a major bluff.

"By the way, Maria, what kind of a uniform is that?" asked Yule, pointing to the trident on her sleeve. "Did the hospital give it to you?"

"No," said Maria proudly, her face suddenly aglow and beaming. "This is my father's uniform. He wore it while in the army."

"Which army was it?" Yule asked, feigning ignorance.

"*Our* army. The Ukrainian army," responded Maria.

Yule quickly changed his tone of voice from cheerful to hushed and secretive. "Can we talk privately?" asked Yule, placing his hand under Maria's powerful arm and making an attempt to move her aside. Maria didn't budge.

"I can't leave my post," she complained.

Yule looked at Kolya, who was observing the scene in utter bewilderment. He asked Kolya to move away. Then, Yule started to whisper into Maria's ear. "You might be in danger of being arrested." Maria's eyes became round and large.

"Why?" she whispered back, bewildered.

"This *trezub*, trident, on your sleeve was Petlyura's symbol of the Independent Ukraine. It could, under the circumstances, be interpreted as being anti-Soviet. And I'm sure I don't need to tell you what the KGB could do to you if they see it. Did you know that Petlyura was murdered by the KGB *after* he escaped to Paris?"

Apparently Maria had no clue, as evidenced by her eyes becoming even wider and larger. She turned pale and whispered, "My God… what should I do?"

"Go home immediately and change. Hopefully nobody reported you yet."

She was still hesitant. "If anyone asks about you, I'll tell them that you went to the bathroom."

"*Thank you,*" she said. She quickly disappeared around the corner.

"Did you lie to her?" asked Kolya, who had heard the entire conversation.

"Not really. I mean—it *is* a plausible scenario after all. But never mind that. Let's go in to see my friend."

Marek looked better already; some color had returned to his cheeks. He was sitting up in his bed, propped up by a pillow.

"Did you go to see Vitaliy?" he asked.

"I did, and tomorrow morning Kolya and I will leave for Gorlovka," answered Yule, pointing to his new friend who was still standing in the doorway.

Marek looked at Kolya appraisingly and said, "Another troubled soul, I see. Incidentally, do you two know what you will actually be *doing* in a coal mine?" He moved his eyes from Kolya to Yule and back to Kolya, but there was no response from either. "I'll tell you, then. You will be pushing heavy rail carts filled to their brims with coal."

"That suits me fine," said Yule, undeterred. "I like physical labor. That way, I don't have to exercise."

"What about your friend here? He doesn't look very athletically inclined."

Kolya kept silent, merely resorting to a shrug of the shoulders.

"It'll be good for him," said Yule. "He'll get stronger. Anyway, we have to go before Maria gets back. I don't want any trouble."

That piqued Marek's interest. "What sort of trouble?"

Yule briefly described the scene that had just taken place by the hospital entrance, including the bluff with Petlyura's *trezub.* Marek laughed until the tears started rolling down his cheeks.

"What a rascal you are! Incidentally, her father was Petlyura's orderly, but then both of them disappeared. We know, though, that Petlyura was murdered in Paris, but Maria's father was never heard from again." He stopped laughing and became serious for a moment. "You could've been right though—warning her…

people are frightened and report on one another to save their own skins."

Yule nodded in response. After a brief silence, he said, "Well then. Good-bye, Marek. Until next time brother." They merely shook hands and looked each other in the eyes. There was no need to say anything else; the two understood each other without words.

While Yule was walking through the threshold of the door, Marek called out, "Be careful out there, Yule! Stay safe!"

Marek's kitchen was empty, but Yule knew where to look. He went down to the *pogreb,* the cold basement where butter, eggs, and pickled goods were usually stored in the summer. Yule's conjecture was correct, as there was a cornucopia of food awaiting him down there.

"Can you cook?" asked Yule, holding a box of eggs and a chunk of smoked bacon in both hands.

"I'm a good cook," Kolya answered. "I cooked for an entire summer camp in high school."

"Great, let's have a feast, then! I don't remember the last time I had a decent meal. Besides, cooking has never been my strong point."

Kolya did not lie about his culinary capabilities. The meal turned out to be delicious, consisting of fried potatoes with smoked bacon topped with sour cream. For dessert, both enjoyed dried-fruit compotes. They had also discovered a bottle of local wine, but Yule said that he didn't drink alcohol and left the drinking to Kolya, who helped himself to two glasses.

By the time they finished with the meal and the dishwashing, it was time to go to bed. They chose to sleep in a small upstairs bedroom, already conveniently furnished with two single beds. Yule immediately took a book out of his valise and started reading. Kolya, however, just looked at Yule, seemingly puzzled about the lack of questions.

"Aren't you curious why I have no place to stay?"

"I figured that you would tell me whenever you felt like it. I know that if I asked you, and you didn't want to tell me, you'd just simply lie about it. If you told me on your own accord, however, it would most likely be the truth. It's up to you in the end."

"You didn't tell me your story either."

"Are we going to play a kindergarten game now? *Show me yours, and I will show you mine?*"

"No, well, there's not much to tell, really. My mother died two years ago. My father remarried recently. His new wife had two small children from her first marriage, but her husband was killed in a coal mine explosion. Ironic, right?" Kolya paused. "There is no place for me in the family anymore, so I left."

How simple and concise, thought Yule. Two deaths, three marriages, a stepmother, a runaway teenager… all in practically one sentence.

"What's your story?"

"Similar to yours. Nobody died, though. I have a stepmother, a stepfather, a stepbrother, all of them in addition to my real parents, and no place that I would like to call home."

"But I've heard you talking about going back to Leningrad to finish school. I had to lie about my age—I'm not sixteen yet. Not legal, so to speak."

"Didn't Vitaliy ask for your documents?"

"I told him that I've lost my valise, along with all of my papers. I also promised that I would be getting the duplicates soon. By the time they realize that I am underage, I'll be long gone."

They said their good-nights, both thinking of the next big step that would most likely change their young lives forever.

They woke the next morning to a soft, placid summer rain. At least for Yule, the rain was pleasant. He enjoyed it sincerely. Although it usually made him feel sad, there was always that touch of nostalgia for the places that he had never been to, at least outside of his dreams. The feeling of the ephemeral nature of the here and the now, that everything happening in the present was only temporary and that the future offered so much more, was significantly more pronounced when it rained. Indeed everything, even life itself, is temporary. On rainy days like this one, Yule questioned and pondered the meaning of life to an even greater extent, though the rain never truly facilitated the discovery of some answer.

Vitaliy was already waiting for them by a yellow and white pavilion, one with a severely oxidized bronze plate on its façade. The word CASSA was painted over an old engraving in Polish, but Yule couldn't make out that original inscription.

"There you are," greeted them Vitaliy enthusiastically. "I was beginning to worry that you changed your minds."

He produced from his suitcase a crude brown envelope and opened it, handing both Yule and Kolya three hundred rubles each, along with two train tickets.

"There is your train, I'll walk you over," he continued. "When you arrive at Stalino tomorrow morning, there will be a bus to Gorlovka waiting for you. You can't miss it. The sign on the bus will read *Shakhta Imeny Lenina,* Lenin Coal Mine. A man by the name of Zakon will meet you there. It's a forty-minute ride, more or less. Any questions?"

The boys shook their heads.

"Good! Like I said, there will be other men on the train going to the same *Shakhta*. Look, they are boarding now. Well, this is farewell then! Good luck!"

They climbed the steep steps leading into the train car and, once within, opened the sliding door of *coupe*, sleeping compartment, number four. There were two young men already seated by the window, both facing each other and separated by a folding tray.

"Good morning," said Yule cheerfully. There was no reply, just blank stares that were likely meant to be interpreted as *how dare you interrupt our reverie*. This kind of reception was all too familiar to Yule, usually signifying some impending trouble. If those two would be working in the same coal mine as Yule and Kolya, their lives could very well be made miserable by their existence. It was, Yule thought, time to assert themselves and to take control of the potentially explosive situation. The one sitting on the right had his arms rested on the table, sleeves rolled up displaying a crude tattoo of a baby on the inside of his right forearm. Yule immediately recognized the tattoo. In the world of *Vori*, a tattoo of a baby meant "born in prison." The man was in his early twenties, from the looks of him, with straight black hair, a darkish complexion, and the bulging, thick neck of a wrestler. He was most likely from the Caucuses. It was hard to guess his height, but judging from the fact that his torso towered above the table, Yule guessed that he was relatively tall. The man noticed Yule's obvious interest in his tattoo.

"What are you looking at?" he shrilled in an unexpectedly high voice.

"What prison were you born in?"

The man, clearly caught off guard, named some town that Yule had never heard of. He finally recovered from his initial surprise and said, "None of your business."

"Oh, but it *is* my business," said Yule, continuing to apply the pressure. "If you wear this tattoo, you should be able to back it up. If you are a *petukh* but claim to be a *vor v zakonye,* you should know that punishment will come sooner or later, and it will be severe."

It was a direct hit, and not only to the man's hubris but also to his fear, as evidenced by his eyes and his facial expression. They were difficult to misread. The man was obviously frightened. He did, of course, know, as most people did, that the punishment for impersonating a thief-in-law was, at a minimum, either a severe beating or, in the most severe cases, an untimely death. Even if he was indeed born in a prison, and even if his tattoo was truly genuine, those two elements alone could not earn him the status of a *vor v zakonye*, a designation that also required an actual conviction and time done in prison. Only if one met all of those prerequisites could he earn the "honor" of being called a thief-in-law. The network, which consisted of hundreds of thousands of criminals released after Stalin's death, was tightly knit, despite being thinly spread throughout the country. All former Zeks had possessed the means to communicate amongst themselves, and the news that someone was impersonating a thief-in-law would reach the appropriate ears rather quickly. The response, Yule knew, would be swift and severe.

The man with the tattoo knew it as well, and he also knew that Yule knew it too. There was, therefore, no need for any further explanations. Yule had him; the man with the tattoo of a baby on his forearm was neutered, no longer dangerous.

"So, what's your name?" asked Yule in a much more amicable tone of voice.

"Pliyev," said the man. "Can we talk outside?"

They both got up and walked out of the sleeping compartment. The man, to Yule's surprise, wasn't as tall as he had appeared while sitting down. He did, however, have a long, powerful torso, short legs, sloping shoulders, and short arms.

"You must be a wrestler," said Yule. "Freestyle?"

"Yep, you nailed it." The man was clearly flattered. "I was the junior welterweight champion of Azerbydjan in 1952."

"Should I be scared?"

"No, no… all I want is for you to stop embarrassing me in front of my friend. Please."

"If you really are trying to get respect by making up a prison story, well, don't. It's bound to come back and bite you, no matter where you go."

"How do you know all of these things anyway? You're just a kid."

"Doesn't matter, I just know things. You have to leave my friend and myself alone. If you do so, then this conversation never happened."

They shook hands firmly and returned to the compartment. Pliyev's companion was visibly agitated, standing in front of the sitting Kolya and waiving his arms in front of his face, clearly trying to pick a fight.

"Sit down," said Yule firmly, giving the standing man a steely, icy look, a look that somehow always seemed to work its magic on those that were insecure. It seemingly worked in that instance as well, despite the fact that Pliyev's friend was at least four inches taller than Yule. The man plumped back into his seat, all the while continuing with his agitated fidgeting.

"What is the problem with both of you? Constantly looking for trouble?" continued Yule. Pliyev's friend was in his early twenties. His was an uneducated voice, betraying his banausic ancestry. He had a bony face, beady eyes and, the *piece de resistance*, a long, thin, and crooked nose. His small eyes drilled Yule with the hatred of a trapped animal.

"Let's not fight," said Pliyev peacefully, again assuming his former seat and parking his powerful torso at the table.

"He called me a stupid peasant," complained Pliyev's companion, pointing at Kolya. "Just because I said that 'God will make you suffer for your sins.'"

"Enough," demanded Yule. "By the way, what's your name?"

"Gavrilo," said the man. He then continued his tirade, unable to calm down. "If your friend doesn't believe in God, he shouldn't put me down just because *I* do."

"I agree, Gavrilo. Let's put this to rest."

"Not until he apologizes to me."

"I will not," said Kolya quietly.

Yule was astonished by Kolya's firmness, an unexpected personality trait that he had not noticed before. The situation was shaping up to be an archetypal confrontation between a deeply religious man and an atheist. Elsewhere, in other regions of the country where atheism took a dominant hold for decades, a religious man such as Gavrilo would've been ostracized as an aberrant and openly laughed at. In the Western Ukraine, however, with its deeply seeded Roman Catholic inheritance, religious people were still accepted. Gavrilo stood up and looked down at Kolya.

"I will fight with you until you take your words back," he said.

Yule started to laugh. "What is this?" he said. "A third-grade contest of dare?"

"It may be funny to you," answered Gavrilo. "But to me, it's a matter of principle."

"Have it your way, then. And when are you two going to fight?"

"At the next big station, so that I will have enough time to teach him a lesson."

"The next stop will be Kamenetz-Podolsk. It's a thirty-minute stop, which should be long enough for you to make a believer out of my friend," continued Yule, laughing.

Gavrilo looked at Yule with unadulterated hatred. "Another *bezbozhnik*, a godless man," said he. He was about to say something else, but Yule suddenly stood up, looking at his watch. "We are getting close to the big stop," he said. "Let's continue later." He looked at Kolya, inclining his head toward the door, and went out into the corridor. Kolya followed him within a few seconds.

"Do you know anything about fighting?" asked Yule. "This man is much taller than you... besides, I've heard that he did some boxing in school."

"No, I've never fought for real. But I have a plan."

"Tell me."

"It's simple, really. I will let him hit me. Then, I fall and don't get up. The fight is over."

"Sounds good. One slight problem, though… you'll get a reputation as a wimp at best, but most likely as a *petukh* at worst."

"What does that mean?"

"It means that you will be asked to pick up the soap bar from the floor every time you take a shower."

Kolya's eyes immediately filled with disgust and horror. He didn't have to say anything; his eyes said it all.

"I have a different solution for you," Yule continued. "I will show you how to knock him out with a single punch… all you need to do is learn where to aim."

"And what if he hits me first?"

"Come with me—I need no more than fifteen minutes to teach you that one secret strike."

As they walked toward the end of the sleeping car, Kolya said, "You make it sound as if we are going to a prison instead of a coal mine."

"It will not be a prison per se, but you can be sure that it'll be very damn close."

Next, they entered the space between the cars, stepping above the shaky passage that led to the next car. The passage below them consisted of two metal hitches, a multitude of electrical cables, and a few water hoses that were sliding on top of one another and producing an odd, rattling noise. Yule opened the door and they entered the foyer of the next car, apparently an upgraded version of their own modest accommodations. It was, however, spacious enough for Yule's intended purpose.

"Stand in front of me and look me in the eyes," he said. "Okay. Now, the most important thing is to understand your opponent. The man you are about to fight is a boxer, so he will start with a left jab. At least most boxers are conditioned to do that."

Yule made a fist and threw his left arm at Kolya, aiming directly at his face. The fist abruptly stopped at about an inch away from Kolya's forehead. Yule did the maneuver so quickly that Kolya had virtually no time to react.

"Now *that's* what's going to happen if you stand there like a dummy."

Affronted, Kolya responded, "What would *you* do, then?"

"When you see his left fist coming at you, duck under his left arm and lean slightly forward. Here, I'll do it slower this time."

Yule repeated the motion and, much to his amazement, Kolya grasped the movement after only three repetitions. Perhaps he was skinny and slightly frail, but the fact that Kolya was a quick learner could not be doubted.

"Okay, very good. Now step two: when you are underneath his left arm and *before* he returns it back to his face, you have to make a wild swing with your right fist and hit him in his left ear. Make sure that your *knuckles* make contact, not your thumb."

"In the ear?" inquired Kolya, seemingly puzzled.

"You'll more than likely miss the ear, but so long as you hit him anywhere near or around that area, especially if you land the punch behind his ear, it will result in a concussion. But you have to swing very hard and put the entire weight of your body into that one haymaker. Let's practice."

They spent another ten minutes practicing the technique and again, Kolya had grasped the move very quickly. He was actually enjoying the whole ordeal.

"I think that you've missed your life's calling," said Yule. "You definitely have a knack for fighting."

"Never mind my calling, what if I miss his ear entirely?"

"If you miss, the inertia will turn you around and you should try to face him again. Just try to repeat the whole process. If you're really interested in fighting, I can show you how to perform a *back fist* later, as one of the ways to utilize the inertia after you miss and can't stop your body from spinning around."

"Can you show me now?"

"I don't want to overload your brain with too much information before the fight. Later, I promise."

"Don't worry, I think I'll be fine."

"Your choice. Now, pretend that you've missed the punch entirely, that your fist flew in front of his face and your body continued to spin around. Well, instead of trying to *stop* the spinning, you have to purposely *accelerate* it and, this time, put out your left arm and aim the back of your fist at his face. You won't be able to hit him with absolute precision because he will be behind you, but at least by using your peripheral vision, you can roughly gauge where your fist is headed. In any case, if you hit his face, you may not knock him out, but at least some serious damage is guaranteed."

They spend a few more minutes practicing the back fist technique.

"It's amazing," said Kolya when they finally finished. "I think that I no longer have any fear."

They walked back to their coupe. The two men were sitting in the exact same positions as before, only this time with a third new friend accompanying them, namely a bottle of *Gorilka*, Ukrainian vodka. They weren't completely drunk yet, but looked to be very close to that threshold of the wonderful state of vodka-induced happiness. Yule looked at Kolya and winked; they both knew that a drunken man had no chance to win the fight. The train started to slow down as a piercing whistle was heard in the distance. The train conductor passed by their compartment and announced in the corridor the imminent arrival at Kamenetz-

Podolsk in five minutes. "*Stoyanka tridzat minut*, a thirty-minute stop!" he shrieked.

The Kamenetz-Podolsk *Vokzal*, Rail Station, was an old stone building, apparently in existence way before the railroad tracks were actually laid down. The train hissed angrily about a dozen times, jerked violently, and finally arrived at a complete standstill. Gavrilo looked at Kolya, his drunken eyes already red and senseless from intoxication.

"*Poshlee*, let's go," he said as he galumphed out the door, through the corridor, and toward the outside exit. All three of them stood up and proceeded after Gavrilo who stopped abruptly as they descended onto the platform and told Yule and Pliyev to go back.

"It's between us two," he said, pointing at Kolya. "Maybe you should take a walk in the town. I'll join you in a minute."

Yule just smiled in response and pulled Pliyev by the sleeve toward the opposite direction where an impressive looking castle was set atop a canyon wall. Pliyev complied, but his gait was unsteady and Yule had to make a substantial effort to keep him from falling off the platform.

They managed to make about a dozen steps before a succession of unintelligible screams emanated from behind them, startling both Yule and Pliyev. They both turned around, only to see a flustered Kolya running directly toward them.

"I did it! I did it! He is out, he is down, and he is not moving, come—" he was screaming in excitement, his big eyes both flushed and worried at the same time. Yule and Pliyev followed him into a low grassy area behind the station. In the center of the area lied Gavrilo's body, his face up and his arms open wide. He looked indistinguishable from a typical drunk who had fallen and passed out from severe intoxication.

"What happened?" asked Pliyev, looking at Kolya.

"He was trying to hit me, but I hit him first. He went down and that's all," said Kolya, somewhat regaining his composure.

He looked at Yule and added, "I did it *exactly* the way you showed me, and it worked like magic."

"Showed him what?" asked Pliyev suspiciously.

"How to fight, of course."

"You can't learn how to fight in twenty minutes."

"Obviously, I did," responded Kolya proudly.

"Don't flatter yourself… he would've passed out from being drunk anyway."

"Where'd you hit him?" asked Yule.

"Right in the ear."

"Good! Now let's put him onto the train before we all miss it," said Yule.

They lifted Gavrilo and carried him all the way to the sleeping compartment. He was still out, but breathing heavily.

"Five minutes till departure! Passengers, please take your seats," the conductor kept repeating.

Yule was indignant that he had missed a rare opportunity to see the ancient town up close and to get closer to the abandoned bunkers that were scattered around the area, many of them even visible from the elevated platforms. Yule recalled the long days back at the icy Gulag, days that were filled with reenactments of famous battles. There were times when the entire floor of the *izba* was littered with the miniatures of tanks, personnel carriers, artillery, and, of course, the infantry, hundreds of little soldiers that served as the cannon fodder of the war. The Battle of the Kamenetz-Podolsk Pocket interested him because it didn't fit the stereotypical Soviet portrayal of the Germans as being stupid and their generals as looking and acting like complete idiots. *If they were so dumb*, Yule thought, *how was it possible that most of the European continent had folded like a cheap camera before them in just a few months, that the German Army was victorious in many battles because of the military prowess of its commanders*? Yes, the Nazis were indeed brutal, antihuman, anti-Semitic, and downright despicable. One thing they *weren't*, however, was incompetent or stupid.

A perfect example of sound military strategy was displayed by Generaloberst Hube while he was encircled by the First Ukrainian Front. He had ordered a complete restructuring of his forces in the *kessel*; the four corps were dissolved and reformed into three *Korpsgruppen*. Despite Hitler's manic objection to an attempted breakout (which he saw as a retreat), Hube and his superior, Erich von Manstein, continued to argue with the Fuhrer and managed to convince him that the breakout would save the First Panzer Army from utter annihilation.

Hube decided to break out west, toward Ternopol, where relief forces were to meet him. The distance between Kamenetz-Podolsk and Ternopol was about one hundred fifty miles over several rivers and an uncannily muddy terrain. Thus, Hube divided his forces into two columns and headed westward. The northern column quickly captured three bridges over the Zbruch River and a leftward tributary of the mighty Dniester, while the southern column fought the Russian Fourth Tank Army that captured Kamenetz-Podolsk. The *kessel* kept moving day and night and, finally, broke free in the west. Zhukov and Konev continued to believe that the breakout would occur to the south. Thus, the Red Army kept augmenting the troop density in the southern flank of the pocket, in anticipation of an attack that never came.

Forty-eight hours before the miraculous retreat, at 1300 hours military time, Senior Sergeant Ivan Lomov of the Second Spetsnaz Battalion and his five men had left their Kamenetz-Podolsk barracks and made their way westward, toward the enemy line. Each and every one of them belonged to a highly trained group of specialists, devilishly lethal to the enemy and unwaveringly loyal to the motherland. The muddy terrain had slowed down their progress, but the distance of approximately fifteen miles was covered in a mere three hours. The men were carrying their *PPSh-41* Shpagin Machine Pistols, a sub-machine gun that had a seventy-one-round drum magazine and could fire nine hundred rounds per minute. Each also carried their two-day canned food rations along with American-made SCR-194 portable a.m. radios (each weighing about 25lbs) that were fitted into their backpacks. At every four miles out of the span of 15, one of Lomov's men was left behind in order to form a radio relay, a sort of communication chain. This had to be done because their SCR-194s had a maximum reception radius of only five miles.

At 1600 Hours, Senior Sergeant Ivan Lomov and Sergeant Vitaliy Prishchemikhin had finally reached their destination, an area that was approximately two-thirds of a mile away from the First Panzer Army's fore post. They were so close to the enemy that they could hear the rumbling sounds emanating from the idling diesel engines. They had one hour until dawn to dig a trench, to camouflage it, and to set up their equipment. The brown mud below their feet was sticky and heavy, the layer below rocky and hard. By the time they had finally finished with the trench, there was hardly any time left for any decent camouflage.

Vitaliy Prishchemikhin was a tech wizard, famous for his mastery over the complex equipment. He quickly pulled his SCR-194 radio out of his backpack. That particular model was designed for voice communications only. The plan, in sum, was to relay any information about the enemy's plans back to Kamenetz-Podolsk by utilizing the point-to-point network formed by Lomov's people, each spaced four miles apart. Although the SR-194 wasn't equipped for coded communication, Spetsnaz learned how to whistle code into the microphone when interference prevented clear voice reception. Vitaliy could set up his radio in less than a minute. Ivan Lomov watched with pleasure as his comrade quickly and efficiently pulled out the set with his huge and powerful hands, gently placed it onto the ground, plugged in the headset and the microphone, and flipped the switch to Coil "B" (to operate on channels twenty-six through sixty-two), all in under a minute. There were a total of sixty-two channels, each separated from the next by four hundred kilocycles, and before leaving the headquarters, they were assigned one specific channel on which to work. Vitaliy then pulled out and extended the antenna to the length corresponding to the coil being used, screwed it into the top of the lid, and turned the filament toggle switch on. It took him another thirty seconds to calibrate the set—he turned the channel dial to the red mark nearest to the assigned frequency. A hissing sound flowed from the unit, but after adjusting the calibration knob, the sound stopped abruptly. Vitaliy turned off the calibrator switch and turned the dial to the assigned channel.

"*Sosna, Sosna*, do you copy?" he whispered in a low voice into the microphone. The reception was good and the response was immediate. "We are in position, stand by."

Meanwhile, Senior Sergeant Lomov was peering through his powerful binoculars at the idling German tanks and personnel carriers, trying desperately to figure out the direction of their next move. The tanks, however, were not lined up in any particular direction but, rather, were positioned in an odd semicircle, some facing outwards, others sideways. In the predawn foggy light, Ivan Lomov, though he couldn't be completely certain, thought that he saw some movement, perhaps even the reflection of a binocular lens on the ground level to the left and slightly in front of the tanks. It could've just been a chunk of ice reflecting the light, though there was absolutely no way to be certain. Just as an added precaution, Lomov kept his binoculars fixed to the spot. He continued observing the area, but the reflection never came back.

"Try different frequencies," suggested Ivan Lomov. "Maybe we can get some information from their communications."

Vitaliy Prishchemikhin spoke German and was well versed in the technological terminology utilized by the Nazis. He started turning the frequency knob. Since it was an a.m. radio with only a limited range, the only other transmission, if any, would be coming solely from the Panzer group in front of them. He reached the last channel without any success and then flipped the toggle switch to Coil "A." As soon as he approached channel three, they heard the harsh, hushed voice of a German operator. He was transmitting logistical orders to the far flanks of the massive tank group about the fuel, the weather, and the ammunition. There was, however, one phrase that caught Vitality's attention.

"*Stunden Neunzehn—Richtung Sud-Ost*," said the operator. "*Kommandeure in den bunker.*" Then the voice repeated it twice.

Sergeant Vitaliy Prishchemikhin couldn't believe his luck—that's what they were here for, this precious piece of information.

"They are moving… southeast at 1900 hours," he whispered excitedly.

"Are you absolutely sure?"

"They repeated it three times."

"Then send this information to Kamenetz-Podolsk. Our mission is complete."

It was snowing heavily on March 31, the day that Hube's army started moving westward. Despite low supplies and heavy snowfall, the troops were moving in good order and obeying discipline. It was a stark comparison to the panicked situation within the Stalingrad encirclement. By the fifth of April, Hube's Army had reached the Strypa River, and on the sixth, near the town of Buczcz, they were united with the Housser's SS Division. The First Panzer Army had managed to escape encirclement while suffering only moderate casualties. The operational planning, the masterful use of the art of disinformation in the radio transmission, and the skill and resoluteness of Hube had resulted in two hundred thousand troops escaping the fate of Stalingrad.

On May 17, The Field Court Marshall of the First Ukrainian Front had sentenced Senior Sergeant Ivan Lomov to death by a firing squad, to be carried out immediately. The verdict was treason. Ivan Lomov was executed the next morning against the wall of the ancient Kamenetz-Podolsk castle. He fell to the ground, freshly covered with the morning snow, his last breath purportedly sounding like "*why*?" Sergeant Vitaliy Prishchemikhin had received ten years of hard labor and was sent to one of Kolyma's goldmine camps, in Shturmovoy.

The train jerked suddenly, hissed and moved, breaking Yule's trancelike state of reverie. The old, dilapidated station started to slowly move backwards, away from sight. The four young men sat quietly, digesting the events of the last thirty minutes. Gavrilo was holding his head in both hands, looking confused and apparently forgetful of everything that had happened in the town. His left ear, both flaming red and twice the size of its normal proportions, served as an omnipresent reminder. The sweet combination of *gorilka* and a punch to the ear had allegedly given him an excruciating headache. No one said anything and the rest of the journey went by rather peacefully. The train was cheerfully traversing the Western Ukraine, winding its way past the multitude of former Polish towns and villages that dotted the landscape. Yule was looking out the window at the *kolkhozy*, the collective farms with their broken bridges and narrow roads that were primarily built for the horses. Yule recalled that Nikita Khrushchev had made some efforts to produce more food. He made concessions to the peasants, which made it a little more worthwhile for them to work hard and to show some enterprise. But the lack of capital investment, coupled with an incoherent agricultural policy and the absence of an educated leadership, produced very few results.

The next stop was in the town of Proskurov, recently renamed Khmelnitsky. It was notorious for the vicious anti-Semitic pogrom known as the "Proskurov Massacre" of 1919. In a fleeting span of four hours, approximately sixteen hundred Jews were killed

by the Cossacks under the con
Although there were no official
the most Jews per hour, the town
World War record.

Four hours later, the train had fi
Vokzal, a sprawling two-story classi
windows, yet another product of th
had shared the same destiny as Stan ... ov. The
town was founded in the fourteenth-century by Prince Algirdas of Lithuania. Its history, not unlike many of the other formerly Polish towns and cities, was both rich and diverse. The town was systematically raided by Tatars, was later passed on to Poland, and, eventually, was ceded to the Russians in the 1790s. Naturally, one of the first moves made by Russians was to expunge the town of its Roman Catholic faith. The Catholic churches in Vinnitsa were converted into Russian Orthodox Churches virtually overnight. This information was about to leave Yule's lips but after second thought he stopped himself from saying anything at all. Gavrilo was still in a somnambular condition, Pliyev was drunk, and Kolya was still giddy with excitement about his newly acquired skills. *None of them*, Yule thought, *would probably make a good audience*. Yule stepped out onto the newly paved platform, which still exuded the pungent stench of fresh tar.

"Only twenty minutes," howled the conductor from somewhere behind Yule's back. Some passengers were still boarding the train. An old woman in a shawl and a black velvet coat was trying to push a huge, bulky suitcase up the steep stairs of the car. She was struggling with its immense weight, yet the conductor, who was standing right above her on the summit of the narrow stairway, seemingly had no intention of helping her. It seemed, on the contrary, that he was enjoying the struggle in front of him. Yule, who had already advanced toward the station building, turned around and said, "Aren't you going to help the woman?"

e too many of you and only one me." The conduc-
gged and disappeared into the darkness of the corridor. quickly walked back to the car just in time to stop the suit- se from falling down onto the old woman's head. He pushed the suitcase up into the landing, climbed up, and gave the old woman his hand, helping her to navigate the steep steps. She was completely out of breath, holding her hand against her chest and unable to speak. She sat on top of the suitcase and leaned her back against the wall.

"What is it," asked Yule, suddenly concerned. "The heart?"

"Oh, no," said the woman, shaking her head. "My heart is fine, I am just not as strong as I used to be. Just give me a minute."

Yule looked at the woman closely. She was in her seventies and had the face of a person who had seen a lot of suffering in a lifetime, yet it was simultaneously a very dignified face. She was probably beautiful in her youth, evidenced by her expressive hazel eyes and fine, aristocratically shaped nose. Her white hair was pulled up tightly and bunched up into the back of her head, held together with the help of a beautiful bronze pin with a Scythian motif.

She got up and took the monstrous suitcase by the handle.

"I'll take it," said Yule. "Where is your seat?"

They walked through the corridor to the last compartment; it was unoccupied. The other passengers must've exited in Vinnitsa. The woman told him that her name was Fannie and that she was going to Dnepropetrovsk, the next large city to the east of Vinnitsa, where her children and grandchildren lived. The suitcase contained home-cooked food, partially explaining its uncanny weight. She informed Yule that she made the long trip a few times a year.

"Can't you have someone help you with the suitcase?" asked Yule.

"I don't have any one to help me," answered Fannie quietly. "I live alone."

"Why not join your family in Dnepropetrovsk, then?"

"My husband is buried here, and I will stay with him for as long as my time on this earth remains."

Yule, who was already beginning to regret the conversation, became silent and made a feeble attempt to switch the topic when Fannie said, "He was the one in that infamous photograph, *The Last Jew of Vinnitsa,* the photo that captures a member of the German Einsatzgruppe D executing a kneeling man before a mass grave."

They sat in silence for a few minutes.

The old lady broke the silence again. "They killed almost thirty thousand Jews. My husband had sent me away with the children right before they came. When I returned to Vinnitsa, the mass grave was reopened, and I found his body. I reburied him at a Jewish cemetery."

She fell silent again.

"He was a kind and caring man, always ready to help. Just like you, in fact."

Quickly detecting the onset of another awkward silence, Yule changed the topic. "How are you going to carry this monstrosity in Dnepropetrovsk?" asked Yule, pointing at the suitcase.

"My son will meet me there," she said. "He has a car." Her eyes lit up with pride. It was a rarity to have a car.

"He must be an important man, to have a private car."

"No, it's not a private car, but his employer has given him one. My son, he is a nuclear physicist and also works on some kind of a secret project with the military," she stopped talking abruptly, perhaps realizing that she had said too much.

"There is plenty of military work in Vinnitsa," said Yule. "Why can't he work next to you?"

"You should know, young man, that people in his position don't have much of a choice when it comes to the place of work."

Dnepropetrovsk was indeed the birthplace of the infamous "UR," *Universalnaya Raketa* or Versatile Launcher, which could serve both as a carrier of nuclear weapons and as a space booster. Here was another brilliant Jewish mind working to make the Soviet Union an even stronger, more potent superpower.

One hour later, the train pulled into the Dnepropetrovsk *Vokzal*, a massive gray stone building with pretentious Corinthian columns. A well-dressed man, wearing a double-breasted gray suit and a paisley-patterned tie, had entered the compartment.

"This is my son, Ilya," Fannie introduced him, "and this young man helped me with the suitcase."

"*Spasibo*, thank you," said Ilya and turned to Fannie. "Are you trying to kill yourself, Mother, by dragging this Pullman with you? We are not starving here."

Fannie looked at Yule apologetically, seemingly embarrassed by her brilliant son. Yule said good-bye and quickly departed, leaving the two alone. In his compartment, the silence was only interrupted by Gavrilo's thunderous snores. All three of his fellow travelers were sound asleep. The sight of it made Yule realize that he too felt tired after a long and tumultuous day. He climbed onto the vacant top cot, fleeting thoughts of Zoya, Marek, and little Vova ushering him to sleep.

In his dream he flew again. It was one of those rare dreams where the liftoff was effortless and the flight was pleasant. He saw his train down below, snaking its way through the Ukrainian Steppes. The Black Sea was the color of charcoal and looked rough, despite the clear sky. Although it was still dark, Yule could see a large ship, flying a Turkish standard. The ship, it seemed, was caught in some violent storm. He covered the distance between the Crimea and China in just a few minutes, soaring over the snowy peaks of the Caucus Mountains and then following the Great Wall of China that entered the northern part of Manchuria and continued his flight northeast toward the city of Magadan. He crossed the white, silent expanse of the Stanovoy Mountain Range and then the familiar watchtowers of the Shturmovoy goldmine. Before Yule knew it, he was soaring over the barracks, the commander's house, and even his own izba. But he continued further, toward Professor's distinctive izba with its tiny fenced backyard. Professor wasn't home, but Chook and Cha were. They were still little cubs, with soft, orange fur on their foreheads and on the tips of their snouts. They started whimpering when they saw Yule, clinging to him as he ran his fingers through the blanket-like fur on their backs. He noticed how emaciated they were. Yule looked everywhere inside the house but couldn't find anything edible to give them. He went outside to go his house in order to fetch some food and took the usual path by which he had travelled a thousand times before, always for his daily lessons with Professor. It was strangely quiet with not a soul around for what seemed like miles. After a minute of walking, he noticed a smallish man on the path walking toward him. The man was holding a double-barreled shotgun aimed directly at Yule. As the man got closer, Yule recognized Semion, dressed in a fur coat that looked like it was made out of wolf skin. The hunter, aiming his gun at Yule's chest, bared his rotten teeth. Semion squeezed the trigger and a loud hissing sound filled the air. The bullet struck Yule hard in the right shoulder—

"Get up, get up," said Kolya, shaking Yule's right shoulder. "We are in Stalino."

Reality slowly crawled back into Yule's mind. He looked at his wristwatch: 5:15 a.m., the train was on time. Gavrilo and Pliyev were already standing on the platform outside, looking around. Massive slag-heaps, called *terrikons*, were everywhere, no matter where you looked and for as far as the eye could see. "Great," said Yule, pointing at the *terrikons*. "The recruiter never told us that we would be surrounded by mountains of toxic coal waste."

A bus with a sign that read *Shakhta Imeny Lenina*, Lenin's Coal Mine, was parked next to the station. An older woman and a burly man, who was dressed in a black suit, white shirt, and a black necktie, stood by the bus door. Both of them held notepads and pencils in their hands. The man had an aura of superiority about him, one that was almost palpable. The only detail that was missing was a halo above his head. The man was checking the names of the new recruits against the roster. He looked vaguely familiar to Yule, or perhaps he was just the generic, stereotypical embodiment of a Communist Party representative, assigned to virtually every organization in the Soviet Union to make sure that every citizen was in line with the ideology.

"How old are you?" he asked Yule. "It looks like you aren't even shaving yet."

"I look younger because I was cryogenically frozen for many years."

"You *what*?" The man's eyes became narrow, peering into Yule's face. The word was unfamiliar to him, but to show his ignorance or to admit his lack of a sense of humor was to tarnish the Party's name. "Get in the bus. I'll talk to you later."

Surprisingly, the bus was almost full. Yule and Kolya sat down in the very last row of seats, next to an older man wearing a navy, white-and-blue striped *telnyashka*, undershirt. He was clean-shaven and smelled like a very popular aftershave called *Shipr*. Yule knew the scent much too well, as Vladimir had used it daily. If it weren't for the faint smell of alcohol on the man's breath (apparently from the previous night), he would've made a good first impression. A large anchor was tattooed onto the inside of his forearm.

"Sit down, *younga*," said the man, leaving no doubt about his naval connection. The term *younga* was the name for a naval cadet.

"What ship are you from?" asked Yule just to be polite. He did not, however, expect to hear an entire episode from the history of the Soviet Fleet.

"What? Do you know all the ships?" asked the man.

“Most of them, especially those that took part in various battles.”

“Have you heard of *Novorossiysk*?”

“Yes.”

“What do you know?”

“She sank in Sevastopol Bay about three years ago under suspicious circumstances. It took with her about six hundred crew members.”

“I was there when it happened,” said the man, “watching her capsize and not being able to do anything.” He sighed deeply. “You see, I broke my arm a few days earlier and was recuperating in the hospital across the bay when the explosion happened. That’s why I survived, unlike most of my navy brothers.”

Kolya, who was sitting next to Yule, leaned over closer to the old man, in order to not miss his story. Pliyev and Gavrilo also became quiet and were looking at the man. Two older men in the seat in front of them also turned around in anticipation. Quite suddenly, the man had an audience.

“How did you know the ship?” asked the man, looking at Yule. “The event has been kept secret from the general public.”

“I have a relative who is a naval doctor. He was stationed in Sevastopol at the time of the explosion and told us about the event.”

“Did he tell you that *makaronniki* blew up the ship?” The man used the derogatory term for Italians in order to show contempt for the German ally, a sentiment common in post-war Russia as the country was still reeling from the enormous loss of lives and devastated infrastructure.

“No, he didn’t. He said that it was an explosion from a German sea mine, placed by the occupying Nazis right before they were kicked out of Sevastopol Bay.”

“That’s a pile of crap,” said the man excitedly. “That’s what *they* want you to think,” he added, lowering his voice to a whisper. “Here is what *really* happened. You probably don’t know that Novorossiysk was originally an Italian battleship, the *Giulio*

Cesare, and was ceded to Russia in 1949 as part of war reparations. The Italians, however, had a very difficult time accepting the loss of their navy's flagship. On the twenty-eighth of November, 1955, the elite special operations unit *Decima Flottiglia MAS,* known as the "frogmen," had been dispatched for a top secret operation. The following morning, at approximately one a.m., an enormous explosion, equivalent to one that would result from twelve hundred kilograms of TNT, had pierced all the decks of the *Novorossiysk* from the bottom plating to the forecastle deck. It was brutal."

"What proof do you have that the *makaronniki* did it, old man?" asked Pliyev, interrupting the narrator with his suspicions. "It sounds like one of *Babushka's* fabricated tales."

"What proof, you ask," said the man, raising his voice in indignation as his eyes narrowed. "What if I told you that exactly one week after she was sunk, a small group of Italian Navy frogmen had received the highest military awards possible in the Italian armed forces? Now think about that. There was no military action for years. So I ask you, what were those awards for?"

The bus went silent.

"He's got a point," said Gavrilo, his left ear still flaming red and swollen.

Most of the listeners nodded in agreement.

The bus, meanwhile, was rolling south through a rural area, between Stalino and the coalmining town of Gorlovka, which was a relatively young town that started as a Cossack settlement at the end of the nineteenth century. The village grew into a small town when it became the home for railroad workers constructing the Kursk–Azov Railroad. Although Gorlovka did have its own railroad station, not all trains stopped there. The outskirts of the town could be easily recognized by the omnipresent terrikons. In the early hours of a foggy morning, the massive *terrikons* looked like a heard of giant prehistoric creatures. The low clouds above the terrikons slowly drifted east, creating the illusion that the giant creatures were moving westward.

For Yule, the seemingly interminable journey that had started ten days ago in Leningrad had finally come to an end as the bus drew to a two-story dilapidated building. A plaque on the edifice, crookedly hanging next to the peeling entrance door, read *Obshchezhitiye,* Dormitory. An imposing figure of a man, dressed in a black, crudely-made coal miner's uniform and a hardhat with a flashlight, appeared in the threshold of the narrow doorway. He also held a roster in his hand, just like everyone Yule had met thus far at the facility.

"*Dobro pozhalovat*, welcome," said the man. "My name is Klim, and I am in charge of training the newcomers." He then proceeded to observe every single candidate appraisingly, notably fixing his eyes on Yule's face for a little longer than he was wont to do with the others. He continued, "After you settle down in your rooms, you will be free till tomorrow morning. At six o'clock, the bus will take you to the mine."

He read the names, one by one, checking them off in his roster and making some notations next to each name. At the end, after the last name had been called, he turned around and yelled into the hallway, "Dusia, *davay formu*, bring the uniforms!" Dusia, a tiny woman lacking two front teeth, showed up in the doorway, carrying a large bundle of black uniforms. She opened the bundle and started handing out uniforms to the men whose names were read by Klim. Apparently, the notes he was making were size estimates. He turned out to be pretty good at it, too, as the uniforms fitted almost everyone perfectly. The rooms within the dormitory were double occupancy, each with two metal beds equipped with spring mattresses. Some of the springs were visibly protruding through the fabric of indescribable color. The single window had no curtains, thus offering an uninterrupted view of yet another *terrikon*.

Yule looked at his watch and then at Kolya. It was only ten o'clock in the morning, and the two had an entire day ahead of them with no obligations to interrupt it. It was, Yule decided, time to see the town, which was situated about five miles from the actual coal mine. They hitched a ride in a huge ten-ton UAZ dump truck loaded with coal. The two sat in the huge cabin, right next to the driver. They were at least ten feet above the ground.

"Fresh meat?" asked the driver, looking at them and, to his chagrin, not finding any enthusiasm in their eyes. He clarified himself. "I mean new *recruits*."

"I guess we are," answered Yule, "but then, wouldn't that make you a hunk of stale meat?"

The driver looked at Yule in astonishment. Whether it was incredulity at the boy's boldness or just sheer amusement, Yule could not tell. The driver paused for a second, the cabin becoming awkwardly and almost frighteningly silent. After a few moments, he started laughing hysterically, banging his formidable fists on the steering wheel. Yule smiled.

"You are good, boy," said the driver, wiping the tears from his eyes. "Very good. You have a very sharp tongue, I see. But you have to be careful. We've got some mean characters working out there, straight from prison. Some of them have no sense of humor, or, at the very least, a sense of humor that is substantially different from yours or mine."

"He can take care of himself," responded Kolya confidently. "What's your name, by the way?"

"Vladek, but everyone calls me Vlad."

"Vladek is clearly a Polish name," said Yule. "*Czy znasz Polski*?"

"Yes, of course I know Polish! I was born in Lvov, when it was still Poland," responded Vladek in Polish. "How come you speak Polish? You're clearly not from this region. You're from the North, aren't you?"

"You're right, I am from the North, but I have a friend who lives in Stanislawow and who taught me Polish."

The driver paused again, as if he were digesting the news. His face turned more solemn, almost concerned. He looked at Yule, the silence only penetrated by the deep, rumbling sound of the truck's motor.

After the brief pause he said, "I feel compelled to tell you—and please don't take this the wrong way, but it's just that I think this job isn't for you. Now, I'm not trying to earwig you into running away, but you seem to be different from the people who are normally recruited for this type of work. If you have already made up your mind to stay, then I see that nothing I say can change that. Just think about it and stay safe." He drew his monstrous dump truck to the curb, right in front of a gray, faceless building.

"Well, this is where I drop you two off. *Do zobaczenia*, see you," he said.

The plaque by the entrance into the building where Vladek had dropped them off read *Gorsovet*, City Council. An enormous granite statue of Lenin dominated the square in front of the building. Lenin stood on a large pedestal that looked like a turret of an armored vehicle, his hat crumpled in one hand, his other hand in the pocket of a long overcoat. His chin was held high; his eyes were set deeply into his high cheekbones. The eyes were looking into the horizon, focused on something far in the distance. *What does he see?* thought Yule.

But Yule, like many others, already knew the answer to that question. Lenin was looking toward the bright future that never came, at the hard labor camps built for those who didn't agree with his vision, at the deaths of millions of innocent people, toward the uncontrolled printing of the ruble that lead to hyperinflation, at the glorious vision of forced labor, nationalization, and price control... But of course, no Soviet authority would agree with Yule's assessment. Most likely, they would cite Lenin's own words if asked the question; that he was looking toward a bright future where "every housekeeper will be running the State."

"Let's take a walk," said Kolya, interrupting Yule's thoughts. "I'm hungry."

The city was small, with a well-defined main street containing government buildings, two very green parks, and the main Orthodox Church. The church dominated the city's landscape. It was a massive and formidable structure; its most notable characteristics included a large dome and a bell tower with a tall steeple. Atop the steeple was a cross. To be able to see the entire structure, Yule and Kolya had to go to the opposite side of the street. The view, however, was magnificent. Even Kolya, who didn't share Yule's passion for architecture, had to admit that the church was beautiful. Although it was too early for church service, a small group of older women, wearing traditional Ukrainian headscarves, were already congregating in front of the entrance. They were discussing something using low, hushed voices, almost whispering.

"I'm hungry," Kolya repeated.

"Tough it up and stop whining," responded Yule. "You don't know what real hunger is." Kolya didn't say anything. "Besides," continued Yule while glancing at the prodigious church, "suffering purifies the soul." They looked at each other and burst into laughter.

A small, seemingly inconsequential building on the next block had a crookedly hanging sign above its entrance that read *Stolovaya*, Dinette. As was the case with most of the public eateries, it was a self-service type. The time of day was the somewhat quiet and uneventful period that spanned the time between breakfast and dinner (in Russia, *dinner* traditionally took place between midday and one p.m.). Since it was still before noon, the place was virtually empty. The room was rather bare, containing nothing but a few tables with chairs that were lined up against the walls and a kitchen counter at the far end. Behind the counter was an opening that lacked a door, which apparently led into the actual kitchen. The walls were painted in an unappealingly yellow color and were absolutely bare, except for a lone poster next to the kitchen entrance promoting "tasty and healthy food." To Yule's dismay, however, the proclamation was a stark contrast to the actual food that was served to the customers. The meat patties tasted somewhat like a wet book, and the mashed potatoes were watery and had no taste at all. Yule poked at the food with his fork, had a few bites, and pushed the plate away. Kolya, who was hungrier than Yule, managed to get through half of his patty but didn't touch the mashed potatoes. A middle-aged, pleasant looking woman behind the counter had been watching them with interest. Finally, she approached their table.

"Looks like the food is not good enough for your aristocratic tastes," she said sarcastically. "But it is all we have."

Yule ignored the sarcasm and asked, "Do you have anything that wasn't cooked here, for instance, biscuits or pastries?"

The woman turned around, walked through the door-less opening behind the counter, and disappeared into the kitchen.

"You just insulted the cook. I hope she's not the one," said Kolya nervously. "Or maybe she's talking to the cook right now. Get ready for some combat."

The woman returned in less than a minute, carrying a small plate loaded with homemade cookies.

"Here," she said, "these are from my house. I also put a kettle on—the tea is coming in a minute."

She looked at them, most likely detecting a trace of incredulity, and added, "I have two boys. The younger just turned eighteen. He was drafted by the navy and sent to Murmansk approximately two weeks ago. The older one is twenty-two and works the night shift at the coal mine. I hardly see him."

She had, Yule observed, kind and sad eyes. Not a word was mentioned about her husband. It was probably an old story, the same one that rang true for so many families throughout the Soviet Union. Yule assumed that either the war or the coal mines had claimed him from his family. Regardless, he decided not to ask.

The lady's name was Magda, and she was originally from the Carpathian Region, next to the Hungarian border. Magda brought three empty cups, a teakettle, and a few lumps of sugar. She poured some tea for both Yule and Kolya then asked, "Have you heard the news today?"

The boys looked at each other and shook their heads. She sighed deeply, a trademark of Russian women, the eternal sufferers, and said, "They hanged Imre Nagy and his associates in Budapest today."

"Imre Nagy," repeated Kolya. "Wasn't he the one that led the uprising in Hungary a few years ago?"

"It was in summer of 1956," added Yule. "I lived in Stanislawow then and still remember the thousands of tanks that passed through the town en route to Hungary."

Magda's eyes filled up with tears, and Yule sensed that his musings about her husband would soon be fulfilled. She lifted up a corner of her apron and delicately wiped her eyes, one at a time. The boys tactfully kept quiet, looking at her and waiting for an explanation. She blew her nose into the other, still dry corner of her apron and, sure enough, offered the story that vindicated her sadness. She explained that her husband and his brother were among the Hungarian rebels. The husband was killed by the Russians. His good friend, Miklos, a journalist, was captured, tried, and executed along with Imre Nagy and two other comrades.

"There is a small Hungarian community here," she continued, "and people are seriously troubled by these executions. When I take my lunch break later, I'll go to the city church and get more details."

"Is that the church we just passed, about a block away from here?" asked Kolya. "We saw a group of older women gathered in front of it, whispering."

"That's the one. People have to be careful and watch what they say, so sometimes we must resort to whispers."

An idea suddenly hit Yule. "Do you have a short-wave radio?" he asked. "We can listen to the BBC news or even Radio Warszawa to get more information."

"My older son has a brand new *Baltica* radio. It starts with twenty-five-meter bands and has an anti-jamming device," responded Magda enthusiastically.

At that moment, someone stepped through the door. Magda lowered her voice and said, "Radianska Street fourteen, just around the corner. Come after three."

At precisely 3:15, Yule knocked on the door of a small corner house. Magda opened the door and took them into a small room in the back, apparently her older son's bedroom. The room itself consisted of a metal-framed bed in the corner, a nightstand, and a brand new-looking radio with the name *Baltica* sprawled across its yellow-clothed front panel.

"Here it is," said Magda, pointing at the radio. "Do you know how to work it?"

Yule approached the nightstand and turned the knob. Almost immediately, following the faint popping sound of a click, the resonance of an accordion filled the room. All three of them sat on the bed, listening attentively to the most recent station apparently listened to by Magda's son.

"Let's try the BBC," said Yule as he moved the pointer to the 25.1 meter frequency, where he knew the BBC was. As expected, the execution of Imre Nagy and his three associates dominated the news. A man's voice permeated through the speaker, dispassionately reading the news and informing the world of the execution. Yule was trying to simultaneously translate but was able to convey only the main thrust of the news. The subject was complicated, and there were political terms not familiar to him, but he did his best.

Hungarian émigrés and Nationals have attacked Soviet Embassies in Germany and Denmark.

Lord Lansdowne in the House of Lords has placed on record "the horror and indignation which this latest shameful act has aroused."

There were also many quotes from the leaders of the Hungarian Democratic community in the West condemning the execution. Even the famous British Communist lawyer, D.N. Pritt, called the act "unduly trenchant."

That was the world's reaction, as delivered by the BBC World News. Yule switched the radio off and looked at Magda.

"How well did you know your husband's friend, Miklos?" he asked.

"I didn't know him that well, but my husband was very close to him. Miklos was one the best journalists in Hungary. He always spoke the truth. He was with my husband when he was shot by the Russians. He died in Miklos's arms."

Getting back to *Shakhta Lenina* was much more difficult than leaving it. Yule and Kolya had to wait for almost an hour at a bus stop until a beat-up, dirty bus had finally pulled over. A cheerful young man with a peasant Ukrainian accent sold them two tickets, closed the door behind them, and pulled away at full throttle. The engine backfired, emitting a painful sound not unlike the explosion of a canon and then spitting out a heavy black plume of smoke, part of which gained entry into the bus through the open windows, thereby throwing the passengers into a frenzy of sneezing and coughing. But all of that didn't result in a dizzying speed. Quite the contrary, the bus merely jerked violently, nearly stalled, and slowly started to creep forward, bobbing up and down into and over the plethora of deep potholes.

The first night in the unfamiliar, uninviting dormitory was terrible. Although the mattress itself was relatively soft, the protruding springs were merciless, pricking Yule's body as if he were sleeping on a bed of needles. The pillow was filled with lumps of raw cotton and, as a consequence, had bumps that were as hard as stone. It took Yule a good two hours before he could finally drift off into one of his flying dreams. This time, he dreamed of being in the middle of a massive field surrounded by *terrikons*. The *terrikons* were converging on him, moving slowly and deliberately. They were red hot and exuded an intolerable heat that could be felt from a great distance. Yule expended all of his energy in an attempt to lift off. After repeated efforts, he finally succeeded but couldn't climb high enough to escape the blazing, unendurable heat.

He woke up sweating, his throat painfully dry. It was, to Yule's consternation, only four in the morning. The dorm was uncomfortably hot, releasing back the heat that was absorbed from the sun during the day. The chance of falling back to sleep was rather remote and, as usual, the solution was to read a book. The book that he borrowed from the library earlier was about the history of the Donbas, written in Polish and, therefore, not subjected to censorship. He learned that the Donbas, which stood for the Donets Coal Basin, was a large mining region in the southern end of eastern Europe. Yule read that it stretched all the way from the Donets Hills in the North toward the Don River, and across the low Azov Upland and coastal plains to the Sea of Azov in the South. The region was part of the Eurasian Steppe, a belt of open grassland that extends from Hungary to Manchuria. Yule remembered from his time spent with Professor that Eastern Slavs called the area the 'wild field.' It was a historical theatre of continuous military operations in which the Slavs, Kipchaks, and

Tatars fought long and bloody battles for many centuries. Yule put the book down and tried to imagine one of his war games played out on a huge map of the Donbas. The map would be dominated by figurines representing the warriors of a mass of different cultures, each wielding a vast array of horses, fire throwing catapults, and deadly cannons that would wreck havoc on the enemy's horsemen. Yule gradually fell asleep holding the book in both hands, images of war and glory racing rampantly through his mind.

He woke up with a start to the sound of a morning siren that sounded more like the wailing whistle of a steamship from the previous century. His wristwatch showed five o'clock, thereby explaining the darkness outside. Kolya was fast asleep, oblivious to the call of the siren. A few moments later, there was a hard knock on the door.

"Get up! Get up, boys! It's time to break the production records." The voice clearly belonged to that toothless, scrawny creature by the name of Dusia.

"Quick, someone has come to see you," said Yule, shaking Kolya's shoulder and pointing with his other hand at the door. Kolya jumped off of the bed, still not completely awake and most likely not fully aware of where he was. He was utterly naked, save for his boxer shorts. Kolya ran to the door and opened it. Dusia, who had worked amongst the predominantly male coal miners for a very long time, appeared completely unshaken by Kolya's appearance.

"Good morning, *Stakhanovets*," she said, giggling.

She was, of course, referring to Alexey Stakhanov, a miner who used to work in the neighboring coal mine. On August 31, 1935, he allegedly hewed one hundred two tons of coal during his six-hour shift; the tonnage represented fourteen times his quota. He purportedly had no help and used only a jackhammer to accomplish this miraculous feat. The occurrence was celebrated by *Pravda* as a World Record, and the Communist Party naturally launched the *Stakhanovite* Movement. Stalin, seizing the moment, stated that such records were possible only in the "land of socialism." After Stalin's death, the artificiality of the movement was acknowledged and, a few years later, the record was debunked as a fraud. A number of witnesses had stepped forward and testified that the production of Stakhanov's co-workers had simply been added to his own total to create the astonishing amount.

Alexey Stakhanov's name had become a complete joke, especially in coal mining circles. It took Kolya a few extra seconds to get it and, finally, all three of them laughed, albeit cautiously and quietly. After the events of the autumn of 1956 in Hungary, the Soviet government took back some of the liberties which Nikita Khrushchev had given to the country earlier. Freedom of speech in private situations was still a novelty to the Russians; the machinery of thought control was not completely dismantled. It merely became less effective as the memory of Stalin receded. Ordinary people had been feeling their way cautiously forward and, at first, found it hard to believe that it was possible to speak openly about politics without danger, even to joke about the artificial heroes of Stalin's era in the Soviet Union without fear of political retribution.

"Don't forget to put your pants on," said Dusia playfully before moving toward the next room. "The bus is already waiting."

They were ready in five minutes and went outside, walking to the stationary bus that was parked directly outside of the dormitory. Dressed in black miner's overalls, the two looked like twins. The bus was already chock-full of new recruits, all looking like a flock of rooks perched atop the wraparound wooden benches, tense in the face of the unknown.

The ride was short, as the mine was situated just behind the *terrikon* that was visible outside of Yule's dormitory window. It was an old mine and, despite the advances in mining technology that were pioneered by the English and the Americans, still employed manual labor, utilizing the room-and-pillar method and jackhammers to excavate the coal seam. Yule and Kolya stepped into the opening, feeling as if they were standing in the threshold of a massive beast's mouth. The feeling was further augmented by the deep, rumbling sounds that emanated from within, sounds from the belly of the beast. *The mine*, Yule thought, *is a carbon copy of the gold mine in Siberia, just substantially larger.*

They piled up into a large cage with a wooden floor and descended about two hundred feet into the void, finally reaching a large underground space with a low ceiling. The entire space was seemingly supported by pillars. The group was then led through an interminable enfilade of smaller rooms and, finally, into the last one, where it seemed that most of the action was. From first glance, it appeared as if the coal was, with the use of large shovels, loaded into shuttle cars, which were then pushed along their rails by hand toward the belt that would bring the coal to the awaiting dump trucks. The role of the new and unqualified recruits was twofold: some were sent to shovel the coal while others were asked to push the shuttle carts toward the belt. Yule and Kolya were selected for pushing the carts, a job that required two people to overcome the inertia of a fully loaded cart. The challenge, however, was not only to get the laden cart to move, but also to stop it later without losing control over it. Surprisingly, however, pushing wasn't as difficult they had expected—the real difficulty came when an empty cart derailed and had to be lifted back and the wheels required realignment with the rails. It happened three times during their shift and expended an extraordinary amount of energy from them, so that by the end of the day they were rendered unable to even *talk* to each other.

During the bus ride back to the dorm, Yule was trying to find a rational explanation for the inhumane conditions in the coal mine and the absence of the modern technology that he read about. Was it because labor was so cheap, or was the principle culprit the fact that the ruble was being printed without any corresponding value in gold at the Soviet treasury? It was, Yule concluded, probably a combination of the two factors. He always remembered Professor's theory about the character of a nation. It was possible that the answer lied in the fact that the Russians never bothered to engage in a long-term study of the realities of money as did their Western counterparts. Professor always did say that Russians had an immature attitude toward money, but at the same time saw the Western preoccupation with it as somehow ignoble.

Dusia greeted the boys with a cheerful wink but did not receive any reciprocation or acknowledgement from them, so she quickly moved down the corridor. In a feeble attempt to motivate the enervated boys, she called out from the other end of the hallway and said, "Don't worry! In a few days it will be as simple as pissing on your own two fingers!" They were too tired to react to the profound bestowal of wisdom and went into their rooms, collapsing onto their beds without even bothering to take off their sullied uniforms.

Yule woke up at one o'clock in the morning from his thirst; his throat was dry and his eyes were itchy. The washroom was at end of the long corridor, adjacent to the communal toilet that consisted of multiple openings in the cement floor that had no partitions separating them. Yule drank out of a faucet and then saw his reflection in a cracked mirror. An ashen-colored face peered back at him. The only part of his face that he recognized was his still startlingly bright blue eyes, which were even more salient due to their contrast with his ashen face. There was no soap and no hot water in the washroom, so Yule washed his face and his hands as best as he could. The coal dust, however, was very stubborn and seemed to have permeated his skin. There was, to Yule's dismay, no towel either. By the time he got back to the room, his skin was already dry. He collapsed again, only to wake up to the irksome call of the morning siren. Kolya was already awake but still in his bed, merely looking quizzically at Yule. Although he did not say it, the question was clearly painted in his eyes: *Is this how we will live the rest of our lives*?

That night, Yule's dreams were full of phantasmagoric events. He was taken by the toothless Dusia into an elevator but not the same one they had used earlier to get into the mine. This one was special, constructed of steel with a wraparound window made of bulletproof glass. The elevator silently and speedily flew down a shaft that penetrated the earth's crust. The ride, Yule realized, was like traveling through time itself, with each layer of the earth's history clearly visible before him. First they entered the ring that corresponded with the last hundred thousand years of earth's history, containing the remains of our hominid ancestors that shared a resemblance with modern humans. The altimeter on the wall showed -0.5 miles. When they reached the negative one mile mark, the scene outside the window had gradually changed; there were traces of the mass extinction everywhere, most notably, the well-preserved carcasses of huge animals that were imbedded in the rocky walls of the shaft, clearly corresponding with the Cretaceous—Tertiary period about sixty million years ago. Dusia was busy with the control panel and paid no attention to the view. At the depth of -1.5 miles, the carcasses had become substantially smaller; the dead creatures were rodent-sized and had a variety of strange shapes. The descent continued through the period of the Cambrian Explosion and, eventually, they reached the period dominated by microbes. Yule was distracted from his observations by the realization that the temperature within the elevator was rising substantially as it approached the liquid core. Yule turned around to tell Dusia that it was time to go back but, to his horror, realized that she wasn't there. He looked at the control panel, trying to figure out how to reverse the descent, but the panel was dismantled and all he saw was a bunch of twisted wires. As the elevator continued its unrestrained free-fall, Yule thought he heard a manic laugh from somewhere above. Terror gripped him as the temperature continued to climb, a sense of hopelessness descending over him. Breathing became more and more difficult, the temperature nearly unbearable.

He woke up. Kolya was standing next to his bed, shaking his shoulder violently.

"You were screaming," he said. "Something about hot magma?"

"I had a nightmare about going deep down into the earth's crust and reaching the hot core. I was about to be burned alive right before you woke me up."

"You can thank me for my bravery later. It's only two in the morning, let's get some more sleep."

Kolya went back to his bed and, in about thirty seconds, started snoring lightly. Yule just stared at the dirty ceiling, observing the burned matches that were stuck to its surface. *Why was the dream so familiar*? The underground descent in the elevator had an obvious connection to the coal mine, but the part about the earth's crust being presented as tree rings by which the entire life of the tree could be read was not as easily explained. He remembered the definition of a dream as an "unusual combination of past events, real or imagined," given to him by Dr. Stein back in the snowy Kolyma region.

Yule's many and racing thoughts accompanied him as he also fell asleep only a few minutes later.

The workweek at the mine was Monday through Saturday. Sunday morning was spent lying in bed till noon, nursing aching muscles and joints and reading borrowed books from the library. By one in the afternoon, Yule and Kolya were hungry and bored.

"Let's go see Magda and have something to eat there," suggested Yule. "The food's not that great, but it's still better than what's offered at the dorm's cafeteria."

On their way downstairs, they bumped into Gavrilo. He was almost unrecognizable from the last time they saw him and looked dreadful, with dark circles underneath his eyes, sunken cheeks, and a bandage wrapped around his head. Both of them stopped, looking at Gavrilo in silence while comprehending his appearance. Gavrilo had a guilty look on his face and a faint smile.

"A piece of ceiling fell onto my head," he explained without being asked, reading the silent expressions on Yule's and Kolya's faces. "But I'm fine now."

"How is Pliyev doing?" asked Kolya. "We haven't seen him since our arrival."

The smile instantly disappeared from Gavrilo's lips, replaced by an angry snarl. "Pliyev split on the second day," answered Gavrilo, with bitterness in his voice. "But before he did so, he also decided that it was worth his time to take my three hundred rubles with him."

"Son of a bitch!" exclaimed Yule angrily. "How are you surviving without any money?"

"I was in the hospital till yesterday—they fed me." He paused. "Now, I don't know."

Yule reached into the back pocket of his pants and extracted a few banknotes. He counted thirty rubles from the pile and handed the money to Gavrilo.

"Thank you," he said quietly. "I'll pay you back as soon as I get paid, I promise."

"You don't have to pay me back immediately. You can do it in installments, if that'll be easier for you," said Yule, walking away and gesturing to Kolya to follow him. "We'll see you around."

When outside, the two looked at each other. This time, however, there was no laughter.

"It's a sad story," said Yule, summarizing Gavrilo's predicament in one simple sentence.

They started walking toward downtown Gorlovka; it looked as if the buses weren't running on Sunday. Regardless, it was a beautiful midsummer day, not too hot yet, so it felt remarkably good to be able to breathe fresh air that was not contaminated by the noxious coal dust. Thirty minutes later, at around one o'clock, they entered the *Stolovaya*. The lunch hour, which Russians referred to as their 'dinner break,' was over. Magda was scrubbing the tables and humming a melody that sounded to Yule's ears like one of Chopin's Polonaises. She was visibly happy to see them and, without asking, went back into the kitchen, only to emerge with a tray of cold cuts and some leftover cabbage pie.

"I always make cabbage pies on Sundays," she explained, "but there are not so many customers as on the weekdays, so I had some food left."

The two young men had downed the entire tray in less than a minute. Magda sat across from them, elbows on the table and supporting her chin with folded hands. She looked not unlike a mother observing her hungry children eat. After satisfying their hungers, Yule and Kolya looked embarrassed at what must have seemed like their ravenous gluttony, but Magda ignored their looks and brought two cups of tea, along with her already familiar homemade cookies.

"How much do we owe you?" asked Yule, breaking the awkwardness of the moment.

"Don't be silly," she said in a chastising though not unkind manner. "It was my pleasure to feed you. You look undernourished and unkempt, *clearly* a motherly hand is needed."

They spent the rest of the day in town, most of it in the library and the last two hours in the local movie theater named the *Zvezda*, Star. They were showing Don Quixote, based on Miguel de Cervantes's novel. According to the announcement on the screen, the film had won first prize at the Cannes Festival the previous year. The film turned out to be much more serious than the novel itself, and the main events had been moved around, but despite the alterations, it was an enjoyable movie, especially thanks to the great acting.

They walked back to their dormitory in total darkness, giving credence to the fact that Ukrainian nights were notoriously dark.

The only source of light was the faint, almost alien-like glow that emanated from the *terrikons* in the distance. They made it to the dorm without any problems, barring an unpleasant encounter with a drunken miner who was demanding some kind of restitution for his lost health and calling for a national revolt. He was harmless, though.

Despite the fresh air and a blissfully peaceful previous day, Yule had a strange dream. It was one of his flying dreams, but this time there was no amorphous danger to escape from. Instead, he had flown to a place that he had never visited before. When he had gained an unusually high altitude, he noticed the silhouette of the Eiffel Tower ahead and flew straight there. To the right of the tower was the Hill of Montmartre with its Boulevard de Clichy stretched between Place Pigalle and Place Blanch. To the left of Place Pigalle was a wide spread of Boulevard Batingole, and to the right, behind Place Blanch, was Saint Antoine, a blue-collar suburb. The crowds of laughing people, the bright lights, music everywhere, the restaurants, cafés, bars brimming with all sorts of different people… Yule was entranced by all of it, almost falling out of the sky due to his ephemeral mental lapse. The surroundings appeared both Ruritanian and vaguely familiar. He looked for a place to land and to join the merry crowd, when all of a sudden a high, shrill whistle pierced through the sky. Yule woke with a start, the morning siren blaring into his ears. He stayed in bed for an extra minute, contemplating the dream, one that offered a pleasant reprieve from his current situation.

As soon as his shift had begun, he noticed Dusia standing by the conveyor belt, talking to the foreman who was angrily arguing and flailing his arms. Both of them were glancing at Yule and, finally, the foreman shrugged his shoulders in resignation and gestured toward Yule to approach.

"You have a visitor," said Dusia. "The director sent me to bring you out. Let's go."

Yule's mind was racing through all of the possible visitors. Was it Zoya? Perhaps it was Marek, or even Aunt Sophia with little Vova? Then Yule's mind turned to less pleasant thoughts, such as the possibility that the "visitors" were the authorities, coming to arrest Yule in the event that Konstantin didn't make it.

The door into his room was open wide. Yule's face transformed into an expression of bewilderment as he glimpsed his father sitting inside, flipping through the pages of one of Yule's books. It was a pleasant surprise to see Efim. *He actually cares*, was one of Yule's first thoughts.

They said hello to each other but didn't move. Yule merely stood on the doorstep, Efim continued sitting. Hugging and kissing were never a part of their family culture.

"How did you find me?" asked Yule, knowing that it was a silly question. He merely wanted to break the awkwardness of the moment.

"Your mother called, she was looking for you. I took a plane to Stanislawow first-thing and filed a missing person report, but they already knew all about you because of your affair with Konstantin, so they sent me to your recruiter."

"You could've asked Marek."

There was a long pause, perhaps the longest pause that Yule had ever felt in his life. Somehow he knew what was coming and understood what he didn't want to understand. He tried to reject it, to cast it from the recesses of his mind and to never think of it again, but alas, the inevitable answer came.

"Marek is dead," whispered Efim. "He died the next day after your departure. I didn't know him, but I understand that you two were very close."

Yule had to fight back the tears. A strange sensation of heaviness settled over him, as if some massive weight had been dropped onto his chest and had exerted an unfathomable amount of pressure. Yule had experienced the untimely deaths of people close to him before, but he never felt as alone or as miserable as he felt in that moment. Marek was more than *close* to him; he was the closest thing that Yule ever had to a best friend, to a big brother even. A void filled Yule's being, as if a vital component of his life had been crudely and forcefully extracted from him. He mumbled something incoherent and wandered over to the window. His father remained politely silent, again flipping through the pages of Yule's book.

Finally, after an interminable amount of time, Yule turned around, feigning composure. "How long will you be staying here?" he asked.

"I am not staying here and neither are you. I have two train tickets, and we are leaving for Leningrad at six p.m."

"I can't leave. I owe the three hundred rubles of start up money."

"It's already taken care of, you have no further obligations to this place." Efim paused. "You don't belong here, son."

Yule didn't answer, but he knew that his father was right. His last few days were filled with doubts bordering on depression and an endless torrent of questions about whether he had made a mistake by coming to Gorlovka. Luckily, his father was a silent man who had spared Yule from lecturing and moralizing. He just took him home, apparently understanding very well the predicament that his son had found himself in.

Hello, beautiful Leningrad! The city seemed even more magnificent in the stark comparison with the destitution and dust of the Donbas coal mines. It was only a mere two weeks since Yule's hasty departure for Stanislawow, but it seemed like an eternity. The events of the past two weeks were nightmarish in Yule's mind, almost surreal in light of his present surroundings. Nothing had changed substantially at Baskov fourteen, apartment seventeen. Grandma Shifra still kept her unbelievably straight posture and her imperial silence intact, Alex continued torturing his accordion while perfecting the "Saint Louis Blues," and the apartment looked very much the same. A sense of familiarity settled over Yule, making the events at Stanislawow and at the coal mine seem distant. The streets were empty as July was a summer month and all of his classmates were away for summer vacation. Since there wasn't much to do, Yule decided to continue his exploration of the city. His thoughts immediately wandered toward Irina Alexandrovna. Who better to tour the city with than her? Yule knew that she usually stayed in town during the summer breaks, tutoring pupils for the upcoming college entry examinations.

Yule knocked on the heavy oaken door, using the massive bronze knocker that hung from the mouth of a lion's head. A more modern electric doorbell was there too, but it was all too tempting to lift the massive ring and to throw it down. The thump was deep, loud, and inexplicably satisfying.

"Who's there?" He heard Irina Alexandrovna's voice, muffled by the massive door.

"Yule."

The clicking sound of a heavy spring releasing a deadbolt lock followed. The door slowly opened.

Irina Alexandrovna gasped. "You look *awful*," she said. "Have you been eating at all? I was beginning to worry about you, but now that you're back a month earlier, I'm even more worried. Come in. Sit down… I'll make some tea."

She went to her antique breakfront and took out the pleasantly familiar white and cobalt teapot, along with two matching cups and saucers. Then she went into the kitchen and extracted from the refrigerator a sugar cone filled with yellow custard.

"Fresh from the cafe Nord," she said. "Your favorite, as if I knew that you were coming."

They settled down at the table vis-à-vis each other, and Yule proceeded to describe the remarkable events of the past two weeks.

Irina Alexandrovna listened intently, without interruptions. Her only displays of emotion came whenever she widened her eyes in horror, specifically when Yule had described the episode with Konstantin and, later on, the coal mine. When he finished, Irina Alexandrovna sat silently, her steepled fingers underneath her chin and her eyes closed. Yule continued to sip his already lukewarm tea and to crunch on his empty sugar cone.

She finally broke the silence and said, "How could you *possibly* leave your mother with that man?"

"She made her choice, coming to his defense and scolding me for getting involved," responded Yule, taken aback by the unexpected response.

"Getting involved is one thing. Putting him in a hospital is quite another."

"What was I supposed to do? Wag my finger at him and say, 'you are such a naughty man, stop breaking my mother's arms?'"

"You know, with all of your intellect and your encyclopedic knowledge of many areas, deep down inside, you are still a boy who doesn't know anything about the complexities of women."

That wasn't something he had expected from his friend. For a moment, he even lost his usual legerity.

"You're probably right, I do know very little about women in general, but I *know* my own mother very well," responded Yule quietly. "I know her well enough to discern whose side she's on."

Irina Alexandrovna's grim expression turned softer as she reached over the table and put her hand on top of his, just like Zoya used to do. Only his mother's hand felt like velvet with her soft and smooth skin, while Irina Alexandrovna's felt dry and firm. It was a comforting gesture nonetheless.

"I am sorry," she said, looking into Yule's eyes. "I didn't mean to upset you. There's been enough misery in your life without my lecturing you."

Yule decided that it was high time to change the subject. "Why don't we take a walk along Nevsky? You could tell me all about the churches that we haven't visited yet," said Yule, getting off the chair.

"I'll do it with pleasure, just not today. I have several tutoring sessions this afternoon, but I'm completely free tomorrow, if that's fine with you." Yule nodded his consent.

She waked him to the door. "See you around eleven," she said. And with that, Yule left her apartment.

It was drizzling outside. A fine, almost imperceptible mist pleasantly kissed Yule's face, cooling it from the summer heat. It was typical Leningrad weather, which Yule enjoyed very much.

He took Nevsky Prospect all the way to Mayakovski Street, turned left, and walked approximately one mile to Baskov Pereulok. As soon as he crossed the street to enter the front courtyard of his building, he noticed a little figure under the far arch leading to the smallest courtyard in the back. The boy was standing there, wiping his bloodied nose with the sleeve of his shirt. Yule immediately recognized Maria Ivanovna's son, Vladimir.

"Putka!" said Yule. "What happened to you?"

"*Kosorotik*, Crooked Mouth, pushed me into the wall." Kosorotik was an older boy who lived in the last building of the furthest courtyard. He had a birth defect; his mouth was significantly off-center, pulled closer to his left ear. The children teased him mercilessly, and every time one of the children called him *Kosorotik*, he would go after the perpetrator. It was a game that kids played, not realizing that it was both cruel and hurtful to the boy whose real name was not even known.

"Why did he do it?" asked Yule, already certain of the reason but wanting to elucidate it for Putka.

"I don't know," said Putka. "I just called out his name and he pushed me."

"Did you call him *Kosorotik*?"

"What else can I call him?"

"But that's not his name. It's actually a very hurtful and derogatory term that describes his illness. By the way, what *is* his real name?"

"I don't know. Everyone calls him *Kosorotik*."

"Just becomes everyone else calls him that doesn't mean that you should. Please, find out his real name from your mother and the next time you see him, use his real name and you've got yourself a new friend. Will you promise to do it?"

Putka nodded in agreement and started skipping toward his apartment where his mother would most likely scold him for a badly stained shirt.

Grandma Shifra was home alone. Efim and Dina were at work, while Alex had left for a special summer camp on the Sea of Azov to receive treatment for his TB-related condition.

"Sit down," said Grandma in her usual stern manner. "I have to talk to you."

Detecting an oncoming lecture, he sat by the window, overlooking the courtyard. The courtyard was dark even on a sunny day due to the shadows from the surrounding buildings, but on rainy days it was especially gloomy. Tall stacks of firewood were casting shapeless shadows onto the cracked asphalt.

Grandma continued, "What possessed you to go to Donbas to work in a coal mine instead of coming back home?"

"I didn't feel that I was particularly missed here."

"Now *that* is a stupid thing to say; your father and I love you, more than you can imagine." She went silent for a moment. "It's your mother's feelings for you that I would question."

"And why would you say that?"

"You're probably not aware of the fact that your own mother had abandoned you when you were only two years old. She left your father and you without any explanation."

"If that's indeed the case, then how was I ever reunited with her?"

"A year later she returned to kidnap you and, shortly thereafter, left for Kolyma. For many months we had no idea where you were."

Yule sat silently, digesting what he had just heard. It was not altogether surprising, at least not as surprising as it should have been. Some pieces of the puzzle had fallen into place as a matter of fact. He and Zoya had never discussed the pre-Kolyma period of their lives; any time that he had asked a question about that period of his life, Zoya would ignore it altogether or just switch the subject.

"Maybe so, but as far as my father is concerned, I feel that what he did for me was more out of an obligation, a duty, rather than love, especially now, when he has his new family to take care of. I don't want to feel like a liability."

"He is a man of honor and yes, it is indeed his duty to look after you. But judge him by what he did, not by what you think, and besides, you are altogether forgetting about my existence. It is true, though, that nobody loved you more than your grandpa Sam, but he is gone. Nevertheless, you should remember where your home is, and it is not in Stanislawow nor certainly is it in the Donbas."

She looked straight into Yule's eyes with her long and penetrating look, as if to seal the statement and to sear it into his consciousness. She then turned around and went into the kitchen.

On the thirteenth of May, 1960, Yule was only three months shy of his seventeenth birthday, as well as two weeks away from his graduation ball at Regional High 194. His father and stepmother were annoyingly insistent on him going into the study of dentistry upon graduation, primarily because it was a very lucrative occupation in the Soviet Union. A dentist could see private patients and, unlike in most other professions, could make a decent living.

Yule hadn't heard from his mother since that fateful visit last summer, one that now seemed distant, as if a remnant of some terrible dream. He had attempted to call her a few times since then but to no avail. Telephone calls outside of the city limits were considered "inter-city" and required a trip to a special "communication center," where such calls were handled by an operator.

Yule was lying in bed that Saturday morning, running through his thoughts the possible arguments that could be made to his father in order to express his desire not to study dentistry. Granted, it was a lucrative career, but somehow Yule couldn't envision himself bending over his patients for the whole day, chastising them for improper oral care and drilling holes in their rotted teeth. On top of all that, Yule just lacked any interest in the subject. Grandma Shifra interrupted his thoughts as she walked in, holding a single sheet of paper in her hands.

"Are you awake?" she whispered quietly and gently. Upon seeing that his eyes were open, she continued to speak in that very uncharacteristic manner, one that disconcerted Yule. Her usual stern and meticulous speech was replaced by a softer, more mitigating whisper. That change alone conveyed the magnitude of what she was about to say.

"Yule," she continued, not knowing how to proceed. "A terrible event has happened in your life."

She didn't have to continue; a heart wrenching, dizzying sensation settled over Yule as his chest constricted and his breath became stuck in his throat. He hoped beyond hope, beyond anything that he had ever wished for, that his conviction would not come into fruition, that the terrible thing would be something, *anything*, else. Grandma handed the paper to him and said, "It is Zoya."

He looked at the letter, written in the familiar handwriting of his mother, but couldn't bring himself to read it. The last two lines of the letter sloped toward the right corner and were completely illegible. He placed the letter on his chest face down, the last remaining remnant of his mother's life. As he closed his eyes, an unstoppable wave of thoughts, chaotic and completely irrelevant, had poured into his mind. There was no way of shaking them off, and the only clear outlet was to follow through that maze of crazy associations. It took him a few moments to finally garner the courage to read that fateful letter. It was brief, confirming what Yule had already known. She hastily wrote the letter after taking a fatal dose of narcotics. She wrote about being completely lost and alone, about seeing no reason to continue to trudge through life in her abject misery. Her only request was for Yule to look after his younger brother. It was apparent that the drug had already taken effect by the end of the letter; the last two sentences were incoherent and the ink was a watery yellow, most likely from the fallen tears. The envelope was stamped with the date of mailing, namely five days ago.

Surprisingly, the tears would not come. It was the one moment in Yule's life when he actually wanted to cry; yet his body would not afford him that respite. His first thoughts were about Konstantin, that had he not poisoned Zoya's mind, Yule's mother would have still been alive. There was no doubt in Yule's mind that the next time he would chance upon seeing Konstantin, the vermin would die.

That very evening, Yule boarded a night train to Lvov, where he transferred to the next available Stanislawow-bound train. That following evening, he knocked on the door of his apartment. There was no answer, so he tested the door by gently pushing it forward; it was unlocked and the apartment was empty. There was no sign of Aunt Sophia or his little brother. The strong scent of pine permeated the interior, indicating that the coffin had been in the apartment for quite some time. Pine branches were traditionally used to decorate coffins during the viewings, as evidenced by the dry, fallen pine needles that were scattered throughout the apartment. He went outside and walked over to the taxi stand across the street. The line was relatively short and, a few minutes later, Yule was seated inside of a *Pobeda* sedan with ripped upholstery and a strong smell of gasoline permeating the entire interior. The driver, an old man wearing a small straw hat and a *papirosa,* a cigarette, hanging out from his clenched teeth, simply looked at Yule and raised his eyebrows.

"The Funeral Bureau," said Yule.

The man artfully moved the *papirosa* to the other corner of his mouth, somehow without unclenching his teeth.

"What, did someone die?"

"Yes, my mother, if you don't mind, and I am not in the mood for small talk so please *drive*."

The taxi, which had already moved forward a few feet, stopped abruptly. The driver managed to turn his torso around so much that he faced Yule, who was seated behind him.

"Are you Doctor Zoya's son?" he demanded, staring at Yule with a cold, harsh expression. Yule nodded, taken aback by the driver's aggression. "Where were you when she died, huh?" he continued angrily. "Total *strangers* had to bury her."

"Her aunt and her husband were both living with her," responded Yule angrily, irked by the driver's implied accusations.

"You didn't know anything about your mother, did you?"

Yule went silent.

"It's a small town," the driver continued, "and your mother was loved by all the folks. All of us knew that she was being abused by that swine of a husband. Your grandaunt took your brother and left for the town of Khmelnitsky."

"Do you know where Konstantin is now?" asked Yule.

"No one knows. He bolted even before the body was discovered." The driver pressed his foot down hard on the accelerator, the knee-jerk reaction a demonstration of his anger toward Konstantin. The sound of the screeching tires pierced the air.

The taxicab pulled over to a small, dingy-looking building with a sign on the door that read *Pochoronnoye Buro*, Funeral Bureau.

"My name is Boris," said the driver, extending his hand toward Yule. "You can always find me on the corner of Rynek, if you need any help. Well, this is your stop. Good luck, you'll definitely need it. You know, that venomous husband of hers practically *diseased* your mother." Yule nodded his thanks and reciprocated the gesture by shaking the driver's hand. He left the taxi, slamming the creaky door behind him with a loud *thump*.

Yule went inside the building. The interior of the relatively large room was as dingy as the building's façade, and the man in the dark gray suit sitting behind the huge metal desk was a perfect match. He was writing using a fountain pen with gold and blue enamel encrustations, scribbling numerous entries into a large, leather-bound journal.

"*Dah*," muttered the man, without so much as looking at Yule.

"I am the son of Zoya Kiseleva."

The man slowly put down his pen and peered at Yule. "You are late. Your mother was buried the day before yesterday—I couldn't keep her body any longer, as our refrigerator is out of order."

"May I see the grave?"

"Stefan!" yelled the man. Stefan appeared through the back door in less than a second. He was the male version of Dusia, that scrawny, toothless creature back at the coal mine in Donbas. To Yule's amusement, it looked like he was missing the same teeth as Dusia, namely the two central upper incisors, as well as the two on the bottom, probably a result of opening bottles with his teeth for most of his life.

"Show this youngster where the doctor is buried," said the man as he again lifted his pen, dismissing both of them. Yule followed Stefan, who led him through the backdoor and then through an iron gate with a sign still in Polish that read *Cmentarz*, Cemetery. After walking past the gate, they wandered down along a winding gravel path until they stopped in front of a freshly dug grave covered with a patch of black soil, slightly raised, with a small wooden cross on top.

"Is that your mother down there?" asked Stefan. Yule nodded. "How old was she?"

"Thirty-six."

"Such a young woman," said Stefan, "and a doctor..." He paused and stared at the grave then started saying something before Yule interrupted him.

"Is there a plot number or a name assigned to this grave?"

"Not yet, we do that much later. If you want, let's go back to the office so we can talk about the finer details."

"Thank you. Let's go back."

The man behind the desk was still scratching some notes into his leather-bound journal. Judging by the sheer quantity of notes, business at the funeral home must have been good. "Sit down, please," he said, pointing at the single chair with a stained seat cushion standing in front of his desk. "We have to decide what to do with your mother's tombstone—if you want one, of course. I know that you don't live here, but in about six months, after the ground settles down, I need to know what to do."

"How expensive is it?"

"Well, *that* will depend on your choice. We can build a mausoleum for you, or it could be just a plate on the ground."

"I need a few days," said Yule. "I have no money now, but I will get some to pay for the stone."

"How are you going to get it?"

"There's a lot of furniture in the apartment, along with some rugs and other trinkets. I will try to sell some of them."

The man's eyes got a little wider, indicating some interest in the contents of the apartment. "Do you mind if I take a look at some of those things in the apartment?"

"Not at all. We can do it now, if you could come with me."

"Stefan!" yelled the man again. "Crank up the hearse."

Stefan, in addition to being the gravedigger, was also apparently the company driver. He pulled up to the door in a black ZIM, converted into a hearse. Yule was placed in the back, on a side seat facing a massive wooden coffin made of oak. "It's empty," said Stefan, tracing Yule's nervous glances toward the coffin.

The smell of pine in the apartment was still strong, despite the opened windows. Since his arrival the previous night, Yule had virtually no time to look around in the apartment, let alone to take inventory of its stock. Most of the furniture and the rugs seemed to be there. As far as the valuables were concerned, Yule was skeptical that Konstantin had left anything of any worth behind. The man from the Funeral Bureau quickly toured around the apartment, briefly pausing by the sofa and looking at the rug that hung on the wall right under the ceiling and cascaded over the sofa all the way down to the ground. It was a valuable Persian heirloom, purchased by Zoya upon her return from Magadan when she and Vladimir had some money to spend.

"This rug will be more than enough to pay for a decent gravestone," said the man, looking at Yule. "Unless, of course, you want to keep it for yourself."

"No, I don't. It's difficult for me just to look at it, let alone to have it in my possession."

"It's a deal then," said the man. "Come back with me to choose the stone. Stefan!" he yelled again, even though Stefan was standing right next to him. "Put the rug in the hearse." Gravedigger, driver, mover—under different circumstances, Yule might have been amused by the Renaissance qualities of Stefan.

Yule walked over to the sofa and sat down on it, feeling the fine texture of the rug with his fingers. He recalled the days when he had played on it with his little brother. Occasionally, they would fall asleep together on a silky-soft section of the rug, hugging each other for warmth and comfort. Yule stroked the rug, running his fingers through the fabric. Something, he realized, was underneath the rug, a small metal object of some sort.

Much to his delight, Yule pulled out his mother's gold watch, the one with the brown leather wristband. The scent of Zoya's perfume still emanated from the watchband. In his haste, the odious vermin must have missed the watch when he had collected the other valuables from the apartment. Yule brought the band closer to his face and inhaled the familiar fragrance of the *Podarochnyi* perfume. Both Stefan and the man watched the scene in silence; what they saw required no explanation.

Yule stood up and pointed at the rug. "You can take it," he said then walked outside. He needed some fresh air to escape from that scent of crushed pine needles. Stefan emerged from the building only a few minutes later, carrying a rolled up carpet on his shoulder, leaning forward under its formidable weight. The man in the gray suit followed directly behind him. "Come back to the Bureau with us to choose the tombstone," he repeated again. "That way, you don't have to return in six months when the ground settles."

The rest of the day was a complete blur. Yule must have done everything right, but later, he could not remember doing any of it at all: choosing the stone and engraving, engaging the next door neighbor to look after the apartment, visiting Marek's grave, and finally boarding the Leningrad-bound train in Lvov. He tried to read but caught himself reading the same paragraph over and over, not grasping its meaning or retaining anything he read. The reality was slowly setting in, an overwhelming sense of guilt accompanying it. Countless unanswered questions were hovering into and out of his mind. *Was little Vova okay? What to do with the apartment? Who would look after the grave?* The thoughts were intrusive and, worse, unanswerable still. He pulled his mother's watch out of his pocket and inhaled the fragrance—it was as if Zoya was still there, sitting right next to him on board that train.

Realizing that the rampant thoughts would drive him to insanity, Yule redoubled his efforts to read. It was, as always, his only escape and solace. He opened a thick binder containing loose pages of a scientific paper from the University of Alma-Ata. The paper was given to him by his school biology teacher. The author, Pavel Marikovski, had advanced an interesting theory on 'flying dreams,' which continued to haunt Yule in his sleep. The author came to the conclusion that we, especially in our youths, often fly in our dreams because of the 'fingerprint' of a distant past when our human ancestors lived in the rainforest and, like many modern apes, used vines that hung high above the ground to fly from tree to tree. It was, Yule thought, an interesting theory, which did not necessarily contradict any of the previous explanations.

The reading had distracted him for at least a short while, but inevitably, the intrusive thoughts came back, storming his mind with a vengeance. Having no support and virtually no advice from his family when it came to questions regarding his mother (a taboo subject of sorts), he had to decide what the next stage of his life should be. By the time the train had pulled in under the roof of the Vitebski Rail Station in Leningrad, the decision had been made. Proud of his ken beyond his tender age of seventeen, Yule yielded to the parental insistence on becoming a dentist. In the USSR, it was possible to become a dentist in only three years, as opposed to a higher-level specialist, a stomatologist, that required five years of medical school. The dentist could perform all of the procedures other than surgeries. The choice would allow Yule complete independence in only three short years. By the second year, however, he had realized that dentistry was a mistake. The prospect of fixing teeth for the rest of his life was utterly unfathomable. Thus, another crucial decision had to be made, preferably one without any major mistakes or blunders. There were several options for remedying the situation: the first and the most obvious one being to just drop out, the second option to join the army. Although he was, as a student, freed from his military duties, he could still volunteer and thus choose to waive the academic privilege, and that was precisely what he chose to do.

Immediately following the conclusion of his second year of study, Yule made the trip to the *Voyenkomat*, a recruitment place, where he had to pass a battery of tests and physical examinations. As a result, he was drafted into the airborne forces, his departure to be as soon as the following day. It was rather unusual to be drafted into the airborne forces on the spot. Normally, airborne recruits were pre-selected while still in high school, where potential candidates went through a military- specific physical examination and were sorted out as per "applications;" those in top condition were labeled the "cream" and assigned to the airborne forces or the marines, while the rest, referred to as the "sediment," went to the army. In Yule's specific case, it was a last-moment decision. Since there was virtually no choice in assignment, he, like every other recruit, was at the mercy of the *Voyenkomat*. The interview with the colonel, a giant of a man in a battle fatigue and a blue paratrooper's beret, was, at the very least, an enlightening experience. After Yule had been offered a seat in the colonel's office, a lieutenant, who also wore a paratrooper's uniform, placed a sizable dossier on the colonel's desk. Yule sat too far from the desk to be able to glimpse the contents of the dossier, but according to the colonel's barrage of questions, Yule could glean that the information it contained was startlingly comprehensive. There were questions about his life in Siberia, especially his close-combat training with Shamir Mamboev. They knew about the beating he had administered to Konstantin because a copy of the police report from Stanislawow was in his file. There were, to Yule's astonishment, references to some other seemingly insignificant events, many of which had no apparent witnesses. The interview was becoming more and more Kafkaesque; Yule received the distinct impression that his entire life was under the piercing gaze of some omniscient and invisible eye, that an invisible hand documented everything that the eye saw regardless of the magnitude or the significance of each event. Naturally, there were also questions that pertained to Yule's nationality as a Jew followed by a lengthy explanation that the *Voyenkomat* was making a privileged exception in his case. Yule was made to understand that the majority of the airborne personnel, or VDV, *Vozdushno-Desantniye Voyska*, consisted of Slavs and, as the colonel so eloquently put it, that very few "other people" were even allowed to join. The colonel, however, claimed that because Yule had demonstrated an exceptional strength of character and uncanny fighting skills, a special dispensation was being made. The interview, which left Yule both dazed and confused, ended with a strong handshake and some hearty congratulations.

The location of the training center was not disclosed, but rumor had it that the training base would be in close proximity to the city of Pskov, in some village called Cheryokha. That, Yule knew, was where the 226th Airborne Training Regimen was situated.

Yule had no intention of going home at the moment, for he wanted to prolong the inevitable and to avoid breaking the news to his father. Eventually he would have to, but the plan was to do it as late as possible in order to make the parental reaction as short-lived as plausible. As he was increasingly wont to do in precarious and uncertain situations, Yule decided to visit Irina Alexandrovna, to see her one last time prior to his departure. She opened the door and immediately, without so much as a *hello,* demanded to know what sort of calamity he had gotten himself into now. "I can see it in your eyes," she said, "and it does not look good."

As usual, she listened patiently and attentively, keeping her fingers steepled under her chin.

"Do you really hate dentistry that much, to the extent that you want to sacrifice *three years* of your life serving in the Soviet Army?"

"First of all, I do not see service as a *sacrifice*. Besides, I'll use this opportunity to make some sense of my life and to make myself useful. So far, I feel like I'm facing a cul-de-sac."

"You misunderstand me, Yule. I never meant to imply that service in the armed forces is a waste of one's life. My late husband, after all, was a professional military man. I was referring to you specifically, *you* who are capable of accomplishing great things in your life."

"Thanks for your confidence in me, but I really feel like I have to regroup and rethink my life."

"I am sure that when you return, you will know what to do with your life."

Yule didn't know whether that was stated sarcastically or whether she sincerely meant what she said, but he didn't think that it was worth his time to ask. Thus, he stayed in her apartment for another hour. They drank the, now customary, tea and ate the delectable pastries that Yule had grown to love so much. Alas, however, the inevitable time had arrived, and the two parted. Yule took one last walk along Nevsky Prospect before going home, partly to delay the inevitable even further and partly to revel in some nostalgia.

His Grandma took the news calmly and predictably. She merely sat down and, in a dramatic gesture, placed her right hand onto her chest. She did not say anything, just walked away while wiping some tears from her eyes. When Efim got home, he already knew; Grandma had apparently telephoned him.

"So, you just wasted two years of your life, and now you're about to waste another three," he said quietly with his usual sarcastic smile. He then added wistfully, "You are capable of much more than that," in a tone that implied that Yule had somehow shattered his father's dreams. Luckily, that was the full extent of his parental disapproval. Early the next morning, Yule said his good-byes to everyone and proceeded to walk all the way to the *Voyenkomat*, enjoying the sublime beauty of the awakening

Nevsky Prospect along the way. Finally, he joined about a dozen other recruits that were also headed for the VDV basic training.

Among the twenty-seven conscripts from Leningrad, Yule was the only one who did not have any prior jumping experience. The two recruits with whom he became friendly with, Nikolai and Vitaliy, had received rather substantial training at the local DOSAAF (Voluntary Organization for Cooperation with the Army, the Air Force, and the Marines) paramilitary center and were ready to jump from any height without trepidation. Whether it was an oversight or whether it was done on purpose, after just three short days of practice jumps off of a ten-meter tower, Yule was taken eight hundred meters into the air (the standard height for a paratrooper's jump) in a windowless, converted version of the Antonov-10, a model known as the "Ukraine." It had a seating capacity for eighty-plus paratroopers. Yule was hooked up to the static line along with the rest of the new recruits. In what seemed like a matter of seconds, the green light went on and the jump sergeant yelled, "*Poshly! Poshly*!" Go! Go! Yule was fifth, right behind Nikolai, whose wide back blocked the view of the open door. The intervals between the jumps were hardly more than two seconds apart, and before Yule had a chance to comprehend what was happening, a gaping hole materialized directly in front of him as a fatherly slap on his behind, administered by a smiling jump sergeant, served as a reminder that his time had finally come. Yule tentatively looked out the door for the first time. His reaction, however, was rather unexpected; a distinct sense of *déjà vu* settled over him. Almost immediately, his flying dreams came to mind, those numerous times when he had soared above the Earth and looked down upon the snowy villages and their tiny, seemingly inconsequential inhabitants. Surprisingly, the familiarity of the view down below had completely removed any sense of fear or trepidation—the ground below simply did not look real. Yule took a step into the void, the initial euphoria of the free-fall quickly interrupted by the deployment of the parachute. The tight, rough sensation that resulted from the parachute becoming taut as the line stretched to its limit served as a reminder that the jump was indeed real, not some distant or harmless dream.

Up until that point, the jump was a textbook exemplar. Yule was taught not to jump but rather to *step* out of the plane close to the fuselage but not *too* close so as to avoid being rammed against it by the wind. He did just that. The ground below was relatively flat, with no trees obscuring the target zone. The landing, therefore, promised to be normal—or so he thought. To Yule's dismay, the wind had unexpectedly picked up speed as he became buffeted by a strong gust that carried him sideways, away from the landing area. He pulled the straps down and lowered the edge of the round dome in an attempt to maneuver back toward the designated area. Due to his lack of experience, however, he yanked on the straps too hard. As a consequence, the wind carried him backwards and even farther away from the target zone. At the same time, the downward movement continued, and Yule suddenly found himself just a few feet above the ground, which now looked very real. Since he was moving backwards, his stretched legs did not do much to cushion the landing. He landed squarely on his behind and was dragged a few feet in a sitting position; an unpleasant burning sensation on his behind accompanied the awkward drag. The phenomenon had caused several trainees to stop and watch. Some pointed at him and laughed. The tips of Yule's ears turned red as he painfully attempted to get back onto his feet. It was downright embarrassing, as flawed a landing as humanly possible.

Back in the barracks, shortly after dinner, a brawny and blockheaded recruit by the name of Bukhteev had accosted Yule. The man was short, stocky, bowlegged, and lacked a neck, a stereotypical Greco-Roman wrestler. He had an air of superiority about him, one that verged on complete arrogance.

"How's your ass?" he asked. "Got any skin left on it?"

Yule realized that the first test of his character had arrived, the moment that would determine his place among his new pack. Time had proven to Yule that the differences between a prison or military culture and the mentality of a wolf pack were marginal at best, that in any rigid organization there were alpha wolves and submissive ones. If he let Bukhteev accost and humiliate him without consequence, Yule would quickly and surely fall to the ranks of a submissive, and he was not about to live the next three years of his life in utter humiliation. Bukhteev, whose nickname was "The Bull," was indeed a renowned and a feared bully, perhaps the unofficial leader of the battalion. It was said that The Bull even dominated the battalion's sergeant, whose name was Gavrilov.

Yule, who stood at a meager five feet nine inches tall and weighed only one hundred sixty pounds, must have seemed like easy prey to the powerful two-hundred-plus pound, barrel-chested wrestler. Furthermore, Yule's quiet and unassuming conduct during his first week at the training facility was a stark contrast to the mostly raffish and rowdy behavior of his comrades. That alone could send the wrong signal to someone like Bukhteev, who must have perceived the composure as timidity.

"Would you like to see for yourself?" asked Yule innocuously, looking straight into Bukhteev's slightly bulging eyes. "I can show you my ass right now."

He pretended to unbuckle his belt, as if he was about to follow through with his offer. The silence in the dining room became palpable, almost deafening—the entire battalion was looking directly at them. Bukhteev's ears turned a deep shade of crimson, and his eyes had bulged even more. He did indeed resemble an angry bull, warranting his nickname in at least his appearance. His lessons at the Gulag taught Yule to look into the eyes of an opponent, in order to detect any indication of his intentions. There was no doubt that an assault was coming; even the most inexperienced fighter could see that. The distance between the two was about ten feet, so a punch or a kick was out of the question. The only remaining alternative for Bukhteev was to quickly cover the distance between them in a mad charge. This pre-fight assessment took just a fraction of a second in real-time, though to Yule it seemed as if time had slowed to a near standstill. Bukhteev was clearly embarrassed and very irate, which made Yule's task much simpler. A mad opponent, he learned, was an irrational opponent, one that would give into blind rage over calculated composure.

Bukhteev charged, his arms spread wide and his head aimed squarely at Yule's solar plexus. A cry reminiscent to that of a wild animal filled the dining room as The Bull charged ahead. All Yule had to do was to step aside by pivoting his body around his left foot and letting Bukhteev fly past him. Yule could have ended it at that, by letting The Bull simply fly past him and let his momentum slam him hard into the wall. For good measure, however, he shoved the attacker from behind, casting him head-first into the cast-iron storage shelves mounted onto the brick wall. Bukhteev's head met the corner of the unit, splitting his forehead down the middle. Blood splattered the floor and covered Bukhteev's uniform. Surprisingly, the man did not initially fall to the ground. Rather, he straightened up and stood there, a look of dumfounded disorientation displayed clearly across his face. His eyes were covered with blood, most likely blinding him temporarily. After a few seconds, he took a few steps forward and collapsed. Sergeant Gavrilov immediately got onto the phone and called the hospital unit, located just behind the dining barrack. In about thirty seconds, a doctor and two soldiers carrying stretchers had arrived.

Yule stood there quietly, observing the ensuing chaos; everyone seemed to have forgotten about him. A few minutes later, after

Bukhteev was taken to the hospital barrack, the trainees returned to their seats to finish their meals in silence, occasionally glancing at Yule, who had also returned to the table and was calmly finishing his oatmeal. Yule, however, knew that the incident was just the beginning of his troubles, that at any moment an authority would show up to chastise him for his misconduct. Yule thought back to his incident at school, specifically to his confrontation with the hockey player in the classroom. He recalled being summoned into the principle's office after the incident. The similarity of the two scenarios amused him.

The authority did indeed show up in the form of Sergeant Gavrilov. The sergeant entered through the main door, pointed at Yule, then pointed toward the door. Yule stood up and walked out, his every step under the piercing gaze of a hundred eyes.

"Captain Horobetz wants to see you," said Sergeant Gavrilov.

"Who is he?" asked Yule. He had never heard the name before.

"He is the *politruk,* the political leader of the battalion."

They continued walking in silence. Going before the politruk meant that Yule would only receive a lecture as opposed to a few days at the *Gauptwachta,* military brig.

Captain Horobetz was a smallish man. When Yule walked into his office, he found the captain neurotically pacing the room back and forth, touching his long jet-black hair in an attempt to keep the longer strands behind his ears. He had a long and massive nose. That, coupled with his neurotic pacing, made him look like a sparrow caught in the rain. In fact, his last name, Yule realized, was the Ukrainian word for *sparrow.*

"Yule Fine," said the Captain. He was not addressing Yule directly, nor was he asking him to confirm the name. Rather, he said it as if only to test the sound of the name, although he pronounced the letter *F* in a soft Ukrainian manner, making it sound more like *HV.* There was something distinctly unmilitary-like about it, which put Yule at ease.

"Tell me what happened," he continued, cutting directly to the point.

"Comrade Captain," started Yule, properly addressing the politruk. "Private Bukhteev attacked me, so I just stepped aside to avoid being knocked off my feet."

"*That's not true*, Comrade Captain," jumped in Gavrilov hastily. "He also *pushed* Bukhteev in the back."

"Is *that* true?" asked the Captain, staring at Yule with his piercing dark eyes.

"It was just a friendly tap on the shoulder," answered Yule, all the while looking straight at Gavrilov.

"Sergeant Gavrilov," said the Captain, sensing the mounting tension. "You are free to go."

Gavrilov saluted, turned about and left, giving Yule a highly distasteful look while exiting.

"Sit down, Private," sighed Captain Horobetz, pointing at the single metal chair in front of his metal desk. He flipped open the already familiar to Yule dossier, spent a minute reading through several pages, closed it, and asked, "How did you manage to get here without a single previous jump?"

"I do not know, Comrade Captain. They just asked me if I could do it, and I said yes."

"So you lied."

"No, Comrade Captain. I *knew* that I could do it."

"Well you certainly showed us that you could, with some modifications at least," remarked the captain sarcastically.

"I have learned from my mistake, and my next landing will be a textbook example."

"I like your confidence, Private Fine. Just be careful with expressing it. Some trainees have already complained about you as being arrogant and looking down at them, but besides that, I have a different subject to discuss."

He consulted Yule's dossier again and said, "You have completed two years of training in dentistry and our current dentist's tour of duty is about to end. He will be discharged in October, so we will need a replacement. I am planning to transfer you over to our Military Hospital next week, so you can familiarize yourself with the type of work that the current dentist does."

"Comrade Captain," said Yule, getting visibly upset. "If you look closely at my file, you will see that I *volunteered* to join the military despite the fact that I was a full-time student and could have easily served just one year after graduation as a lieutenant."

"I know that," said Captain Horobetz. "Your file is an interesting read. Unfortunately, I have no choice but to transfer you."

"I do not want to work as a dentist, Comrade Captain. That is precisely the reason why I volunteered in the first place."

The captain nervously placed a strand of black hair behind his right ear. His eyes showed signs of mounting irritation. "Do you know what disobeying a direct order means?"

"Yes, Comrade Captain."

The Captain was visibly taken aback, startled by Yule's easy acceptance of the punishment. "Are you saying that you'd rather go to the brig than to work as a dentist?"

"Yes, Comrade Captain."

"Have it your way, then. Personally, I think that you are out of your mind, but I have no choice in this matter. Private Fine, you just got yourself three days in the *Gauptwachta*."

Yule remained silent.

"*Sergeant Gavrilov*!" yelled the captain toward the closed door. It took less than a second before the door flew open. Sergeant Gavrilov was no doubt eavesdropping on the entire conversation, judging from the gleeful look on his face.

"Take Private Fine to the *Gauptwachta*—he got himself three days."

"Yes, Comrade Captain!" Gavrilov enthusiastically saluted, clicking his heels. "Let's go," he barked, addressing Yule this time.

The brig was only a short walk from the captain's office. It was a small, one-story, freestanding brick structure without windows.

The *Gauptwachta* had a massive cast-iron door, one with no lock on the outside of it, only a substantial deadbolt.

"Give me your belt and the contents of your pockets. You will get everything back in three days. That is, if you don't do more stupid things and get yourself more time," said Sergeant Gavrilov.

Yule complied and, when the guard opened the massive door, stepped inside. The tiny cell, no more than ten by ten feet, had no windows; the only source of light was a weak bulb behind an iron-cast grill mounted onto the low ceiling. The air was stuffy, and there was no visible ventilation device or any opening. It took Yule's eyes about thirty seconds to adjust to be able to determine that he was not alone. A short and powerful figure of a man wearing a white hat moved away from the wall and stopped about five feet from Yule.

It was Bukhteev, only this time with a fresh bandage wrapped around his head.

In the small confines of the room, he looked even wider than before, almost as wide as he was tall. Bukhteev was looking at Yule without blinking, silent, like a cobra preparing to strike. He was clearly enjoying the situation, convinced of his physical superiority, looking for signs of fear from his prey. Yule did not oblige, only remained silent and looked directly back at Bukhteev.

"So, what are we going to do now?" Bukhteev broke the silence.

"Are you stupid enough to start a fight here?" asked Yule.

"There will be no fight. I will crush you before you can say *mama*."

Several options presented themselves to Yule at that moment. He could knock on the door and ask the guard for protection. The second and the most outlandish option would be to submit and apologize to Bukhteev, to placate his wounded pride. The third one was to fight. Yule dismissed the first two options immediately, but a conventional fight was also out of the question—Bukhteev was about fifty pounds heavier and a decorated wrestler. Kicking him in the groin most likely wouldn't be effective either because the man most likely had brass balls. A kick in the head wouldn't be effective for the same reason, as demonstrated by the brute's slam to the head earlier that day. Yule looked at Bukhteev's neck—it was thick, a wrestler's neck, but his Adam's apple was prominent enough to make a target. Yet again, it took Yule just a second to perform the assessment, but the momentary lapse also allowed Bukhteev to advance a few feet closer. It was crucial to avoid close contact, which would afford the Bull the opportunity to grab Yule and to utilize his brute strength.

Yes, he is stupid enough, thought Yule as Bukhteev made one more step forward, both arms raised in a wrestler's stance which left no doubt of his intentions. Yule took a deep breath to calm his nerves and, without warning, faked a left jab aimed at Bukhteev's stomach. That prompted Bukhteev to instinctively lower his arm in order to block the punch. That left the Bull's thick neck exposed, albeit for only a second. While faking the left jab, Yule allowed the momentum to keep moving his right shoulder backwards, pivoting his body around his left foot. When Bukhteev's arms reached the lowest point of defense, Yule twisted his right shoulder forward, throwing the edge of his right hand directly at Bukhteev's neck. The base of Yule's right thumb hit the Adam's apple hard. Yule had no intention to break the windpipe, just to stop the brute and to discourage further aggression, but he had apparently miscalculated the force of his strike. The silence was pierced by Bukhteev, who was gasping for air. His eyes rolled in terror as he held his neck with both hands, unable to breathe. He finally managed to breathe in some air and a high- pitched scream came out of his mouth.

The door flew open as the guard stuck his head in. He immediately realized that something was wrong and called for help. The same medical crew that had carried Bukhteev away earlier burst into the room, stretchers in hand.

Yule sat down on the floor—there were no beds or benches or anything else to sit on, just an empty room with bare walls. Since plumbing was a luxury, the only "toilet" was a hole in the ground, directly behind the barracks.

A few hours went by. He heard the trumpet signaling for the commencement of supper. Soon thereafter the door slowly opened. A new guard, carrying a tray with a bowl and a mug on top of it, walked in. This guard was older than the previous one and had a sergeant's chevrons on his shoulders. He looked at Yule with suspicion and anxiety in his eyes. Yule also noticed a second guard standing outside, holding a paratrooper's edition of the AK-47, one with a skeleton stock. He was positioned in close proximity to the door. The sergeant placed the tray on the floor and retreated backwards, quickly shutting the door behind him.

Yule looked at the tray; it contained a bowl of oatmeal porridge, a piece of black bread, and a mug with milk. The food looked almost fresh and, under different circumstances, would have even been enjoyable, but at the present moment, Yule had no appetite. He did not know how much time had passed, not until the sound of the trumpet signaled that the camp was on lockdown for the night. Surprisingly, no one came for Yule. He was restless that night, first trying to find a comfortable position on the cement floor and then attempting to sit in a corner. He fell asleep only when the first rays of the morning light penetrated through the minuscule gap underneath the door.

His sleep, however, was short-lived. He heard his name being called, as if from far away, but when he opened his eyes, the already familiar figure of the colonel from the *Voyenkomat* was standing in front of him. Yule immediately stood up and made a feeble attempt to salute, but quickly realized that since he was not wearing a hat, it would have been in violation of military etiquette to salute. He drew back his hand.

The giant colonel stood in front of Yule, looking down from his height of at least six and a half feet, an expression of curiosity in his intelligent eyes.

"Follow me," said the colonel, turning around and leaving the brig. The guard on duty made an attempt to follow them, but the colonel waved him away. The short walk to Captain Horobetz's office was silent. Yule walked behind the colonel, who still wore the same paratrooper's fatigue and blue beret, trying to figure out all of the possible consequences of yesterday's events. As soon as the colonel entered the office, Captain Horobetz stood up and saluted.

"At ease," said the Colonel. He sat down in the chair that was promptly vacated by the captain and waved toward the side chair, inviting the captain to take a seat.

Yule stood in the center of the office, bracing himself to hear some harsh words and a possible discharge verdict, but once again, the unpredictability of life, the vicissitudes of fortune, surprised him.

Captain Horobetz spoke first. "Private Fine. Due to this unusual set of circumstances and your conduct, I have decided to contact Colonel Matushenko to help me decide what to do with you." He looked at the colonel as if inviting him to take over. Colonel Matushenko was flipping through Yule's file, which had become substantially thicker since the last time Yule saw it. Finally, the Colonel lifted his head and looked at Yule, as if reassessing him in view of recent events. The colonel kept his eyes fixed on Yule's face for a few seconds longer.

"You have managed to put my best wrestler out of commission, twice in one day," he said. "Would you like to share your secret with us?"

"There is no secret, Comrade Colonel—I was just protecting myself."

"I understand that," said the colonel, showing some slight irritation with Yule's political answer. "You could have ran or even asked for help… instead, you fought a stronger man and prevailed on both occasions." He again consulted the file in front of him and looked at Yule. "You clearly have received some training. Where was it?"

"It was in Kolyma, Comrade Colonel. To be precise, in the Magadan Region's *zona* where I lived with my mother."

"I see," said the colonel, apparently satisfied with the answer. Although the information was in Yule's file, he wanted to hear it from Yule himself. Any mention of the word *Gulag* was treated with the utmost suspicion and required an explanation. Yule offered an abbreviated account of his time in Siberia and noticed that the colonel was making notes in his file.

Twenty minutes later, Colonel Matushenko closed the file.

"Have you heard of Spetsnaz?" he asked.

"Yes, Comrade Colonel. It is every soldier's dream."

The statement was a slight exaggeration, but Yule sensed an opportunity for escape and went for it. He knew perfectly well that fresh Spetsnaz recruits would be put through the most rigorous trials. The entire philosophy behind Spetsnaz's training was to instill in the soldier a belief that, before having the ability to *give* orders, one must first be able to *receive* them. The officers and sergeants of the Spetsnaz training units were a special breed of people who derived great pleasure from giving orders, orders that served to make or break the strongest of characters. The bright side of the ordeal was that after five months of harsh training, the soldier received his sergeant's stripes and either returned to his regular division or joined a special fighting unit. The journey, however, was no petty task.

The colonel was clearly pleased with Yule's answer; his eyes had assumed a much softer, almost fatherly expression. As a professional soldier and a combat veteran, Colonel Matushenko obviously loved his profession. "Settled then," he said. "Go back to your barrack and get ready for departure. Tomorrow, at four hundred hours, you will board the plane with two more recruits. You're going to a Spetsnaz training battalion." He stood up and shook Yule's hand with his bear-like grip and walked out without saying another word. Colonel Matushenko was a man of action, not words.

On the third of November, at the break of dawn, Yule and two other soldiers boarded a single-engine AN-2 biplane, lovingly nicknamed by the pilots as "*Annushka*," Sweet Little Ann. The cockpit of *Annushka* was not separated from the passenger area, so Yule could clearly see the back of the pilot, an older man with gray hair. His co-pilot was substantially younger, a soldier in a blue beret. It turned out that one of the two other recruits going to the Spetsnaz training facility was Nikolai Oberemok, whose last name clearly implied a Ukrainian origin. The second recruit was unfamiliar to Yule. He was blond and had a thin, almost ascetic face, which offered a sharp contrast to his powerful shoulders and bulging biceps. His name was Stepan Zubov.

The engine of the plane sputtered a few times before settling into a steady, rhythmic hum. The AN-2 was one of the most reliable bi-planes in the world, with a remarkably short take off and landing distance and a seating capacity for twelve. This particular variant was the AN-2TD, equipped with a static line and a jumping signal light. After a short and bumpy run, the plane took off, circled over the airdrome, and settled in an eastern-bound direction.

"Do you know where we're going?" asked Yule.

"Not a clue," answered Nikolai. "But it can't be too far—this plane has a range of only four hundred miles."

He was right—they landed very soon, within thirty minutes of their takeoff, at a very small, seemingly inconsequential airport that looked more like a cornfield. The surroundings were those of a small village in the middle of nowhere. The new recruits looked around in utter bewilderment, expecting some sort of clarification from the pilot. He did not offer an explanation but just told them to wait. A small, crooked sign in the distance read *Promezhitza,* clearly the name of the God-forsaken village. A few minutes later, a green military transporter with a canvas top materialized on the hill and descended, eventually merging into the landing strip while stirring up thick clouds of brown dust.

The Spetsnaz training grounds were located just behind the low hill and consisted of half a dozen brick barracks, a three-story headquarters building, a fenced transportation and equipment area, and an intimidating obstacle course. The transporter drew up to the headquarters building where a stocky man wearing *Starshina's* stripes greeted them with the standard *dobro pozhalovat,* welcome. The three recruits were led inside where, on the second floor, in a dusty office, they were made to sign a document, one that would alter Yule's destiny forever.

SPETSNAZ

ANY MISSION, ANY TIME, ANY PLACE.

SPETSNAZ MOTTO

Yule grasped the cold pen in his hand, rolling it between the tips of his fingers as he eyed the document in front of him. It was an agreement of non-disclosure, one that had to be signed by every single fresh Spetsnaz recruit. The document made it convincingly clear that a Spetsnaz recruit had absolutely no right to inform anyone of where he served or what that service consisted of. At most, the agreement limited the soldier to a public acknowledgement of serving in the Soviet Airborne Corps; otherwise, the nature and the details of Yule's service would have to remain secret forever. The document also stated that any unsanctioned or illicit disclosure of Spetsnaz's many secrets would be treated as high treason, punishable by death in accordance with the Soviet Criminal Code, Article Sixty-Four. Signing the document would seal Yule's fate; it would effectively alter the course of his life forever, but for better or for worse, he could not say. Those thoughts in mind, he placed the tip of the pen on the paper and signed his name; the pen produced a faint scratching sound as it glided over the line.

When each recruit signed the agreement, *Starshina*, Master Sergeant, Zotov, the man who greeted the new recruits upon arrival, led the three of them to one of the brick barracks. The guard in front of the entrance, upon seeing the *Starshina*, clicked his heels and saluted.

"At ease," said Zotov casually. "Fetch me the lieutenant."

The guard disappeared into the brick structure only to reappear a few seconds later accompanied by the lieutenant, a good-looking, tall, and athletically built man most likely in his mid-twenties. He stopped directly in front of the new recruits and looked at each appraisingly, his face betraying nothing of his thoughts or intentions. He did, however, keep his piercing eyes fixed upon Yule's face for a little longer than he was wont to do with the other recruits, or so Yule thought. Perhaps the lieutenant was already briefed on the unusual circumstances surrounding Yule. As before, however, the expression was unreadable, as reticent as the lieutenant himself.

"I am Lieutenant Sur," he began, his voice faintly raspy yet unexpectedly pleasant. "I will be your platoon's training commander for the next several months, for as long as it takes to train you up to my standards… that is, assuming that you even make it all the way to your sergeant's stripes. Meanwhile, *Starshina* Zotov will escort you to your accommodations. Dismissed." He turned about and disappeared into the dim interior of the barrack in one graceful motion.

The recruits followed *Starshina* Zotov through a short hallway, one that was flanked on both sides by gun racks. The hallway terminated with a wide opening into the washroom, a large windowless space equipped with a plethora of sinks and toilets. There was, Yule noted, no sign of any shower stalls. After turning left, they entered a wide and lengthy space. It was the sleeping area, as evidenced by the two-tiered metal bunks that were lined up on both sides of the room, each perfectly perpendicular to the walls. The beds, Yule noticed, were immaculately made, without so much as a single wrinkle to disturb their smoothness. The entire place, as a matter of fact, was exceptionally clean and smelled of soap. At the very end of the sleeping area, Yule glimpsed a door bearing a small, shiny brass plate that read *Lieutenant Sur.*

All three of the recruits were assigned to top bunks, two of the three directly next to each other and the third at the far end of the room. To Yule's relief, he was placed in the bunk immediately next to Nikolai's. The bottom beds were obviously occupied by the *Stariki*, the old soldiers, while the top ones were for the *Salagi*, the young ones, in an informal display of rank that was religiously upheld at the facility. Yule, as one of the new "small fries," stood no chance of sleeping on the more preferable bottom beds. The Cult of the *Starik*, old soldier, was very strong throughout the Soviet Army, zealously enforced and recognized by the recruits as well as the commanding officers themselves. Although there was no clearly defined line or boundary that demarcated whether one was to be considered a *salaga* or a *starik*, it was generally accepted that any soldier who served for even a few months longer than another soldier would be considered a *starik* relative to the latter.

Each barrack housed one platoon, and each platoon was defined by its own unique culture, traditions, and even methods of punishment. The individualized customs were largely determined or, at the very least, *permitted* by the platoon sergeant or, as in Yule's case, the *Starshina*. In terms of formal rank, the *Starshina* succeeded the senior sergeant and preceded the junior lieutenant. Regardless, each platoon was a microcosm of an autonomous culture within the greater framework of the entire armed services.

Quite suddenly, the thunderous sound of a multitude of heavy footsteps disturbed the silence, heralding the arrival of the platoon as it stormed into the barrack, evidently returning from a brutal ten-kilometer run. The soldiers looked utterly exhausted, a look augmented by their sheer dirtiness. Each solider was covered by a filthy film of brown dust, to the extent that it was almost impossible to make out any distinct facial features. Without so much as stopping at the bunks, the entire platoon rushed into the adjacent washroom. Virtually nobody paid any attention to the newly arrived recruits, barring a few quick glances in passing. To Yule's limited understanding, this particular platoon was formed just a few months ago. In fact, it was manifest that the entire training facility was a very recent endeavor, as it had no official name or number other than the name of the neighboring village.

The members of the platoon washed themselves and changed into fresh uniforms with remarkable alacrity and dexterity. Afterwards, with everyone in pristine order, it was time for dinner.

Starshina Zotov barked an order to form a double file then marched the soldiers into the dining barrack. It was quite a site, the entire procession of soldiers marching in a singular, uniform, and flawless formation. Upon entering the dining room, the Starshina raised his hand, ordering a halt to the march. After a brief pause, he barked "*Zapevay,* sing!"

Almost immediately, a designated soldier, in a melodious yet inherently powerful voice, began to sing "Katyusha," the standard marching song of the Soviet Armed forces.

When the time finally came to sleep, Yule climbed to the top of his bunk and gazed upward, toward the ceiling, using the rare silence to rummage through his thoughts and to think about the future. Many unanswerable questions still plagued his mind. Doubt washed over him as he heard his father's criticisms echoing within the deepest recesses of his mind. His chaotic and haphazard thoughts then focused onto Zoya, and with that, his eyelids slowly slid shut over his tired eyes as sleep overtook him, his muddled reverie gently accompanying him as he made the transition from the conscious to the unconscious realm.

Yule's eyes abruptly shot open. It was, he realized, still pitch dark outside, virtually impossible to tell what time it was. But why did he wake up so suddenly? As he slowly regained his senses, a musty smell penetrated his nostrils: a dirty and smelly blanket was thrust hard onto his face immediately followed by a blow to the shoulder with something that felt like a belt buckle. Yule suddenly realized what was occurring—every *salaga* had to be put into his proper place within the ranks of the platoon. The severe beating of new recruits was a common way for the *stariki* to assert their dominance over the new-bloods, a crude sort of initiation in which the *salaga* had to be humiliated, abused, and dominated physically by the older soldiers in order to be taught a "lesson of obedience." There was, after all, not much of a difference between a prison culture and the traditions of Spetsnaz. Yule muttered a curse to himself for abandoning his attentiveness when he should have known better.

He realized that fighting back would have been futile, so after the first blow, he assumed a fetal position by pulling his knees to his chest in order to protect his vital organs, namely the heart and the liver. He used his feet to protect his crotch, and he covered his face with his arms and his head with his fists. He also turned onto his back in order to protect the kidneys. In that way, he established a sort of bodily fortress that would allow him to withstand virtually any beating without any serious injuries. It was another invaluable lesson that he learned back at the Gulag, specifically from the prisoners who utilized the fetal position in order to survive the beatings by the guards or from other criminals.

The beating continued for several minutes. The attackers resorted to using weapons when they realized that fists would not inflict much damage. Some thrust spoons at him, whereas others whiplashed his body using wet towels. Every time that a heavy towel impacted his skin, Yule felt the urge to scream but recognized that screaming would merely encourage his attackers and would serve to label him as a submissive whelp, one with no tolerance for pain and therefore no place in Spetsnaz. He made no sound, no attempt to escape, just waited until the ordeal was over. Again and again he was assaulted from all sides. From the bunk adjacent to his, he heard the shrill screams of Nikolai, who was obviously faring much worse with the hazing than Yule. The *stariki* finally left Yule alone, clearly disappointed. They did not see any signs of submission.

In the morning, Yule took inventory of his multiple bruises, mainly scattered across his arms and legs. Thankfully, the bruises were the worst of the ordeal. Nikolai, on the other hand, was not as lucky. He had received some serious blows and was bleeding from a deep gouge on his head. They had a brief exchange in the washroom—Yule warned him that there would most likely be another hazing later that night; he had heard the soldiers saying something about "finishing the job."

It was late September, a time when the weather became very fickle. On that specific day, the weather turned abysmal as a downpour of rain buffeted the earth, transforming the dry brown dust into a disgusting dark mud. Although Yule normally enjoyed the rain, the mud wreaked havoc on their daily routine. The thick, heavy, and sticky substance reached, at some points, to above the ankles, adding at least ten pounds to the weight of each already heavy boot. A routine five-kilometer run rapidly turned into a devilish nightmare, especially where a small hill, once covered with mud, became an insurmountable obstacle—it required the soldiers to get down on all fours and to crawl to the top. Occasionally, a recruit would slide back down all the way to the base, only to attempt the near impossible climb yet again. There was no timing, no quotas or timetables to meet while completing the drill. Rather, it was a test of persistence and physical endurance; to finish the course in those conditions was a great success in itself, no matter how long it took to do so. The AKS-47s that the troops were required to carry didn't help either; with their folding metal stocks, the weapons were heavy. As if to add insult to injury, the recruits also carried military rucksacks on their backs, each with rolled up blankets affixed to their tops. That kit alone burdened them with about twenty pounds of additional weight. By the time Yule had finally completed the course, his vision was blurred, and he was hardly able to walk. The trip back to the barrack was almost more difficult than the course itself now that the adrenaline rush had subsided.

Each evening, the platoon was given an hour of personal time. Some spent the time napping, others socializing or playing games. Yule and Nikolai, however, used the opportunity to get out of the barrack in order to have a private conversation. It was still raining hard, so the two decided to seek the shelter of an equipment hangar in order to avoid getting drenched again. Nikolai was quiet and visibly depressed. He had a nasty bump on his forehead and was favoring one leg while walking.

"I don't want to patronize you, so don't take this the wrong way," said Yule, "but try not to scream when they come back tonight."

"Easy for you to say, with all of your fancy fighting skills," he said with some contempt. Nikolai paused for a moment and added, "Not many people believe it, but I have honestly never hit anyone in my life. I never had to, because of my size and all… nobody ever dared mess with me."

"The art of combat is more about skills and strength of character, not size. I've taken down bigger opponents plenty of times. And seeing that you *are* in the Army, you'll eventually have to learn how to fight, one way or another. But for tonight, what you really need is to learn how to avoid being injured."

"Tonight?" responded Nikolai nervously, as if finally comprehending the situation. "Are you certain they'll come back? I mean, maybe you didn't hear them correctly, maybe—"

"Nikolai, calm down. Yes, they're doing it again tonight, that's definite. The question is, do you want to do something about it, or are you going to keep feigning ignorance?"

Nikolai went silent, merely nodding as if in response to Yule's question. The two of them spent the entire personal hour going over defensive techniques. First, Yule gave Nikolai a brief introduction on the human anatomy, followed by a quick explanation of the rational behind protecting one's most vital organs, especially the heart, the kidneys, the liver, and the head. Yule described that the defensive techniques would save those organs from any severe injury but at the expense of the limbs, most notably the arms and the legs. However, as Yule mentioned, a minor fracture or bruise would heal much quicker than a damaged organ. After the abridged lesson in anatomy, he got down onto the floor and demonstrated several defensive positions, and then he made Nikolai mimic the positions. Yule played the role of attacker, feigning punches and demonstrating the effectiveness of the defensive postures.

When the hour was drawing to an end, Yule extended his hand toward Nikolai, to help him get up. "You know, with your physique you could become a killing machine," said Yule laughing. "But instead you choose to be a gentle bear."

"I don't have it in me," said Nikolai, clearly distressed. "I'd have a hard time harming any living soul." Yule could not restrain his laughter. With his hand he made a sweeping motion over the training facility and said, "*Look around you*, Nikolai! I think you might be in the wrong place."

With that, the two walked back to the barrack.

That night, the *stariki* did indeed come back. Only this time, they dragged both Yule and Nikolai off of their upper bunks and administered their beating on the cold, hard floor. The new vantage point allowed the attackers to kick their victims, thus inflicting substantially more damage than they had the previous night. Nikolai, however, did not scream and faired much better, doubtlessly following Yule's instructions. While curled up on the floor, Yule managed to take a transient peek at his assailants from under his blanket; he was able to identify the features of two attackers. The beating was mercifully cut short because *Starshina*

Zotov, apparently awakened by the ruckus, had turned the lights on, causing the attackers to scurry.

It was still raining the following morning. Yule rolled over onto his back and groaned, both from anticipating another harrowing charge through the mud and from the new bruises that he had accumulated the night before. Mercifully, however, Lieutenant Sur had instead ordered a "weapons care" session. In a large room, the one adjacent to the hallway with the weapons racks, the trainees were required to disassemble, clean, and oil their Kalashnikovs. Yule always enjoyed mechanical work, so the process of taking the heavy weapon apart and putting it back together gave him an uncanny sense of joy. The drill also taught him to appreciate the remarkable sub-machine gun, the ingenious invention of a Russian gun maker after whom the gun was named. Yule was startled by the sheer simplicity of the design, along with the reliability of its operation. It was pleasantly heavy, just the right balance of weight and maneuverability. The room was silent, other than the sounds of sliding metal and locking springs. The trancelike, voiceless rhythm was occasionally interrupted by the criticisms issued by the officer overlooking the drill. Each solider performed the task with remarkable dexterity and care.

After about thirty minutes into the "weapons care" session, Lieutenant Sur, accompanied by two soldiers from the mechanical section carrying a large wooden crate, had walked into the room. The lieutenant announced that the Spetsnaz platoon was awarded the honor of testing the new Dragunov sniper rifle. The crate was pried open and a fully assembled Dragunov SVDS rifle was gently pulled out. Lieutenant Sur placed the weapon onto one of the tables. It was, Yule thought, a sleek, elegant looking rifle; that particular model had a foldable stock and a railing, which allowed for the mounting of a scope. With the stock folded, the weapon was only about three feet in length; the barrel was also quite thin. With an unloaded magazine, the rifle weighed only nine pounds— quite suitable for jumping. When parachute jumping, however, both the Dragunov rifle and the AK-47 had to be secured to the soldier's body via several fasteners, in a manner that did not obstruct the deployment of both the main and the reserve parachutes; thus, it was near impossible to quickly detach the rifle or submachine gun from the fastenings. As a consequence, the paratrooper was left defenseless and vulnerable upon landing in hostile territory. That was why each parachutist was required to carry both a pistol and a knife; the small arms enabled a soldier to defend himself immediately after landing. Of course, the paratrooper's personal arsenal also included about half a dozen hand-grenades.

Lieutenant Sur lifted the rifle, placed it onto its butt, and took it apart in about thirty seconds, without the use of any tools or equipment. Yule observed the process intently and realized that the rifle consisted of no more than a dozen simple parts, not counting the ten-round magazine and the scope. Judging from his remarkable adroitness and efficiency, the Lieutenant was truly a professional soldier who clearly had a passion for the tools of his trade.

"Now, would anyone like to put her back together?" he asked, looking around the table.

Yule broke the ensuing silence and said, "I can do it."

The lieutenant eyed him for a few seconds and nodded, handing over the rifle to Yule. It felt cold in Yule's hands, the metal both sleek and polished. Then, without so much as a second of hesitation, he repeated the entire process in reverse, without any significant problems or hitches. He was much slower in assembling the weapon than the lieutenant was in disassembling it, but he still managed to accomplish the feat in under a minute. He stumbled only once while attaching the magazine—it would not latch. Yule quickly realized, however, that one side of it was made completely flat, in order to accommodate the stock when folded. He flipped the magazine around and jammed it into place with a satisfying *click*. Lieutenant Sur was clearly pleased by the effort, but some of the *stariki* didn't reciprocate the appreciation. A few of them glanced furtively at Yule in a very unfriendly manner.

There was another beating that night, only this time they came for Yule alone, sparing Nikolai the pain. Yule anticipated the beating, interpreting the dirty glances during his assembly of the rifle as harbingers of another hazing. That night, therefore, Yule was prepared. In anticipation of the beating, he did not undress while going to bed—he still had his boots on as well as an extra sweater underneath his uniform for additional padding. Yule felt that it was high time to bring the nightly beatings to an end.

About twenty minutes after the lights went out, he heard the excited whispers and murmurings of some nearby *stariki*. Feigning sleep, he caught a glance of the first *starik* out of the corner of his half-shut eye. Yule was ready, and before the all-too-familiar blanket landed onto his face, he kicked the attacker squarely in the head with the heel of his boot, holding onto the metal bar of the headboard as he put all of his strength behind the kick. He heard the *thump* of a falling body. The second *starik* materialized in the aisle, looking down onto his fallen comrade, an expression of utter disbelief painted clearly across his face. He looked up at Yule, raising the belt that he was holding in his hand. Before the belt could impact Yule, he recoiled and kicked the new assailant with both feet, still holding onto the headboard for support. He landed the kick onto the *starik's* ribcage, directly underneath his raised arm. Yule was certain that his kick had broken a rib or two, as evidenced by the man's shrill screams and incessant stream of profanities. The screams pierced the silence of the night, echoing throughout the entire room. Soldiers began to stir as the lights came on and *Starshina* Zotov's face appeared in the aisle. The first soldier, the one who had received the blow to the head, was still out; the second sat on the bottom bunk, holding onto the right side of his chest with his left hand. He was clearly in pain. The rest of the gang had apparently dispersed immediately following the uproar, quickly returning to their beds and pretending to be fast asleep.

Starshina Zotov looked down onto the fallen soldiers, assessing the situation without expressing any emotion or surprise. After a second or two, he walked to the telephone and dialed some number. Yule heard the *Starshina* requesting a medical helicopter to take the two soldiers to a nearby military hospital, somewhere in the suburbs of Pskov.

An hour later, Yule found himself standing in the office of Lieutenant Sur who was casually flipping through Yule's dossier, just like the other commanders had before. The sight was becoming all too familiar. If the lieutenant was upset at being woken from his sleep, he did not show it.

After what seemed like a few minutes, Lieutenant Sur looked up from the dossier and directed his glance at Yule. He paused, as if assessing the recruit in front of him, then asked, "What was the fighting style you used to put two of my men in the hospital?"

"There's no name and there's no style, Comrade Lieutenant," answered Yule. "I just use my intuition and do whatever it takes to survive."

The Lieutenant was clearly not satisfied with the response. "I'm not looking to chastise you, Private Fine," said the Lieutenant, much to Yule's astonishment and delight. "I called for this meeting because I want to know what it is that you do that enables you to put three soldiers into a hospital within one week."

"Honestly, Comrade Lieutenant, I have never *analyzed* what it is that I do to survive, but my knowledge of the human anatomy definitely helps. And most importantly, I choose not to be limited by any rules…" Yule hesitated for a moment, then said, "not to be limited by any rules when I fight. That's why I have no *style*, per se.

The lieutenant smiled faintly, a very rare expression of emotion on his part. "I like your thinking and your attitude. We need people like you—only, next time you get into a fight, please try not to inflict any… permanent damage. Unless, that is, you have to fight a real enemy."

The lieutenant then stood up and approached Yule. He placed his hand on Yule's shoulder and said, "With a name like Fine, you have to be very careful—you have to be *better* than the rest, but you also have to be beyond reproach." Lieutenant Sur looked straight into Yule's eyes and added, "Trust me, I know because of personal experience."

Yule was not completely certain about the implications of the lieutenant's cryptic advice, but asking would have been out of place. He suspected that it had to do with the Jewish origins of his name, so he opened his mouth in order to explain that he was not religious in the first place, but then decided otherwise and closed his mouth, not saying anything in response.

"You already have quite a reputation," continued Lieutenant Sur. "I highly doubt that anyone will be foolish enough to challenge you now, so I wouldn't lose any sleep if I were you. Besides, this platoon was formed only one month prior to your arrival, so the other recruits could hardly consider themselves *stariki*. Now go and get some sleep; we will be having our weekly parachute jump in the morning."

Yule saluted and turned about, ready to leave the office. On his way to the door, he caught a glimpse of a photograph with the corner of his eye. It was standing on a small étagère in the corner of the room. A very thin, bearded black man was looking back at Yule with an expression of intensity in his eyes. He was holding a toy-like white saxophone in his arms. It was not, Yule realized, a personal photograph, but rather a good quality framed magazine illustration.

"Permission to address, Comrade Lieutenant," said Yule, turning around.

"What is it?"

"Is that Ornette Coleman, in that picture over there?"

"Yes," said the Lieutenant, lifting his eyebrows. "How did you know what he looks like?" The inscrutable lieutenant was clearly surprised, his eyes aglow with astonishment.

"I've never seen him before, but I read that he plays a white plastic alto saxophone, so I assumed that it was him."

"That is indeed Ornette Coleman. This picture is a cut–out from the December 1959 issue of Downbeat Magazine." The Lieutenant hesitated for a moment then asked, "Do you like jazz?"

"Yes, I do, Comrade Lieutenant. Very much."

Lieutenant Sur looked at his wristwatch and said excitedly, "It's too late now, but whenever I have the chance, I have to show you my record collection." With that, Yule saluted again and returned to his bed.

It was three o'clock in the morning when he returned to his bunk; he was too excited to fall back asleep, so he spent the rest of the night talking with Nikolai, discussing the events of the previous evening. The wake-up trumpet sounded at five in the morning, its thunderous blare finally putting their conversation to an abrupt end.

It took on average approximately half an hour to get through the entire morning routine, to line up double file, and to march into the dining room. There was only one platoon stationed at that exact facility. The entire platoon had only twenty-four recruits, divided into two sections of twelve each. The sections had differing schedules, so they only met at mealtime and at night. Yule had been assigned to Section I, under the command of *Starshina* Zotov; Section II had no official commander, so Lieutenant Sur fulfilled the role in the interim.

At breakfast, the two vacated seats of the two absent *stariki* were very conspicuous; everyone was quiet, as if pretending not to notice the absence. Yule's section had included the two wounded soldiers. The ten remaining members marched to the hanger, led by *Starshina* Zotov. There, they folded and packed the assigned parachutes and boarded the AN-2. For Yule, it was his first jump after that unfortunate landing, a blunder that had triggered the chain of events leading up to his transfer to Spetsnaz. Yule was determined not to repeat his error again. The events and sensations leading up to the jump were much the same as the first time around, including that strange and conflicting sensation of being in a real, tangible dream. He learned his lesson, however, and the landing was flawless. There was no perceptible wind and visibility was superb. As a consequence, Yule managed to hit the bulls-eye, landing directly in the center of the target zone. *Starshina* Zotov was very pleased; though he did not say anything, he nodded approvingly, his face unreadable as always.

The Spetsnaz of the early 1960s was not officially called as such—the era only marked the beginning of a transition that called for a distinct separation of the special purpose detachments from the main body of the military. In the mid-1960s, however, Yule's platoon was part of the VDV, the airborne division, and much to the chagrin of the trainees, there was no distinctive uniform or any kind of Spetsnaz insignia to identify a Spetsnaz soldier. Spetsnaz recruits wore the ubiquitous camouflage overalls and the blue airborne trooper's beret common to other units. Since Spetsnaz troopers had no tangible identification of their status, they created their own intangible form of identification, manifested in their mannerisms and conduct. A true Spetsnaz soldier, for example, would not get involved in any conversation. Rather, he would keep to the side and would never mingle with other soldiers. The status was also embodied in the soldier's gait; a Spetsnaz serviceman would carry himself with a very distinct sense of pride and would have a discernible spring in his step. Among other infantrymen, a sense of camaraderie was not an uncommon phenomenon. There was, on the other hand, no friendship among Spetsnaz soldiers, a mentality that was promoted and even upheld by the commanding officers. A Spetsnaz officer had to be a leader, and in a combat situation, he would have to have the clarity of mind and the resolve to leave a wounded team member behind—friendship would only become an obstacle to the completion of the mission. The unique culture of Spetsnaz was reminiscent of the functioning of a wolf pack. Yule actually liked it—the silent conduct, the constant challenges presented by the leader, the uncompromising courage… all of it was very close to his heart. If he had a choice in the matter, he would have chosen the wolf as Spetsnaz's insignia. Having lived with wolves in Siberia and watching the pups grow up and develop their remarkable intelligence, endurance, and strength, Yule knew more than most about the propensities and mannerisms of wolves, and to him, their most outstanding characteristic was always their strength of character—a wolf cannot be domesticated or tamed, much less taught to obey commands. Some interpret the trait as a lack of intelligence. Nothing, however, could be further from the truth. The wolf is a creature that will do what it wants precisely when it wants to; that independence, the wolf's unwillingness to submit or to be tamed, is one of the hallmarks of its intelligence. Yule saw many of those characteristics inherent in the Spetsnaz culture.

That same day, after dinner, Lieutenant Sur ordered a "spade training" session. All Spetsnaz soldiers had to carry an infantry spade, a sort of sharp-edged shovel. The spade was not for digging, however; the Spetsnaz version of the tool had a square blade with all edges and corners made as sharp as a razor. According to *Starshina* Zotov, Spetsnaz soldiers never dug; their mission was always to go forward and to attack, not to hide in the trenches like some burrowing critters. Rather, the spade was used as an efficient and noiseless weapon, and the trainees had almost daily practices in the use of it. Yule enjoyed the sessions. They were conducted by the most proficient practitioner of spade use: *Starshina* Zotov. As he demonstrated on multiple occasions, he could split the tiniest sliver of wood or cut a glass jar in half without shattering it by using the spade. The weapon was very flexible in its use; it could have been used as an axe or a la Indian tomahawk for throwing. In sum, the spade was an indispensable weapon for hand-to-hand combat, superior to a knife in virtually all respects. Throwing the spade required a lot of practice, but when the art of throwing it was mastered, the spade became an accurate, reliable, and deadly projectile weapon. Yule was eager to learn *spadesmanship*, as he called it. Joining the platoon a month later than the rest of the recruits, he fell behind in some disciplines. The use of the spade was one of them, but having exceptional reflexes and outstanding coordination, he caught up with the rest rather quickly. He particularly excelled in the art of throwing and was able to split a small tree from a ten-yard distance, no easy feat for even a seasoned practitioner.

The best of the training sessions was the daily close combat lesson taught by *Starshina* Zotov who, in Yule's eyes, was the ultimate warrior. Zotov excelled in many things; there was not a single known weapon that he could not use, nor was there any vehicle or plane that he could not operate. But when it came to hand-to-hand combat, Zotov was the quintessential killing machine. He stood at about six feet tall, rather slim with very powerful arms and long, muscular legs. To watch him fight was akin to watching a master magician in action; he could throw a two hundred pound man down into submission with an almost imperceptible movement of one arm and a slight bend of his leg. Rumor had it that he had spent a few years in Okinawa training American Special Ops in the art of Japanese Judo and Russian Combat Sambo. As far as his weapon skills were concerned, the *Starshina* could throw two knives simultaneously and hit two separate targets. He also demonstrated to the recruits how to hit a target ten yards away with a shooting knife's blade.

One of his fundamental postulates regarding hand-to-hand combat was "to defend only the part of the body that was being attacked." He had consistently demonstrated and repeated the most economical and shortest ways to move in a fight. There were no fancy kung fu dances, no kicks above the belt. He frowned upon elaborate and pointless gestures. Zotov constantly reminded the recruits "not to fight against the air" by swinging at a mobile combatant with pointless and imprecise fury. "Let him come to you," he used to say. Russian Combat Sambo did not have any rules, which made Yule's Gulag survival style very appropriate and fitting. The only problem was that, during the sparring sessions, the soldiers were not allowed to use full-contact strikes. To Yule's mind, the restriction conditioned soldiers to stop short of making a full-force strike; stopping short over a period of time created a habit that was very difficult to overcome. Any hesitation in a real fight would, Yule knew, mean certain injury at best and death at worst.

Being smaller than most of the recruits, Yule's main weapons were his quickness and his knowledge about pressure points and human anatomy. His most indispensable ability, however, was his fighting intuition, one that was innate and very difficult to teach. Now, in those close combat practice situations, he had to follow the rules of training and was not allowed to use the "survival fighting" techniques he was so good at. In essence, he had to learn how to curb his natural inclinations and intuitions. During the sparring sessions, when he was being lifted off the ground by much larger opponents, he had to fight his natural urge to avoid a takedown by sticking his thumb into the assailant's eye socket, or by grabbing the side of his neck and ripping out his jugular vein. On one occasion, he had jokingly complained to *Starshina* Zotov that the Spetsnaz training was ruining his fighting abilities. Much to Yule's astonishment, Zotov took the trivial comment seriously and promised to have weekly sparring sessions with volunteers, in order to properly teach them "survival fighting" without any rules or hindrances. There were, however, no volunteers, so *Starshina* Zotov, being a man of his word, had set up an hour-a-week private practice session, just for the two of them. Unfortunately, it did not work out the way Zotov intended. Yule simply could not bring himself to kick his commanding officer in the groin or put his thumb into the *Starshina's* eye socket, even if he was encouraged to do so by the *Starshina* himself. He was, as a consequence, very hesitant, more often than not, ending up on the ground because of his indecision. After just two weekends, they stopped the private sparring sessions.

"You have to start building muscles," said *Starshina* Zotov, "but not by lifting weights. You have to use your own body weight. Start with fifty pushups, twenty pull-ups, and twenty sit-ups on one leg every morning. Believe me, in two weeks you will be a completely different fighter. You have a great advantage over most of your comrades, perhaps the greatest of all when it comes to survival fighting—I have noticed that you tolerate pain very well."

Meanwhile, the budding grounds of the future Spetsnaz training school had started to take shape. A new tarmac was being laid out about a mile south of the barracks, along with a new and much larger hanger built to accommodate the AN-12 cargo plane, which was capable of carrying a full-sized armored vehicle and a large contingent of troops. The first AN-12 had arrived and was sitting on the new landing strip in all its beauty, the sun gleaming off of its shiny, flawless hull. It was incomparably huge compared with the AN-2 being currently used for the jumping. The aircraft had high mounted wings, an elevated tail, and a very large cargo door underneath its formidable frame that allowed for the para-dropping of large pieces of military machinery. Unfortunately, the cargo cabin was not pressurized. As a consequence, the paratroopers had to use individual oxygen masks in order to facilitate breathing. Yule hated the oxygen masks and took them off whenever he had the chance. Once, he was caught by Lieutenant Sur, however, who warned him that if it happened again, Yule would be punished. "I will not allow you to jeopardize the mission," the Lieutenant said. "Every man is needed to be at one hundred percent."

Additional barracks were also being built across the grounds of the training facility, apparently in anticipation of even more Spetsnaz recruits. It had been announced that the two soldiers who were taken to the hospital after that bedside beating would not be coming back. No further explanation had been given. Friendship between the soldiers in Yule's section was virtually non-existent, at least on the surface. With the unexpected absence of the two unofficial *stariki* leaders who had attacked Yule, the juxtaposition for leadership continued in very subtle ways. The commanders implicitly promoted this natural leadership selection by assigning specific tasks and sending the sections on assignment without appointing any section leader. The scenarios allowed the recruits to assume leadership roles naturally, to exert themselves in order to emphasize their propensities toward a managerial role. The quest for leadership was played out on a near daily basis, and over time, a subtly distinguishable hierarchy began to take shape. Yule, being true to himself, stayed away from the eddies of the power struggle. He regularly ignored the name-calling and the snide remarks, often being sarcastically called a doctor, a professor, or a face surgeon, doltishly alluding to the night of the beating, but he would ignore the rude remarks. If a perpetrator decided to test the waters of Yule's patience, he would merely stop and stare into the eyes of the joker for a few extra seconds. The gaze normally sufficed for preempting a potential conflict.

Not every soldier, however, was antagonistic toward him; out of the twenty-two remaining men in the platoon, one particular soldier was noticeably friendly to Yule. His name was Khanov, a huge man from the ancient city of Kazan, approximately five hundred miles east of Moscow. Due to his substantial immensity, he was often referred to as the "Train." He was two years older than Yule and was so big that nobody dared to challenge him. Khanov's brutish proportions, however, belied his character; he was very diligent when it came to the fulfillment of his military duties, well versed in most of the disciplines but rarely exhibiting any sense of enthusiasm. Yule suspected that Khanov was a very kind and placid person; he was absolutely indifferent to the squabble for the top position in the platoon and was uncannily silent, keeping to himself most of the time. Yule, however, saw kindness in his eyes. During the now constant verbal assaults on Yule, Khanov would approach the area of the altercation and simply maintain his ground without uttering a single word. His presence was, more often than not, enough to discourage further conflict. Another remarkable quality was his apparent ability to function without any sleep. He was always the first to get up and, any time there was something unusual going on at night, he was always the first one at the scene, looking fresh and alert.

The normalcy of the ebb and flow at the camp was interrupted one freezing night in November. The entire platoon had been awakened by *Starshina* Zotov, who lined up each recruit in the central aisle of the barrack. Lieutenant Sur was also present, pacing in the aisle back and forth, an unusual look of worry painted across his face.

"We have had an unprecedented occurrence, something that does *not* happen in Spetsnaz," he said, looking into the eyes of each man, starting from the left flank and slowly moving his eyes until he reached the last person in the line. "*Theft*. That is what I am referring to," he continued. He paused again, examining each face in the room, searching for any signs that would belie guilt. "Last night, a personal object of value was stolen from a soldier in our platoon. As a consequence, your bunks will be thoroughly searched… I sincerely hope that none of our men are involved."

The Lieutenant nodded his head toward Zotov, who immediately turned the mattress of the first bunk upside down. The *Starshina* was indeed very thorough in his search; it took at least thirty minutes before he reached Yule's bed. Then, much to his amazement, Zotov extracted a small matchbox from underneath

Yule's mattress. He opened it and removed a gold wedding ring, an object that belonged to a soldier by the name of Pavlov, one of the informal leaders of the platoon and well respected by the men. Pavlov got married one day before being drafted, so he carried the wedding band in his pocket at all times, as no jewelry was allowed anywhere on the body. The astonished platoon grew deafeningly silent, all eyes on the evident perpetrator. No one, however, was more dumbfounded than Yule, who looked at the lieutenant and said in a firm but stupefied voice, "Comrade Lieutenant, I did not take that ring."

"The facts say otherwise, Private Fine. I will have to pass this case over to the Military Tribunal." He looked at Yule with an expression worse than anger, one of regret and disappointment. Finally, the Lieutenant shook his head and muttered, "Dismissed."

As the men started to disperse, Khanov stepped forward and, in a stern voice that pierced the deathly silence and commanded everyone's attention, said, "Comrade Lieutenant. Private Fine did not take that ring."

Everyone froze again, this time looking at the Train with apparent incredulity.

"And how do you know that?" asked the Lieutenant.

"Because I saw the man who did, and I also saw him put it under Private Fine's mattress."

For the first time, Yule noticed that the Train had a very slight accent and was visibly nervous; perhaps the accent manifested itself precisely because of his nervousness.

"So, who was it, then?" *Starshina* Zotov jumped in impertinently, violating the rules of subordination. Nobody, not even the lieutenant, seemed to pay any mind to it—everyone's eyes were glued onto the Train who turned to his right and placed his huge hand on the shoulder of the soldier next to him.

Yule could not believe his eyes—the perpetrator was Oleg, the third recruit who accompanied Yule and Nikolai from the

226th Airborne. Yule suspected that Oleg, who everyone knew had come from a good family and was reasonably well read, was jealous of Yule's popularity with the commanders, as well as of his reputation among some of the trainees as being knowledgeable about many different subjects. Yule presented an intellectual obstacle to Oleg, who was most likely accustomed to being treated as an erudite and respectful individual throughout most of his life. Yule had apparently usurped that distinction with his presence. It was not the theft per se that made the crime so heinous. It was the setup itself, which was considered as the worst possible offense, tantamount to treachery.

Lieutenant Sur understood the implications of the delinquency, evidenced by the sternness of his expression; he ordered Oleg to follow him into his office and once again dismissed the men. No one, however, managed to sleep that night—an event of such magnitude had stirred up a lot of emotions.

"Thank you," said Yule to Khanov. "I just don't understand why you didn't tell me immediately."

"I was going to deal with him myself in the morning," said Khanov, banging his right fist into the palm of his left hand, the universal gesture that signified a serious beating. They both laughed. Yule never felt as relieved as he did at that moment.

Surprisingly, Yule did manage to fall asleep in a relatively short span of time. It was not, however, a restful kind of sleep, but rather a very tumultuous one, full of nightmares. He dreamt of being on the plane, getting ready to jump, but right before he stepped out of the hatch, someone behind him had snatched his parachute. Yule was in a dizzying, spiraling free-fall, plummeting toward the earth like a heavy stone. He was feverishly going through all of his survival options, until he remembered that he had the ability to fly. As soon as he came to the realization, the free-fall transformed into a slow and controllable descent. The ground down below did not look anything like the training grounds. He saw a mountain range in the distance, completely blanketed with a thick layer of milky snow. Right behind the mountain, Yule glimpsed a leaning watchtower with a sagging, dilapidated barbed-wire fence at its base. The barracks in the distance had broken windows and the roofs were caved in—the labor camp had long been abandoned.

Yule circled slowly above the grounds that he remembered so well and noticed multiple animal tracks imprinted onto the fresh, otherwise undisturbed layer of snow. He landed as gently as possible. The rucksack, his weapons, and his ammunition made him heavier by at least sixty pounds, so despite the gentle landing, he sank waist deep into the freezing embrace of the snow. Yule took the burdensome equipment off, everything except for his pistol and his knife. He climbed out of his ditch and started a brisk, ginger walk, shuffling his feet so as to not break the gentle crust. Two sets of the fresh tracks definitely belonged to a pair of adult wolves. There were many smaller prints around him, all diverging into different directions. He followed the wolf tracks. To his amazement, the tracks led him to Professor's bungalow, remarkably spared from the ravages of time relative to the other structures within the camp. He paused outside the entrance, an endless stream of memories coursing through his reminiscent mind. Then, after what seemed like an interminable pause, he gently pushed open the door and stepped into the threshold of the bungalow. Inside, Yule was amazed to find Chook, only this time with his happy family, which consisted of three beautiful cubs. The cubs had orange and gray faces; in fact, they looked just like Chook and Cha when he had rescued them. Chook stood up on his lean, powerful hind legs, placed his front paws gently onto Yule's shoulders, and licked him in the eyes. His tongue was pleasantly soft, wet, and warm.

Yule woke up. It was still dark outside. He looked at the wall clock—its phosphorus hands indicated that it was only three in the morning. He had slept for just one hour, but it was a very happy hour, probably his happiest hour since he had joined the airborne. He stared at the dark ceiling, images of the dream passing through his mind. The dream was so vivid and fresh in his mind. It felt more like a vision, as if he had been transported to the camp itself in that short amount of time. He even *felt* the tangible, lingering, and moist softness of Chook's tongue on his eyes. It had been more than ten years since his last encounter with the wolves; it was probable that Chook and Cha were no longer alive—wolves in the wild never live that long. Yule sighed and touched his eyes; they were wet. Only then did he discover the hot tears that were streaming down his cheeks.

The morning routine went on in absolute silence. The platoon was still digesting the events of the previous night. During breakfast, Lieutenant Sur came up to Yule and, without saying a single word, quickly tapped Yule's shoulder and continued walking. It was, Yule thought, a gesture of both encouragement and of regret, specifically for doubting him when Yule swore that he did not steal the wedding band. There was no mention of Oleg, nor was he ever seen again. His name had become almost taboo, synonymous with treachery and surreptitious deceit. Rumor had it that he was transferred to the penal battalion. The rumor, however, was most likely untrue; it did not reflect the reality of the relative liberalization of the Soviet Union and, to a lesser degree, of the Soviet Army. Later, Yule had learned that Oleg ended up in a construction battalion, an infantry unit used for building military and civilian installations. It was obviously meant to be a punishment, but aside from being humiliated by the transfer from Spetsnaz to construction, service in the construction corps was not much different—hard labor and no weapons, just a shovel.

Yule was summoned to Lieutenant Sur's office one morning during the following week. Before Yule could issue the mandatory declaration of arrival to his superior, the Lieutenant stopped him with a wave of his hand and ordered him to sit down. His behavior, Yule thought, was highly irregular. Subordinates were required to stand in front of the commanding officer, unless indicated otherwise. The lieutenant's desk was, as always, remarkably neat and minimalistic; its only contents were a desk lamp and a fountain pen on a desk bladder. This time, however, there was also a square piece of paper with the word *Telegramma* printed across it in bold letters sitting atop the near empty desk. The rest of the text consisted of a small print that was illegible from Yule's distance. The text was written across thin strips of paper, generated by a telegraph machine and glued to a larger, single sheet of paper.

Lieutenant Sur lifted the telegram and flicked an invisible speck off of its surface, his gaze averting Yule's eyes. Then, without saying a word, he handed the document over to Yule. The telegram had just one sentence: *Grandmother Shifra died, come home for the funeral.*

Yule could do nothing but stare at the telegram, utilizing all of his willpower and composure to stem the impending stream of tears welling up inside of him. He was still cognizant of his surroundings, and he did not want to show any signs of emotional distress or weakness in front of his commanding officer. It was almost impossible to bear yet another loss of a loved one in what seemed like an endless chain of unfortunate and tragic events in his life. Lieutenant Sur stood up and expressed his condolences.

He sounded sincere in his sadness. Yule just nodded, fearful that speech would release the dam within his eyes. "Unfortunately," the Lieutenant added, "I cannot let you leave, even for a day. Tomorrow is the beginning of a joint military exercise, and I need every single man to participate. As you know, we are three men short as we are. I am sure you understand."

Yule knew that arguing would have been futile, and that begging would only serve to damage his reputation. So instead he saluted and, with some effort, croaked, "Yes, Comrade Lieutenant."

He felt both powerless and depressed. The trainees were not allowed to use the battalion's telephone. Going to the village was out of the question. Furthermore, intercity calls were extremely expensive, too expensive for his meager monthly allowance of four rubles and fifty kopeks. Yule hated the sensation of being powerless, of not being able to do anything about the situation, and so, the only thing left to do was to say a private good-bye to his Grandma, uttered within the deepest chambers of his heart. One thing that Yule realized was that in life, it was oftentimes necessary to desensitize oneself to a variety of circumstances and factors, but no matter how often a loved one passed away, Yule could never desensitize himself to the feeling of immeasurable sadness and regret that followed.

It was the twenty-third of November. An inch of fresh snow blanketed the tarmac, but for the AN-12, the coating presented no problems. The takeoff was perfect as the plane gradually angled itself upwards toward the cold sky. For this mission, a total of fifty-four men were aboard the cavernous AN-12. The group consisted primarily of both sections of the battalion, the lieutenant, the *Starshina*, a new sergeant, a flight crew, and a support section. Most of the space, however, was occupied by an armor-plated personnel carrier equipped with a multiple-tube portable rocket launcher known as the GRAD-V. The remaining space was filled with tents, a field kitchen, and boxes packed with food. All in all, it looked as if the impending military operation was going to be both serious and lengthy. The trainees had no idea where they were going or what their assignment was; they merely lived in the moment, taking orders as they came and doing what was required of them. In addition to the regular assortment of personal weapons carried by each man, there were two small grenade launchers and a mysterious box labeled *STRELA-2*. If it did indeed contain a weapon, none of the trainees had ever heard of it. Despite a lack of knowledge about the mission's specifics, Yule couldn't help but feel slightly tense, a feeling only augmented by the evident importance and magnitude of the mission.

It was a long flight, one that far exceeded three hours. Based on the position of the sun, they were flying south. Most of the men remained silent. The only sound was the rhythmic buzz of aircraft's formidable engines.

"We should have passed Moscow already," said Yule, turning to Nikolai. As soon as he said it, *Starshina* Zotov appeared in the aisle, announcing that the cargo would go first, followed by the men immediately afterwards. The gathering spot on the ground was identified as a red barn. Alas, after what seemed like an endless flight, the operation had begun. The AN-12 was circling the ground at a low altitude, discharging out of its huge underbelly first the personnel carrier, followed by dozens of large and small boxes. The personnel went last.

It was, Yule guessed, approximately ten in the morning. The sky was clear and the visibility was good. From the near-two-thousand-foot altitude, Yule could just barely make out a large city approximately twenty miles to the south of their position. The tallest structures were unmistakably churches, with their steeples stabbing deep into the clear blue sky. On the ground, about halfway between the drop site and the city, there was an airbase with hundreds of military planes lined up at the airpark, all of them easily recognizable from the air. It had finally dawned on Yule that the city in the distance was Tula. The joint maneuvers that Lieutenant Sur had alluded to earlier would no doubt be conducted together with the 106th Airborne Division, north of Tula.

The disembarkation went relatively well, if not to count Khanov who landed on top of one of the ammunition crates and slightly twisted his ankle. Khanov's personal weapons included a newly introduced PK machine gun, another brilliant invention of Mikhail Kalashnikov. The gun was heavy, at least twenty pounds without ammunition, and the two boxes accommodating the feeding belts, each containing two hundred fifty rounds, were also rather burdensome. Whether that additional weight had contributed to Khanov's awkward landing was hard to tell. According to Khanov himself, the burdens made it difficult to maneuver his parachute. Nikolai landed flawlessly, despite the fact that it was his first jump after he was designated as the battalion's sniper and thus started carrying the brand new Dragunov rifle. Nikolai was an outstanding shot, but the Dragunov rifle turned out to be extremely sensitive to the touch and, as a consequence, presented a challenge in the long-distance target practice sessions. Nikolai was very distraught with his inability to hit a bull's eye outside of the range of one mile, blaming his inaccuracy on the shortcomings of the gun's design. Yule knew that Nikolai was a superior marksman, so he tried to help him figure out the reason for the bullets wandering off target over the long distance. He recalled his days in Siberia, when he had participated in hunting expeditions with his stepfather. He always wondered why Vladimir held his rifle by putting his left hand underneath the magazine instead of grasping the hand guard. Vladimir's explanation was that the warmth of the hand would transfer into the barrel and would expand it ever so slightly, sufficiently enough to change the thickness of the grooves. That, in turn, would prevent the bullet from wandering off its trajectory over a substantial distance. Nikolai decided to employ the suggested technique and was immediately chastised by the new sergeant who told Nikolai that he was handling the rifle "like a girl." The criticism, however, was withdrawn almost immediately after the targets had been checked for accuracy—each shot was a bulls-eye.

The gathering place, a bright red barn, towered very conspicuously over the snow-covered field. The barn itself was designated as a storage facility, so two large tents were erected: one that served as a kitchen and an eating place, the other for sleeping—something the men would get very little of.

A section of the 106th Tula Airborne Division was in the process of converting themselves into a paratrooper-fighting unit, one that was, in essence, not much different from Spetsnaz. The joint maneuvers were designed to introduce the new paratroopers to field operations and to test their freshly acquired combat skills.

The platoon spent both the entirety of that day and the next "digging in." Hundreds of containers had to be pried open while equipment needed to be sorted out, assembled, and installed. The field was stacked up with boxes upon boxes of ammunition. Special care was given to the anti-personnel mines and the grenades. On the third day, the already fatigued men were awakened at four in the morning to finally commence the military escapade; they were all greeted by a good six inches of freshly fallen snow, which had accumulated over the frigid night.

Lieutenant Sur's briefing was simple and concise, namely to capture one of the designated sections of the airfield and to use all necessary means to do so. The platoon was divided into four subunits. At 0500 hours, Yule and three other men in the unit, dressed in snow-white overalls and carrying rucksacks with food rations, personal weapons, and ammunition, started their three-mile trek toward the designated target, near Tula. Their principle task was to circumvent the airfield and to attack if from behind. Two other units would also circle the perimeter of the field, invading the "enemy" territory from both sides. The main unit would attack from the front. That, at least, was the strategy developed by Lieutenant Sur, who was one of the rare officers assigned to Spetsnaz without any special training. The majority of Spetsnaz officers were graduates of a highly specialized training facility at the Higher Airborne Command School. Lieutenant Sur, on the other hand, had only an engineering degree. His major was heavy weapons design, but his exceptional talent as a military strategist, as well as his passion for weapons, had prompted his superior officer to recommend him to Spetsnaz.

A team of neutral observers was also dispatched by the Tula Military Regional Headquarters. Their task was to determine the soldier's "manner of death," specifically whether a participant in the drill was eliminated as a result of being shot or from falling in hand-to-hand combat. The bullets utilized in the exercise were hollow, but the bayonets on the AK-47s were, Yule knew, very real. When detached, they could effectively be used as knives. The objective of the drill was to *silently* capture the airfield, thus limiting the use of guns. As far as hand-to-hand combat was concerned, the instructions were to use full contact in order to take down an opponent.

Since Yule's unit was ordered to approach the airfield from behind, it had to cover the longest distance in order to penetrate the target area, specifically the runway. The task was to install a Strela-2 on the tarmac, a portable missile launcher with a mechanical timer. The missile was a curious weapon; after the clock wound down, the sound detector would activate itself, listening to the distinct sound of a roaring aircraft engine. Upon hearing the sound, the heat-seeking warhead would be launched and would follow the aircraft until impact.

The virgin snow was fresh and soft, blurring the surroundings into a near indistinguishable sheet of brilliant white. It was also very bright as the sun reflected off of the surface. The men had to squint continuously in order to assuage the intense brightness, virtually eliminating any peripheral vision. Yule's unit had decided to enter a small birch forest in order to gain a tactical advantage. They hoped that the trees would provide some semblance of cover and would camouflage their advance. Within that forest, however, the unit was ambushed by a waiting "enemy" accompanied by several of the observers. The trap may have been effective, but the men were overeager and, as a consequence, made the basic mistake of opening fire onto Yule's unit with their AK-47s upon first sight. By doing so, they gave away their positions prematurely. Yule's unit, upon hearing the echoing and rhythmic *thuds* of machine gun fire, immediately scrambled and took cover behind the birch trees and the piles of snow, blending in perfectly with the environment due to their white overalls. It was clear that the ambush was performed by inexperienced men—to compulsively open fire and to consequently give away one's position, instead of waiting patiently to draw out the enemy, was definitely not the best strategy.

Yule waved to his men to stay down and to not respond to the enemy's gunfire. The idea was to lay low for as long as it took and to eventually draw out the enemy. Then, the unit would engage the unsuspecting soldiers in hand-to-hand combat. Timing was critical. If they were to reveal their positions prematurely, the enemy would have the chance to retreat and to hunker down, most likely resulting in a lengthy and noisy firefight. After about five minutes of silence, Yule noticed a gentle movement behind a tree in a small ravine about thirty yards ahead of him. He steadied his breathing, trying to eliminate as much noise as possible. In the ensuing silence, Yule heard the soft and faint crunch of snow. Then, after a few more seconds, a man in white overalls materialized a few yards away, crawling toward Yule and obviously unaware of his position. The man's AK-47 was on his back, its gunmetal contrasting with the brilliantly white snow, not unlike a shark's fin floating ominously above the water. Yule allowed the man to get closer and, when the distance between them shrunk to about ten feet, he stood up. The man was startled; he scrambled up onto his feet and faced Yule. He was a large man with the face of a teenager, one that looked as if it had never felt the touch of a shaving razor. He was probably relieved to see that his opponent was smaller in stature. Since it was too late to use firearms, the inexperienced soldier went for a high kick, aimed at Yule's head. Yule could almost see the man's foot rising in slow motion—a high kick was the most inappropriate choice under the circumstances as the deep snow and the burden of the weapons and ammunition made it close to impossible to aim. Yule could almost hear *Starshina* Zotov's hallmark admonition against uselessly fancy kicks above the waist. He caught the rising foot with both hands and, with his left foot, swept the attacker off of his remaining leg. The big man went down with a soft and muted thud, both legs flailing up in the air, and landed on his back. In retrospect, he was lucky that the snow was soft enough to break his fall. Otherwise, with the Kalashnikov mounted onto his back, the fall could have been injurious or even fatal. Yule leaned over the man, took out his knife, and made a faux stabbing motion. As soon as the soldier, who looked quite embarrassed, got up and attempted to walk away, the voice of one of the observers bellowed through a megaphone, ordering the fallen solider to stay put until he was properly marked as "dead." Yule smiled and continued on with the completion of his mission, this time without any surprises or unexpected hitches.

In the February of the following year, Yule Fine and Nikolai Oberemok were, at the request of Colonel Matushenko, returned to the 262nd Training Airborne Division. They both boasted brand new sergeant's stripes upon their successful completion of Spetsnaz training. The night before departure, Lieutenant Sur summoned Yule to his office.

"I am going to fulfill my promise and show you my record collection," he said. He opened a closet door and pointed at the bottom shelf, where he kept his collection of jazz records. There were numerous LPs and some forty-fives, mostly with Columbia Records labels affixed to them. The middle shelf contained an RCA record player, a luxury in the 1960s. Catching Yule's puzzled expression, the Lieutenant gave a brief explanation of the events that had led him to the acquisition of such an invaluable trove of musical treasures. Specifically, Lieutenant Sur was in Cuba in 1962 where he had acquired the stereo and the jazz records. He carried only a small suitcase when he left Cuba, so he could bring only a limited number of records back with him. Limited by the constraints of the suitcase, he chose only his favorites, which included Miles Davis, Dizzy Gillespie, and Charlie Parker. The showpiece was not a record, but rather a tape that Lieutenant Sur promptly loaded into a small *magmnitophone*, a tape player. "This," he said, "is Ornette Coleman with three other musicians. Listen to it and tell me what you think."

At first, Yule could not understand or make out what he was listening to. It was, he observed, not jazz in the traditional sense—it had no apparent structure or chords. Coleman's saxophone was screaming and groaning, sliding in and out of tonality, changing tempo, each instrument playing what seemed to be a completely different tune. Yet the result was *not* a disjointed cacophony. Somehow, the multiple and distinct parts blended together to form a complete whole. The music was so intense that, when it ended, Yule was breathless. The Lieutenant stopped the tape and looked at Yule, his inquisitive eyes awaiting Yule's judgement.

"I don't know what that was," said Yule, "but it was mind-boggling. I have to listen to more of it." It was a momentous and incredible conclusion to an even more indelible journey.

Upon reassignment to the 262nd Airborne Division, both Yule and Nikolai had immediately assumed command of their respective sections in the newly formed platoons. In total, there were five platoons with a combined might of approximately two hundred fifty fighting men. Their old platoon, the one in which they had started their military journeys during the September of the previous year, was still there. The men, especially those who had once clearly disliked Yule, were very cautious in exhibiting their feelings. It was, Yule thought, good to have authority. It was almost liberating.

Colonel Matushenko met with the newly promoted sergeants the next day and congratulated them.

"Are you still as contumacious as you were when you first arrived, Sergeant Fine?" he asked while shaking Yule's hand vigorously.

"Yes, Comrade Colonel," said Yule, smiling.

"Good. Now you will see what it's like to command people like yourself. As a matter of fact, we have a few interesting specimens in your section," he added, smiling all the while.

One cold and dreary morning, some time in the middle of March, approximately two hundred men boarded two AN-12s, both of which took off with a thunderous roar and headed in a southeastern direction, two deadly birds laden with troops and equipment. Yule was among the men who were all participating in a mission of some import. The previous day's briefing for the commanding personnel regarding the purposes of the expedition informed Yule that the endeavor was a "humanitarian mission to help the ethnic Uyghurs" who'd escaped to the Soviet Union from China's Xinjiang Province.

"Instruct your men to stay as close together after the landing as possible," ordered Colonel Matushenko during that briefing. "The terrain will be mountainous and rough. I will personally assume command of this operation." He paused for a few seconds, then added, "The order came from the Kremlin." A deafening silence penetrated the room. Those two variables alone, the fact that the Colonel was assuming command over the operation and that the operation itself came from the highest ranks of the Soviet government, conveyed the tantamount importance of the mission. The sergeants and officers merely sat there without discussion, digesting the magnitude of what they had just heard. It made sense, Yule thought. There were persistent rumors that Khrushchev and Mao shared a mutual dislike for each other, especially after China had tested their nuclear warhead about a thousand miles from the Soviet rocket installation in Kazakhstan.

The Uyghurs, a Turkic–Muslim minority group in China, had become pawns in the insatiable game for power. Driven by starvation and prosecution, the disgruntled group sought refuge in the Soviet Union by consistently spilling over across the border into Kazakhstan, Kyrgyzstan, and other Central Asian Soviet Republics. Now, however, it appeared as if the migration had manifested itself in unprecedented proportions; tens of thousands of Uyghurs were simultaneously crossing the Soviet-Chinese border. Naturally, the Chinese government had immediately accused the USSR of subverting the Uyghur population and, as a consequence, started dispatching troops closer and closer to the border. At the same time, the Chinese government was *encouraging* the Uyghurs to leave China, a typical example of the duplicity that epitomized Mao's politics. The fickle and somewhat truculent relationship between China and the Soviet Union was not a new phenomenon; the border tensions stretched back all the way into the seventeenth century, when Russians occupied the Amur River region north of Mongolia. The conflict throughout the 1960s, however, differed substantially from the previous relatively trivial disputes; it had manifested itself into a potentially dangerous antagonism with far-reaching consequences. Specifically, the difference stemmed from the nuclear capabilities of both nations. China, furthermore, used every possible opportunity to demonstrate their nuclear arsenal. In the October of 1964, a nuclear bomb was tested at the newly constructed Malan nuclear test base, known also as *Base 21.* It was a vast area of approximately fifty thousand square miles. Chairman Mao, emboldened by China's nuclear arsenal, went as far as claiming that Vladivostok and Khabarovsk were both built on territory that, by rights, had belonged to China.

The irrepressible paranoia and the consequent military buildup on both sides continued throughout the 1960s. The Soviets, in essence, had a *carte blanche* to intervene militarily whenever one of the countless Muslim revolts took place. The situation was also exacerbated by the existence of a very strong antagonism between Han Chinese and Muslims. To top it all off, there was a deep-rooted division between the Chinese and the Turkic Muslims. The region was a dormant furnace, fueled and ready for that one spark to set it off.

The red light in the back of the plane started to flash, interrupting Yule's reverie; it was time to jump. Yule's section went first. He stepped into the threshold that divided the plane and the open sky, peering down onto the terrain thousands of feet below. From his high vantage point he saw a river winding its way between two steep cliffs as well as a small town upstream that was straddling the river. Next to the town, he glimpsed some kind of a compound, one resembling a military installation. When he was cleared to jump, he took a deep breath and stepped out of the aircraft. Both AN-12s, after emptying out the contents of their enormous bellies, slowly wiggled their wings back and forth, a longstanding airborne tradition that symbolized *good-bye* and *good luck*. The two behemoths then set out in a northwesterly direction, back to their starting base; there was no airfield large enough to accommodate the aircraft anywhere nearby. Colonel Matushenko had landed not too far from Yule who could not help but marvel at the Colonel's almost artistic and masterful landing technique. Unlike Yule, who employed the more conventional "landing fall" technique, Colonel Matushenko always managed to land upright, a landing that always terminated with a very brisk, short run. He was a maestro at his craft, and Yule never managed to figure out the secrets of his dexterity.

At the post-jump briefing, Yule discovered that the town they had landed next to was identified as Naryn, a small Kyrgyz settlement north of the Soviet-Chinese border. The assignment was to secure the Torugart Pass, which connected Xinjiang, where the Uyghurs were escaping from, with the Naryn Province of Kyrgyzstan. The pass soared over the Tian Shan mountain range at an altitude of twelve thousand feet above sea level. The snow already started to melt in mid-March, but at that higher altitude the snow blanketed the Torugart Pass until May. A small convoy of personnel carriers was waiting for them by the jump site, parked along the road. The road, which led to the Torugart Pass, was in reasonably good shape. Thus, about half an hour later, the convoy reached the town of Dostuk, the last settlement before the Chinese border. Yule looked around, taking in the stunning surroundings. Mountains stretched in all directions, the gargantuan colossi towering over the earth, their jagged peaks piercing the clear blue sky like so many knives stabbing deep into the heavens themselves. In about two more hours, after passing by numerous sparsely situated and scattered yurts set deep within the valleys of the snow capped mountains, they finally arrived at the Torugart Pass.

Yule, for the duration of the trip, sat within the cabin of a truck, high above the ground. It was, he realized, the same model as the one he rode in while working back at the Donbas coal mine. The driver was from the local military base, the one that Yule had seen from the air. He was small and dark-skinned, most likely Kyrgyz. It was highly unusual that someone served that close to home. Then again, his knowledge of the treacherous terrain probably made the Military Personnel Office bend the rule every so slightly. He handled his huge transporter expertly and with ease, anticipating virtually every twist of the road. After the first thirty minutes, Yule began to wonder whether the driver had a voice. Almost on cue, the driver started to sing in a very quiet, soothing monotone:

Zuleika-hanum

You are the only one

I am dreaming of and

Always sing of

Oh, my Zuleika-hanum

No wonder that ashugs

Sing that there is no defense

Against her eyelashes

She just looks and my heart

Is set on fire

Oh, my Zuleika-hanum

The song was familiar to Yule—he had heard it multiple times before, but only then did he remember that it was sung by the prisoners in the Zona. The images associated with the song were disturbing, so he started looking out the window to distract himself. The scenery, although breathtaking, was very repetitious, so Yule found his mind wandering yet again. He closed his eyes and attempted to take a little nap, when the driver startled him by speaking. He pointed to the top of one of the many cliffs along the road and said, "The Golden Eagle." Yule followed the direction of his finger and saw a large stone eagle perched on the very top of the cliff.

"It is a sacred bird in Kyrgyzstan," the driver said. "It brings good fortune."

After a brief pause, Yule said, "My name is Yule. What's yours?"

"Bagu, Comrade Sergeant."

"Bagu," repeated Yule. "What does it mean in Kyrgyz?"

"A deer, Comrade Sergeant," he said with a discernible degree of pride. "I am from the Bagu tribe, the descendants of the Mother Deer, from the banks of the Yenisei River."

"Tell me more about your tribe. And please, drop the whole Comrade Sergeant thing, just call me Yule."

"We have a legend that goes back a thousand years," said Bagu, looking at Yule with his narrow, deeply seated intelligent eyes. "And it is a long one."

"As long as it does not take a thousand years to tell, I am ready."

They both laughed. As the ice was broken, Bagu began to tell the legend he was so proud of. To Yule's delight, he turned out to be a great storyteller, using elaborate metaphors and detailed descriptions of nature and people. It took about one hour for him to finish the legend. Yule did not interrupt too often, just occasionally asked for Bagu to translate some Kyrgyz names. The legend was about the original Kyrgyz tribe that settled on the banks of the Yenisei River.

"They were a peaceful people, but their neighbors, a tribe that came from a different part of the region, were very cruel and bloodthirsty. They regularly raided the Kyrgyz people's territory, stole cattle, razed houses, and killed the villagers. One day, the Kyrgyz tribe's leader, Kulchoo, died and the tribesmen prepared to bury him. As the funeral ceremony took place and the entire tribe gathered together to pay their respect, the enemies attacked and killed every single person, one by one. It so happened that two children from the tribe, a girl and a boy, had earlier gone into the woods to gather mushrooms and thus escaped the slaughter. Upon returning, they found everyone dead and their homes destroyed. Scared, they had hid in the woods until dark and then started to search for food and help. After many hours of wandering, they finally saw signs of life at the foot of a mountain. They rushed there only to find out that they were their enemies, celebrating the victory. Nevertheless, driven by hunger, the children went forward and begged for food. An old woman took pity on them and gave them some boiled meat. Some in the crowd recognized the children as Kyrgyz and took them to their Khan. He went into a rage that some Kyrgyz had survived and ordered the old woman to kill the children so no Kyrgyz remained alive.

"She took the children to a cliff overlooking the mighty Yenisei River and was about to throw them down when she heard a voice and saw a large Maral Deer with huge sad eyes and udders full of milk. The deer explained to the old woman that the hunters had killed her own children and that she could nurse the two human children. 'You do not know men and how cruel they are,' said the old woman. 'You are inviting so much trouble by fostering the human children.'

The Mother Deer still insisted on taking the children away. She said that she would raise them and would be a good mother. The old woman agreed and let the children go with the deer who led them a long way away, over the mountains to the lake Issyk Kul where she raised them. They grew up, got married, and had two sons: Tynymsejit and Alesejit. That was the beginning of a new tribe, the tribe of the Mother Deer—the Bagu tribe. Later, Tynymsejit moved his family to the Naryn region…"

"It's a beautiful legend," said Yule when Bagu had finished. "You know, it is not unusual for an animal to raise human children. Even the most vicious carnivores yield to their maternal instincts when it comes to human babies."

"The animals kill only when they have to survive," added Baku. "Unlike us… we kill each other because we are different, at least some of us."

Yule nodded. After a short pause, he asked, "By the way, how did you manage to serve so close to home? Is it because you know the area so well?"

Bagu looked at Yule, obviously hesitant, and then decided that he could trust the young Sergeant. His answer was short but concise.

"Baksheesh."

Yule, who apparently had given too much credit to the wisdom of the Military Personnel Directorate, nodded again, acknowledging the answer. They both fell into silence for another minute, but did not get a chance to continue their discussion—the convoy came to an abrupt halt.

"*Razgruszaysya*, disembark," commanded the colonel, who was somehow on the ground even before the convoy came to a complete stop. The men jumped out and lined up in a single file. At thirteen thousand feet above sea level, on the very top of the mountain range that separated Kyrgyzstan from China, the view was breathtaking. On the Chinese side, the red desert stretched on into infinity, with no apparent boundaries to divide its endless expanse. The road continued into Chinese territory, passing through an *arka* resembling the Arc de Triumph, only with the large Soviet Seal on top.

At the order of Colonel Matushenko, they crossed into the neutral territory and took their assigned positions on both sides of the Torugart Pass. The wait was short – in about forty minutes, the first wave of refugees appeared down below, slowly winding their way up a steep road. Some were walking on foot, leading children by the hand. Others, mainly older Uyghurs, were riding small horses, all with various bags and small pieces of furniture loaded onto carts that had two wheels and had to be pulled by two to four people each. There were at least a hundred of them, all garbed in traditional Uyghur clothes. The women donned long velvet robes and thick headscarves, while the men dressed themselves in light colored, lengthy robes and their traditional four-angled hats with colorful embroidery. The older men had long beards and looked very distinguished, almost dignified, despite their abject circumstances. Some were pedaling full-sized tricycles, the large containers between the back wheels filled with their meager belongings.

From his vantage point, Yule was able to distinctly see Chinese troops also standing on both sides of the road down below, machine guns pointed at the refugees. It was a tense time. Yule remained in his position, at times gripping his gun so hard that his hands hurt from the pressure. His heart was beating rapidly in anticipation, awaiting the slightest indication of any aggression. One shot, whether accidental or purposeful, would transform the area into a killing ground.

Surprisingly, however, there were no incidents. It looked as if the Chinese wanted to get rid of the Uyghurs as much as the Uyghurs wanted to get out. In two hours, the entire ordeal was over; the operation was bloodless and successful. Colonel Matushenko would most likely receive a commendation or a medal for the effort. If that happened, Yule would be truly happy for the colonel, a quintessential soldier who would sincerely appreciate such a commendation.

In the January of 1965, Yule had been transferred to the Eighth Airborne Corps of the 103rd Guards Airborne Division, stationed near city of Vitebsk in Belorussia. The 103rd division was undergoing some restructuring and the general headquarters had requested experienced and well-organized unit commanders to be transferred to facilitate the restructuring. Colonel Matushenko had recommended Yule, who was promptly promoted to a senior sergeant, adding one more stripe to the previous two.

Vitebsk turned out to be a charming old town, situated on the high bank of the western Dvina River and full of the ruins of old castles and churches. Some were perfectly restored, whereas others were in the process of rebuilding. Yule received his first *uvolnenye*, weekend release pass, three months after his transfer—he was allowed to go to town for twelve hours, along with a dozen fellow soldiers who could not contain their excitement in anticipation of meeting local girls at an upcoming dance.

It was an early April morning, a perceptible chill still permeating the air. The contingent of soldiers rode into town in a green GAZ-66 truck, with nothing more than an inadequate canvas top to protect them from the cold, merciless Gulf of Riga winds. The taut top vibrated ever so slightly as it was buffeted by the winds. They were dropped off at the center of town by the *skver*, square, not far from the bridge that could be seen even from a distance. The soldiers jumped out onto the sidewalk, straightening out their uniforms and stretching their legs in order to restore some circulation, happy to be rid of the cramped confines of the GAZ-66. The streets were relatively empty, probably due to the fact that it was still too early for most to be walking about on the crisp Saturday morning. Yule looked toward the square where he saw an old, bearded man crossing the street. The man wore a long black overcoat. He held an ornate walking stick in one hand and his hat in the other. The hat piqued Yule's interest, as he had never seen the likes of it before—it was a tall fur hat with a wide brim, almost like a tall fedora made out of fur. His long, white beard flowed to and fro in the wind, sharing an uncanny resemblance with Zeus's mighty beard and the beards of the Uyghur elders.

One of the soldiers walked over to the man, clearly asking him some sort of a question. Yule, however, could not hear the conversation, which was blocked out by the howling of the wind. It appeared that the inquiry was for directions, as the old man pointed toward the building behind the square. By doing so, he released his grip on the brim of his hat. A strong gust of wind then lifted the hat, carrying it for at least ten feet until it finally landed on its side and kept rolling on the ground. Flabbergasted, the old man started to chase after the runaway hat. When he reached it, he bent over to pick it up, but a fresh gust moved the hat a little further. The soldiers clearly found the sight amusing, expressing their mirth through laughter. The elderly man straightened up and looked at the group with his scornful eyes. Yule was disgusted by the behavior of his soldiers, all of whom were under his command. He jumped out of the truck's cabin, picked up the hat, and handed it back to the old man.

"I apologize for my comrades," he said. "They did not mean to offend you."

"No, no... there is no need to apologize," the old man replied. "They are all so young; it is good to laugh sometimes. Thank you." He placed the hat upon his head and walked away.

The men, seeing their commander's reaction, were clearly embarrassed. Their laughter ceased as quickly as it had commenced, replaced by nervous looks.

"This," said Yule angrily, "is your free lesson in civility. I won't punish anyone, but *know* that each and every one of you has just disgraced those blue berets that you are wearing."

As a Sergeant, he had the power to cancel their leaves and to send them back to the barracks. He thought, however, that the situation, disgraceful and embarrassing as it was, offered a good and valuable lesson. Thus, he merely turned around and started a brisk walk in the same direction as the old man had gone, along Sovyetskaya Street and then to Lenin Street. He turned right onto Frunze Street, which opened up to the bridge that led to the other side of the river. Upon examining the bridge for a few moments, Yule turned right and walked alongside the river, passing a stately building that looked somewhat like a theater. Upon the conclusion of the two-hour walk, he again found himself by the square. There, Yule settled down onto a park bench and opened up the copy of the *Komsomolskaya Pravda* newspaper that he had picked up along the way. It contained the usual assortment of stories, namely pro-Syrian and anti-Israeli articles, reports about the Communist Party Congress, and troubles brewing in the politically unstable Czechoslovakia (whose military leadership wanted more control within the Warsaw Pact). All of it was, as Yule's father used to say, the "usual borsch variety."

"Good day, young man," said someone as a shadow fell over the newspaper. Yule looked up. It was the old man, wearing his strange hat. He was standing directly in front of Yule, bending forward ever so slightly as he dispersed some of his weight onto the cane.

"Hello," said Yule, gesturing toward the bench. "It looks to me like you could use a little rest."

The old man gingerly sat down next to Yule, placing his cane between his legs. It was an exquisite piece, probably very old and very valuable. The top was crowned with a large round ball that looked like it was made of ivory, while the shaft itself was crafted out of some kind of black wood with minuscule pieces of reddish metal, shaped like stars, imbedded throughout its length. It was doubtlessly a museum-quality piece. The old man must have caught Yule's interest in the cane. Without any vocal impetus he said, "That used to be my father's stick, one of the few things left behind from my family's belongings."

"Why was so little left behind?" asked Yule. It was a rhetorical question; he already knew that the answer was war.

The old man pulled out a pocket watch, looked at it, and said, "If you are not in a hurry, I will tell you."

"No, I'm not in a hurry at all. I have about eight hours left before I must return to the base."

"Very well, young man," he said, clearly excited about the prospect of a conversation. Then he added, "You are certainly more polished than your comrades, and your voice sounds much more educated."

Yule decided to ignore the "educated voice" remark, electing instead to say that his comrades were excellent soldiers, albeit slightly uncouth at times. The old man nodded in agreement and asked, "Are you one of those men who jump out of the planes with parachutes?"

"Yes, I am."

"I've always been curious, young man… aren't you afraid of dying every time you jump?"

"Not really."

"Why not, if I may ask?"

"Because dying is much easier than living… I'm sure that you know all about that much better than I do, though, having lived such a long life."

The old man laughed and said, "You sound as if you've lived a very long life yourself. It's amazing; you have the *chochma*, but you are just a boy."

"I'll be twenty-two in August."

"Just a boy," he repeated twice, slowly bobbing his head as if engaged in prayer or meditation.

"I've been told that my age belies my wisdom, but I've had teachers and mentors throughout my life who were as wise as you are. They deserve unadulterated credit for what I am today," responded Yule.

"What is your name, young man?"

"Yule. Yule Fine."

"It's a pleasure to meet you, Yule," said the old man. "Mine is Nachum." And with that briefest of introductions, he told, in his quiet, almost monotone voice, a remarkable story of survival.

Yule's original guess was that man was at least eighty years of age. It turned out, however, that he was ninety-five. Nachum was a Hasidic *zadic*, righteous man, originally from the nearby town of Lubavitchi. He was, right before the Nazi occupation of Vitebsk, appointed as the head of the Yeshiva of the Great Lubavitchi Synagogue, which now lay in ruin. In the July of 1941, the Red Army retreated from Vitebsk and put the town to the torch, burning it to cinders in order to preempt the Nazi occupation. The fire gutted whatever had survived the heavy bombing raids conducted by the German Luftwaffe. Three years later, when the German Army was pushed out of town by Soviet troops, only a handful of buildings still stood, and only a few hundred residents had survived the occupation, among them only a dozen Jews out of the thousands who had refused to evacuate Vitebsk. Nachum was one them; he hid in the basement of a building situated not far from the Lubavitchi Synagogue with a local family who had managed to escape the deadly embrace of the ghetto, where thousands of Jews were later slaughtered.

They lived in the basement for almost three years, supplied with food by sympathetic non-Jewish neighbors and friends. At the time, Nachum was already in his seventies. The fact that he had survived the occupation and was still, nearly twenty years later, alive to tell the tale was nothing short of a miracle.

"So you see," he continued, "I kept this cane and pocket watch with me in hiding. My family had perished in the bombings, and my house was completely destroyed. The only thing that had kept me alive was my faith."

As remarkable as it was, the story was all too familiar to Yule, albeit with some variations; it was similar to that of any Western Ukrainian or Belorussian town where the Gestapo had committed indescribable and innumerable atrocities.

"It is so hard to imagine that one human being could do such things to another," said Yule. "Every time I read or hear about these accounts, my mind struggles with comprehending the reason."

Nachum paused, clearly holding back something and deciding whether he should say it or not. When he gained the courage, he asked, "You are a soldier, Yule. What would you do if you were ordered to kill without question?"

"If it was a war, I would kill on the battlefield, but I would *never* kill or torture civilians or drown little children or bury people alive... I'd rather be executed for treason."

Nachum listened intently to the response, nodding his head approvingly with every word. He was clearly lonely, gladdened by the opportunity to have a conversation with someone who was willing to listen. Although he had followers at the underground synagogue that he frequented on Saturdays, he lived alone in his old age.

"Now, young man, it is your turn," he said. "Tell me your story."

"I am not as good a raconteur as you are," answered Yule. "Besides, I don't like talking about myself."

"Certainly, I understand, but can you please indulge me with just one question?"

Yule nodded.

"What is your faith? Your religion, I mean."

"I do not believe in God," responded Yule.

Nachum sighed. "That is not unusual nowadays, but tell me, how do you know which direction to choose when you come to a fork on the road of life?"

Yule smiled and said, "I have an internal compass. It always shows me the way."

Nachum nodded, though Yule knew not whether it was in agreement or merely acknowledgement. "You are an interesting specimen, Yule, and I would most certainly like to talk to you some more."

"If I get another weekend pass, I will be here, at the same time and in the same place. Unfortunately, I am neither the master of my time nor of my life, for that matter. That is, until my discharge day of course."

"Well then. I sincerely hope to see you again, Yule Fine."

"Likewise."

They shook hands. The old man's hand was big and bony, still strong despite his many years.

Regrettably, Yule never saw the venerable elder again. The following week, the Eighth Airborne was sent to Baikonur and, immediately upon return, on a long and grueling trip to the southern Mongolian border with China. It was a time when the communist bloc became engaged in a fierce power struggle for world domination. The schism between the USSR and China had deepened substantially, ultimately involving Mongolia, which was sandwiched between the two super-giants. Mongolia had taken the USSR's side, primarily because of the great amount of financial and military help received from Khrushchev and from his successor, Leonid Brezhnev. In the January of 1966, the Mongolian government had officially requested the presence of Soviet troops on the Mongolian border with China.

The time for demobilization had finally arrived during the spring of 1966. After a seemingly interminable three years of being away from Leningrad's embrace, the city appeared somewhat smaller upon Yule's arrival, more chamber-like and in a state of noticeable disrepair. His apartment also looked different—all of the beautiful antique furniture collected by Grandpa Sam had apparently been sold, replaced by an absolutely atrocious looking set of "Made in Rumania" furniture, the couches upholstered in a sickening chemical green. Several oil paintings were also conspicuously missing from the walls, most likely exchanged for jewelry or other trinkets. Yule looked out into the courtyard, which was eerily and sadly desolate. The kids who used to play in the courtyard got older, most likely electing to play hockey or football at one of the various sports clubs in the city. To his dismay, Yule discovered that the boy with the crooked mouth had committed suicide, hanging himself in the stairwell of his building. According to his neighbor, he could no longer bear the teasing and the daily ridicule by the kids. Much had changed in Leningrad, and none of the changes seemed for the better. Yule was incredulous at the difference that three fleeting years could make.

Putka, the future president of the Russian Federation, looked more mature and cockier than he did three years ago. Maria Ivanovna was glad to see Yule. She informed him that her son was practicing Sambo at the local sports club, and that he spent most of his free time there. She was glad of it, because time spent at the gym meant time spent away from trouble.

Although saddening, none of those changes matched the magnitude of Yule's discovery upon his visit to Irina Alexandrovna's apartment. As soon as he climbed those massive marble stairs and faced the door, he knew that something was seriously wrong. There were now three electric bells on the door, each with a name tag: Popov, Rudenko, and Sevrugina. The bronze doorknocker was gone. Yule rang the first bell and was immediately confronted by an unshaven and topless man of an undetermined age. His breath reeked of alcohol. The man was tall and very thin, a kind of thinness that indicated many years of heavy drinking.

"What do you want?" asked the man.

"Is Irina Alexandrovna home?"

"Who?"

Yule's heart sank into his stomach as the familiar taste of bile filled his mouth. "Irina Alexandrovna," he repeated quietly.

The man turned his head into the darkness of the hallway and yelled, "Zeena!"

A heavy door slammed within the apartment and a woman showed up next to the man, peering at Yule with curiosity. She was young and chubby and had a pretty face. Yule heard a baby wailing inside the apartment.

"This young man is looking for an Irina Alexandrovna," the man said. "Do you know who she is?"

"She lived here before us," said Zeena. "I heard that she died in the Botkin's barracks, from complications after an infectious hepatitis."

Yule's facial expression had most likely betrayed his pain and sadness, as the couple went silent for a few moments.

"Was she your relative?" asked Zeena sympathetically.

"No, just a friend. Thank you." Without saying anything else, Yule turned around and went downstairs. It was drizzling outside, the fine and pleasantly refreshing Leningrad mist kissing his face, as if the city itself was trying to comfort him in his time of great sadness.

And so, life continued to deliver its unfathomable cruelty.

Yule had spent the last several months before his discharge dreaming about his homecoming. In those dreams, he had flown many times over the city, never dreaming of anything specific, just the mere concept of coming back. Now, however, when his dreams had finally materialized, any sense of happiness was quickly replaced by dread and sadness. The homecoming was, to say the least, disappointing, one of the many lessons in life that taught that the anticipation is always more exciting than the event itself. Yule found Leningrad different beyond comprehension, as if nothing was compatible with the comforting images of his memories. In addition, it was not easy to adjust from a highly structured life to a life lacking any coherent structure at all. The nagging question that burned into his mind was what to do. Continuing with dentistry was, Yule knew, not an option. The only thing that was clear to him was the need to go to college. He considered attending medical school to study pediatrics, but it would have taken more than six years to complete the rigorous curriculum, and Yule's father made it very clear that he would not support his son for such a long period of time. Efim was still clearly upset over Yule's wasted opportunity to become a dentist. He did, however, do very well for himself over those three years. He was appointed the deputy director of a chemical plant that was working for the military, one of the secret plants whose official name was nothing but a P.O. Box. Getting a job, Yule knew, would have been the way to go, but working while in college was a foreign notion in the USSR during the 1960s.

One day, Yule had bumped into someone he knew from his time spent in the military. His name was Yaakov. They had first met in a hospital, not far from the town of Lvov, where Yule was recuperating after he had sustained a leg fracture. Yaakov informed him that a new Department of Speech and Psychopathology had just been established at the Leningrad Pedagogical University, and that he was going to apply for admission. The only barriers were the three entrance examinations, namely a Russian language verbal exam, a Russian language essay section, and a foreign language exam. Yaakov also told him in confidence that, according to his sources, the new department would give preferential treatment to men because the Pedagogical Institute's student body was predominantly female.

"Put on your uniform for the interview," said Yaakov while shaking his hand. "You look good in it. They will not be able to turn you down."

The exams were not that difficult, so Yule did not have to resort to the help of his uniform. Whether his gender had played a role in his successful admission, he did not know, but he was absolutely confident that he had committed no grammatical errors in his essay.

His uniform, with the sole exception of the *telnyashka*, the striped undershirt, went into a huge, dusty chest with metal corners. The chest smelled of mothballs and sat in the hallway of the apartment on Baskov Pereulok. Yule took one last look at the uniform, then he shut the chest with an audible and ponderous *thump*. The uniform was never to be seen again, and yet another chapter had ended in Yule's life.

One day, while walking to a tram station on Vosstania Street, Yule bumped into Genna, whom he had not seen since his high school years. Genna had that typical busy look of the Leningrad Jewish intelligencia about him, but he was overwhelmingly glad to see his old friend. After a brief summary of the last six years of their lives, the conversation circled around current events and plans for the future.

"Are you still into the chess?" asked Yule. "I remember that you were the Junior Champion of the city back in school."

"I am," he responded with a sly smile. "And to prove it, I just whipped Boris Khropov in thirty moves."

"Is he any good?"

"He's a strong player, but I was better, and I played white."

"Ah. So did you open with your signature Queen's Gambit?"

"Why yes, as a matter of fact I did," said Genna in a tone that implied surprise. "I am amazed that you still remember, after all these years."

"Don't you remember how we played in class, under the desk, and how we were kicked out by the teacher?"

"I do, but I also remember that you didn't pay much attention to that game."

"We were lousy students, weren't we?" It was a rhetorical question because both knew that it was the truth.

They promised to keep in touch with each other and parted.

That same evening, when Yule returned home, there was a letter from Aunt Sophia waiting for him in the apartment. She wrote to tell him that it had become absolutely impossible to manage his brother Vladimir, who was already fourteen and out of control. She had no choice but to place him in a residential school for boys. An overwhelming sense of guilt had risen from the depths of Yule's mind, guilt that had been suppressed all those years. He was unable, however, to manifest that guilt into action because he himself was dependent on his father for support and for a place to live. Bringing his brother without having any means to support him was probably worse than a residential school, at least for the present. Yule promised himself that little Vova would join him in Leningrad as soon as he got a place of his own to live in. It was more like a distant dream, but a comforting thought nonetheless.

DEFECTOLOGY

**IN MOMENTS OF CRISIS
ONE IS NEVER FIGHTING AGAINST
AN EXTERNAL ENEMY BUT ALWAYS
AGAINST ONE'S OWN BODY.**

GEORGE ORWELL

On the first of September, the newly created Department of Defectology (a term defined as the teaching of the mentally retarded) and Logopedia (speech correction) at the Hertzen Pedagogical Institute in Leningrad was bubbling with excitement, not unlike any other school on the first day after the long summer recess. The excitement at the Institute, however, was unique. Everyone, from the students to the faculty itself, was new, enlivened about the promises of the future. Professor Ivanov was the dean of the new department, a well-built, medium height man in his mid-fifties with a head full of white hair and a look of distinguished pride etched onto his face. Yule had later learned that Professor Ivanov, a medical doctor, had well-pronounced anti-Semitic tendencies. Rumor had it that he was a Jew who had changed his last name in order to blend in and to facilitate his transition into the scientific world. In a way, his anti-Semitism served in his mind as evidence of his gentile identity. Yule, however, did not like the man from first sight. He felt that Professor Ivanov was too vain and artificial, both in his countenance and in his mannerisms. The Professor's hubris seemed to permeate his entire being. Luckily, however, that temperament was not ubiquitous when it came to the rest of the faculty. Professor Pankratov taught the course in psychopathology. He was likely in his sixties, tall and lanky and with a superlative sense of humor. In an odd way, he reminded Yule of Doctor Stein who would have been the same age as Pankratov had he survived the Siberian labor camp. Although the man was essentially a stranger, the perceived familiarity was comforting to Yule. There also was a young adjunct professor, a man by the name of Valery Kovshikov. He was both scrawny and prematurely bold; his physique (at least from a distance) curiously resembled the structure of a question mark. He looked, as a matter of fact, like Duremar, a character in the Russian adaptation of Pinocchio by Alexey Tolstoy.

The students themselves also exhibited a wide array of personalities. The body consisted mostly of young women and a much smaller population of somewhat nerdy-looking men. Some, however, shared Yule's circumstances, fresh out of the military and looking to take advantage of the opportunities afforded to them by the new department. A few of the other military men, however, had seemingly disparate motives. One of them, a man by the name of Naum, wore his uniform on the first day of school in order "to impress the ladies," as he artfully explained. The insignia that he so proudly flaunted indicated that he served in the artillery branch, where the bottom-of-the-barrel recruits usually ended up.

The first psychopathology class, taught by professor Pankratov, was an utter delight to Yule. The principal subject was neurosis and stuttering. From the very first sentence it became obvious that Professor Pankratov, like David Stein and Ivan Lensky, belonged to a special class of "encyclopedians" or "literati." Pankratov's illustrations of the various types of neurosis were taken straight from Russian classical literature—from Tolstoy, Dostoyevsky and Chekhov. The classiest and most interesting of them all was his analysis of the scene where Anna Karenina had thrown herself underneath an oncoming train. His lecture was animated, both vivid and very easy to comprehend despite the complexity of the subject. At the very end of the lecture, he briefly mentioned condition reflexes and his involvement with Pavlov's dogs when he was a young boy. Yule knew that Pavlov moved his laboratory to Leningrad at the end of his career, only for a few years. A sudden realization dawned onto him; it was entirely possible that Professor Pankratov and Doctor Stein knew each other during their work with Pavlov. That would, after all, explain the congruities between the two men. Yule resolved to ask the Professor during his break.

Thus, when the break had finally arrived, Yule approached the professor's desk and asked him whether he knew of a Doctor Stein who also studied and later taught psychopathology at the First Medical Institute. Professor Pankratov looked at Yule with utter disbelief in his eyes.

"Are you asking me about Doctor *David* Stein?"

"Yes, David Borisovich Stein. He told me that he was just like you, looking after the dogs in Pavlov's laboratory when he was a little boy."

"He *what*?" Pankratov's facial expression was as if he were looking at a ghost. "Mr. Fine, Doctor Stein disappeared before you were even *born*. He could not have told you anything."

"I know. This might seem strange right now, but I got lucky; he came into my life and gave me the kind of knowledge I would not have been able to gain anywhere else, and for that I'm forever indebted to him."

Pankratov shook his head, disbelief still painting his facial expression. He looked at his watch and said, "I have a lecture in two minutes. Can you meet me at four by the entrance?"

Yule flew down the stairs and arrived at the entrance at four o'clock sharp, eager to learn more about the man who was once an apparent colleague of one of his greatest mentors. Professor Pankratov had not yet arrived, so Yule spent a few minutes studying the façade of the building. A freshly hung plaque read *Facultet Defectologii i Logopedii.* The building, Yule thought, was once a good looking classical structure, painted in bright yellow and white, which was evident by the coloring in the large square where the original plague that read *Pokrovsky Institute* used to hang. Now, however, the structure looked dingy and gray, littered with peeling plaster and lacking the gargoyles that once overlooked the main entrance.

Pankratov showed up at 4:05. "Sorry," he said, out of breath. "I could not get away. The dean wanted to know about my opinion regarding the new students."

"About our intellectual capacities or our religious and political inclinations, I assume?"

Pankratov gave Yule a long, hard look and said, "I can see now that you have indeed spent some time with David. It appears that you have contracted what Dostoyevsky called a *revolutionary disease.*"

"Would it not be a counter-revolutionary disease in his case?" asked Yule, almost immediately regretting his question. Although Professor Pankratov did not respond, it was too risky to delve into the subject of political ideations—Yule, after all, had just met the man. The fact that he was once acquainted with Dr. Stein in no way evidenced his trustworthiness. With that, they took a short walk across the street, toward a small café frequented by the students. There, they were offered a wobbly table with a peeling plastic top. They settled down with two cups of suspicious-smelling, hot tea and braced themselves for the inevitably lengthy conversation.

Yule went first, telling Pankratov the story of his time spent in Kolyma with David Stein. The professor listened without interrupting, only occasionally sipping his tea and making hardly audible grunting sounds, as if he were experiencing some minute physical pain.

When Yule finished his lengthy tale, Pankratov stood up and wandered over to the window. Since only the professor's back was visible to him, Yule could not see his face. He did, however, see his hand making a lateral motion by his head, as if wiping something away. Perhaps it was tears, but Yule could not be certain.

After a few moments spent in silent reverie, Pankratov returned to the table and said in a continuous stream of breathless despair, "I begged him not to dispute the diagnosis because those people were already sentenced, and the medical professionals could not stop the NKVD, but he would not listen. No, he was very righteous and then they came for him," he paused, collecting both his breath and his thoughts. "We were childhood friends, you know. We looked after the lab dogs together, went to the same school, and then the purges started and he was taken away. He was a brilliant psychiatrist, a very gifted diagnostician." He looked Yule straight in the eyes and added, "If you think even for a moment that times are different now, well, you are wrong. Especially now that Khrushchev is gone. Just be careful and keep things to yourself." With that, he got up and extended his hand toward Yule. "Thank you for closing this chapter for me." He spun around and returned to the university, leaving Yule to sit alone at the table and to ponder the recent developments.

On the second day of school, the first lecture of the day was defectology. There, Yule learned that individuals with mental retardation were often called *oligophrens*, literary translated from the Greek word meaning "small brain." The coarseness of the language being used to stratify the levels of mental retardation was absolutely shocking; the terms *idiot*, *imbecile,* and *cretin* were used in the official jargon, oftentimes corresponding to certain specified IQ ranges. Yule, however, was not surprised; the terminology had, to a certain extent, reflected what he referred to as "the everyday common cruelty" that most Russians (and now Soviet citizens) were subjected to on a daily and historical basis. In a way, the language was not meant to slander but rather to reflect a certain norm. Despite all of that, however, Russia always had compassionate people in general, in particular the compassionate professionals in the field of defectology. On average, they were people whose hearts and souls were in the right place. As enigmatic and full of contradictions as ever, Russia was one the first countries in the world that mandated and even funded education for disabled children since the 1900s, usually starting from the kindergarten age. Unfortunately, due to Russia's isolation from the rest of the world and the severe limitations imposed onto the scientific community after the 1930s, a serious gap in the understanding of childhood developmental conditions had emerged. The lack of psychological testing, which was prohibited in the USSR, had played a significant role in rendering diagnostic procedures ineffective. The diagnosis of mental retardation was based on clinical, not psychometric, indicators. After the first week of classes, Yule had already formed a basic understanding of the concept that difficulties in the written language were directly connected with difficulties in the spoken language, and that both had to be studied under the context of logopedia and defectology. *That* was the main idea behind the creation of the new department, so that future practitioners would be able to marry the two disciplines and to avoid any further incongruities. The first two lectures in logopedia, however, were solely devoted to the study of the typical stages of language acquisition, namely syllable formation, then syllable blending, then finally the rules of spelling, which are many and complex in the Russian language.

The subsequent lectures were about the Russian language, presented in the context of abnormal development, the area that Yule enjoyed the most. By the end of the semester, he had formed a comprehensive picture of the multiple difficulties in the learning of the written language, such as difficulties in transitioning from letter to syllable, syllable to word, slow reading, double reading, etc. Yule was empirically prepared for the subject through his past experiences with his brother who had language acquisition difficulties until he outgrew them by the age of seven.

Yule found it utterly fascinating that the rivalry between the Leningrad and Moscow linguistic schools had found its continuation in the area of atypical learning. The Moscow "School of Logopedia" was based on the interpretation of reading and spelling difficulties, referred to as dyslexia, as the consequence of complications in the spoken language. The Leningrad School, on the other hand, viewed reading problems as a specific inability to master the skill of reading in spite of perfectly normal intellectual functioning. Yule had quickly developed his own opinion, one which coincided with the Leningrad School. He did not, however, elect the Leningrad School because of loyalty to his city, but because his younger brother was living proof of someone who had difficulties with language while being intellectually intact. The two, Yule thought, were not conditional.

He ended the first semester with straight fives, the highest possible marks, and consequently became entitled to an enhanced stipend. With the unique exceptions of the Dialectic Materialism and the History of the Communist Party courses, the two most revered and simultaneously most boring subjects, the courses were exceedingly interesting and, despite the material being very challenging, technical, and sophisticated, Yule studied with pleasure and looked forward to each subsequent day of classes. Therein laid the difference between his experience as a student of dentistry and as a student of defectology. He immediately realized that defectology was what he truly wanted to devote his life to.

During the subsequent summer, Yule applied for a job at the Leningrad train depot, passed the mandatory physical examination, and was thus hired as a *provodnik*, train conductor. The pay was marginal, but the job could potentially become rather lucrative once he was assigned to work on the southbound trains, especially the ones passing through the Caucuses and the Crimean resorts. The trains were booked in advance and, by the summer months, the seats were completely sold out. The vacationing public, desperate to escape to the sunny beaches of the Black Sea and to get a much needed break from the long, cold, and dark northern winter months, was willing to pay extra to stow away on the upper bunks of the sleeping compartments, normally designated for the storage of luggage.

The first assignments for the new conductors, however, usually took them in the *opposite* direction from the Black Sea, reserving the more lucrative routes for the more seasoned conductors. Yule was assigned to the Leningrad-Murmansk line and then to the Kotlas-Arkhangelsk one, where it snowed even in May and the waters of the White Sea remained frozen until June. Among other things, the duties of a train conductor consisted of letting passengers on and off the train, checking tickets, distributing clean linens, and collecting the used ones for washing. There was also an almost sacred duty to make tea and to serve the passengers in their sleeping compartments with the delectably warm elixir. The trains were running half-empty, as that part of the country was not very popular with the vacationing public. The job was easy and interesting enough, but the financial reward was marginal at best. Yule was beginning to doubt whether that golden opportunity of going south would ever present itself.

One dark and rainy night, the train had made a scheduled stop at a small, quaint little town lost among the many Karelian lakes. The name displayed on the relatively small and peeling station tower read *Loukhi.* There were no passengers getting on or off. A station of that magnitude was not even called a station per se, but rather a *polustanok,* half-a-station. The train had slowly started pulling away and Yule was about to close the door when all of a sudden, two thin hands materialized out of thin air and latched themselves onto the bars on each side of the steps. After a few seconds, a mane of snow-white hair appeared above the platform that covered the stairwell. The man pulled himself higher and asked, "Are you going to Murmansk?"

"No, we are going in the opposite direction," answered Yule and attempted to close the door. Much to his astonishment, however, the man had completely pulled himself above the stairs, a feat which required considerable upper body strength. He bounced off the floor inside the corridor and remained motionless for a few seconds, only to quickly spring back onto his feet. He was, Yule realized, about six feet tall and extremely thin. His skin was dark, but not from any exposure to the sun—it was a darkness that came from a life of alcoholism. His face was long and had a good, well-defined bone structure. The man's eyes evidenced Yule's initial suspicion; they were blue and blood shot. He also reeked of alcohol and other unpleasant odors. Nevertheless, despite all of his flaws, he was not as repulsive as most of his kind. To the contrary, there was something pleasant about him, something that Yule could not place or determine. It was impossible to guess his age, so Yule had approximated him as being somewhere between forty and sixty.

"I do not really care which way you are going," said the man. "I just need to get some vodka for me and my comrades. Our store just ran out." He pulled out a wad of money, mostly single rubles, and showed it to Yule as if to prove his noble intentions. Searching for vodka for the entire village was as sacred as any humanitarian mission.

"I am convinced now," said Yule, "but you are getting off at the next station." He looked at his wristwatch, "In twenty minutes."

"Thank you," said the man as he sat down on the floor, his back leaning against the wall. "What is your name, by the way?"

"Yule. And your's?"

"Konors."

Yule's eyebrows arched up in surprise. "Where did you get a name like that?"

"It was my father's last name. Actually, it was Connors, according to the signed daguerreotype he left behind. It's the only evidence I have of my father's existence, aside from me being born, of course."

Konors was clearly an intelligent man and Yule's curiosity reached its peak, especially after he noticed a blue, crudely-made tattoo of a sailing ship on his forearm. A tattoo that was blue and fuzzy could mean only one thing: the man had been in prison at some point in his life. A sailing ship usually meant that the bearer was a vagrant.

"Connors is not a Russian name."

"No, it's not. My father was an American, from Michigan. He fought the Bolsheviks in this region in 1919. I was born six months after his death."

"Are you referring to the American intervention called the Polar Bear Expedition?"

"That's the one, but no one calls it as such in Russia, as that was the name given to the operation by the Americans. We know it as the Antanta Invasion."

Yule was enlivened by the opportunity to talk to the man, to learn more about the vague events of that period. "You know, Konors, the school books do not teach much about that period. Maybe you can enlighten me. I love history," said Yule, being a little disingenuous by proclaiming his outright ignorance of the subject, but it was very tempting to hear from someone intimately connected to that obscure period in Russian history.

"What would you like to know?"

"Anything that you feel is appropriate to tell me. I, most likely, will never see you again, so I think that it's safe."

Konors was hesitant at first, but the desire to share his information had ultimately prevailed. Finally, after much deliberation, he said, "My mother told her story to a friend and a few years later ended up in the Gulag."

"So, what was her story?"

"She met my father in the winter of 1918. He was a Corporal in the 310th Engineers Battalion and traveled between Arkhangelsk,

Murmansk, and Seletskoe, where he met my mother. They fell in love, and he promised to take her with him to America. In the July of 1919, a few weeks before his battalion was scheduled to leave for America, he drowned while building a bridge over the Dvina River near Arkhangelsk. From what I know, he was twenty-three years old. My mother was only eighteen then, and when I was born, my grandmother took over the maternal responsibilities. The people of Seletskoe thought that she was my mother, as a matter of fact. Eventually, however, the Bolsheviks had won and the Communist Party took over the country. I was five years old when they came for my mother and took her away. Someone had reported to the authorities that she had collaborated with the occupying forces and had an affair with an enemy soldier. I never saw her again. Soon after my mother was arrested, they came for me and placed me in a special colony for children who needed to be… re-educated." He paused for a moment then asked, "How do you like my story so far?"

It was clearly a rhetorical question. "Did the re-education work?" asked Yule instead.

"It did for me," said Konors with a smile. "I hate them more than ever."

Alas, the train started slowing down as the whistle heralding its arrival at another *polustanok* pierced the crisp air. The half-station, not unlike the previous one, was lost in the vast wilderness, situated somewhere between the countless lakes that were scattered throughout the region. Konors jumped off onto the wooden platform below with an audible *thump*, without waiting for the metal cover to be lifted off the steps. He was, Yule observed, very light on his feet, a true messenger of Bacchus, and while running toward the station, he turned around and waved one last time to Yule, as if thanking him for the brief company.

Once the train jerked into motion, Yule closed the door and walked toward his service compartment at the other end of the car, his every breath visible in the cold air that had seeped into the train. Suddenly, the large figure of the train supervisor appeared in front of him. Gregory Nechayev was a big man with a wide, ruddy face and a network of capillaries that crept up along his nose, indicating his frequent participation in Russia's favorite pastime: drinking.

"Is everything in order?" asked Nechayev suspiciously. "I just saw a man running away from your car."

"He was trying to get to the liquor store before closing time."

The explanation was apparently perfectly reasonable and sufficient. Nechayev wished Yule a good night and departed for his compartment, located in the first car. Gregory Nechayev was a man of few words.

The following day, the train made another scheduled stop at a small town by the name of Valdeevo, located halfway between Murmansk and Kotlas. The town's tiny station had liquor for sale. The train sat dormant in the station, prepared for departure and awaiting Nechayev's signal. That was part of his responsibilities as a train supervisor. The signal, however, never came; the train supervisor was nowhere to be seen. All of the conductors merely stood on the platform, each adjacent to his respective car. The machinist was hanging out of the locomotive's window, looking around with an expression of confusion on his face. There was, Yule suspected, only one possible explanation for Nechayev's vanishing: the liquor store. Yule liked Nechayev; the man was a decorated war veteran, an artillery captain with four years experience on the battlefield at Stalingrad and Kursk. He was twice wounded in combat, once in the right leg and once below the knee; both left him with a serious limp and severe pain every time the barometric pressure changed. He was never married, had no children, and lived alone, his liquor his only comfort and companion.

Yule took off toward the station and, while passing by the last car, asked the conductor to hold the departure for five minutes. Yule found Nechayev in a shallow dugout located a few feet beyond the end of the platform. He was curled up and sleeping like an infant, apparently overcome by the alcohol on his way back to the train. Yule tapped him on the shoulder then shook him. When neither yielded any result, he finally slapped him across the face but without any effect. Nechayev moaned a few times but refused to wake up. Time was running out, and Yule had no choice but to carry his drunken supervisor back to the train. He looked down at the man. Nechayev was heavy, at least two hundred pounds, so carrying him back to the train would require a substantial effort. Seeing that no other solutions would present themselves, Yule bent down and heaved the heavy supervisor onto his back with a fierce grunt. He had to labor hard to carry Nechayev for even a few feet. He was completely out of breath by the time he reached the last twenty feet of the distance. Suddenly and unexpectedly, his legs gave way. He would have dropped his load if it were not for the two conductors who ran up to help him. The three of them then lifted their supervisor and carried him into the service compartment. The train immediately moved and started gaining speed, in order to make up for the lost time.

In only a few hours, the train finally pulled into the City of Kotlas Rail Station. From Yule's vantage point, the view of the Northern Dvina River was magnificent. The river was wide, and the port was full of moored cargo vessels with cranes hovering above, like sentinels guarding their precious cargos. The shipyard itself was huge. On the other side of the tracks was a rather steep embankment on top of which stood a white Orthodox church surrounded by four-storied Khrushchev-style cheaply made apartment buildings.

Yule had three hours before the train was scheduled for departure back to Leningrad, so he decided to use the rare opportunity to explore the town. After only a few minutes' exploration, however, Yule realized that the town itself had very little to offer—it appeared as if all of the main activities revolved around the port and the railroad hub, the sights of industry branching out in multiple directions. The elevated sidewalks in Kotlas were wooden and the roads unpaved. The dirt covering the roads was deep and pernicious—once it latched itself onto your shoes or clothes, those articles of clothing would be rendered useless. Disappointed with his brief escapade, Yule turned around and resolved to head back to the train. While passing a masonry apartment complex on Lunacharsky Street, he heard a conversation being conducted in the Polish language between two women. *Poles in Kotlas*, Yule thought? His curiosity was heightened; every Pole he had ever met could not stand even mentioning the name of the town. It was, he thought, highly unlikely that a deported Pole would voluntarily stay in Kotlas if given the choice, given what had transpired there during the Second World War. He turned around and faced the two women, one in her fifties and the other, a younger one, no doubt mother and daughter, as the resemblance was evident.

"*Przepraszam, czy jestescie turysci*, apologies are you tourists?" asked Yule in Polish. The older woman was clearly startled, but the younger one merely smiled and answered in perfect Russian without any trace of an accent.

"No, we live here. In fact, I was born in Kotlas, but my mother grew up in Poland." The young woman was about Yule's age and very pretty with her big, curious green eyes and her light brown hair. The older woman had finally relaxed but had not yet spoken, still resorting to examining the intruder in silence. She was blond and had a small, tired face with high cheekbones. The older woman was not as pretty as her daughter. "How come you speak Polish?" the younger one continued.

"I lived in a formerly Polish land for several years, and most of the people around me spoke Polish, so I guess you can say I learned from my surroundings."

The older woman's eyes sparked with interest. She broke her silence and asked, "What town?"

"Stanislawow."

Quite unexpectedly, a smile manifested itself on her tired face. "It is so good to hear the real name of that town," she said. "It is called Ivano-Frankovsk now. I am from Lvov, but I left it in 1939." She paused and corrected herself. "Or rather, I was *taken* away from my home and ended up in Kotlas." She did not say who took her away, but it was obvious—in 1939, Lvov was under the control of the Soviet Union.

Yule said, "But as far as I know, Kotlas was just a short stay for people on the way to permanent Gulag camps, a sort of intermediary between the camps."

"It was, but there were so many of us taken forcibly from our homes that it took a long time to get us sorted out into the different camps. In my case," she sighed, "I never left."

The younger woman turned to her mother and asked, "Why don't we invite the young man for a cup of tea, so we can talk?"

"My train leaves in two hours," said Yule after consulting with his wristwatch. "But whatever time I have left here in Kotlas, it would be my pleasure to spend it in your company."

The older woman laughed and said, "I have not heard such gallantry since I left Poland. My name is Danuta, and my daughter here is Galina."

"*Bardzo przyjemnie*," said Yule as he introduced himself. The three of them then crossed the street and entered one of the numerous five-storied masonry buildings clustered together in the near vicinity. Despite being relatively new, the building was already showing some signs of deterioration, evidence of its poor construction. The stench of urine also permeated throughout the staircase. The actual apartment had two rooms and a kitchen. The interior itself presented a stark contrast to the uniform state of the surrounding buildings; it was brightly colored and was furnished with good-quality pieces. A plethora of framed prints and photographs lined the walls. One photograph showed an older woman standing next to a good-looking man, blond and tall and garbed in an engineering major's uniform. He looked unmistakably Russian.

"Is this your husband?" asked Yule, pointing at the photograph.

"That's my father," responded Galina. "His name is Nikolai."

"Ah. I see that he is in the engineering division. Is he working at the shipyard right now?"

Galina, who was standing next to Yule, suddenly squeezed his arm as a somewhat dramatic expression painted her face. Then, she looked at her mother apologetically.

"I am so sorry," said Yule. Judging from the mother's expression, he guessed that there was a divorce and that the mother took it hard. "It is clearly none of my business, and I really didn't mean to upset anyone but—"

"My husband was killed in 1945, defending his country." Danuta said it with such an unwavering pride and conviction that Yule immediately recognized that characteristic and unbreakable Polish fighting spirit, one that permeated through the very core of the nation's identity. That fighting spirit was a ubiquitous expression of the innate Polish desire to belong to the fatherland, even if it meant the sacrifice of one's life.

The tea was quickly served and they settled down around the kitchen table, an unshakeable Russian tradition. Yule briefly told them his story, merely the chronology of it, but the dry retelling still managed to make Galina pull out her handkerchief and dab her eyes a few times. Their story, however, was no less remarkable and perhaps even more tragic than his.

Danuta was deported from her hometown of Lvov right after it had fallen under Soviet control. Any Poles that were perceived as any kind of a threat to the Soviets, regardless of how minute, were crammed into boxcars and deported to the network of Gulags via Kotlas, which served as a kind of transit facility. The Polish Intelligencia, the educated and professional elite of the Polish population, as well as those who had merely refused to conform, found themselves arrested under the omnipotent Article Fifty-Eight of the Soviet Penal Code and shipped to the region in order to build the Kotlas-Vorkuta railroad, and were consequently forced to endure inhumane conditions and the brutal cold. Danuta, who was a bookkeeper, got lucky; she was assigned to keep the books in the engineer's office in Kotlas. Her future husband, Nikolai, worked there as the chief engineer and was instrumental in getting her a permanent job and thus exempting her from being shipped to Kolyma or to Kazakhstan with the majority of the deportees from Poland, many of whom later died in the brutal conditions of the Gulags. Galina was born in 1943 and knew her father only from his photographs. The three became immersed in their stories, and as a consequence, the time had passed very quickly. Alas, it was time for Yule to head back to his train. They exchanged addresses and promised to keep in touch.

Once on board the train, Yule walked into Nechayev's compartment, catching the supervisor desperately trying to piece together the events that had led to his severe intoxication. Try as he might, Nechayev was unable to recall the events leading up to his intoxication, only that Yule had carried him back to compartment. He looked embarrassed, his face red from the shame as well as the alcohol.

"How are you feeling?" asked Yule. It was a rhetorical question, a mere nicety.

"I've been better," said Nechayev, his voice still weak. "I appreciate what you did there, back at that station."

"Don't mention it. Just get well," said Yule as he headed back toward the door.

"Wait," called out Nechayev. "Where was I when you found me?"

Yule briefly described the events that had transpired and when he finished, Nechayev had an epiphany. "It was a bad batch of moonshine," he whispered. Yule just looked at him, expecting an explanation. After a brief pause, it followed.

"An old friend of mine, someone I served with during the war, lives in that town. He is an invalid. He had both legs blown off by a field mine and now receives a miserable pension, so he makes some money by brewing *samogon* at home. We always have some when I visit him, and I hardly ever get drunk."

"You don't need to explain yourself," said Yule. "Whatever happened, happened. Let's just move on."

"How did you manage to bring me back to the train? I weigh more than two hundred fifty pounds."

"I slung you onto my shoulder and carried you. How else?"

The train departed as scheduled and, in less than twenty-four hours, arrived at Leningrad. At the Moskovski Rail Station Office, where the next trip assignments were being announced, Nechayev pulled Yule aside and told him that the next route they would do together would be to one of the many resort areas along the Black Sea, a very profitable route. Thus, the following morning, Yule proceeded with the usual preparations in the sleeping compartments, namely distributing the supply of fresh linens, blankets, plenty of tea, lemons, and sugar cubes, all favorites among Russian travelers. Everything was normal. That is, everything was normal *until* the passengers showed up and stormed the train. Yule knew perfectly well about the custom of overbooking, but what he saw materialize in front of him surpassed any of his expectations; it looked as if there were twice as many people than the train itself could accommodate all pouring in like an unstoppable breaker smashing through the rocks. It was hard to tell how many there were because of the chaos that ensued. The door and even the windows were besieged with rabid tourists trying to worm in and, in some cases, people without tickets managed to sneak aboard. To someone who was not familiar with the inner workings of the southbound trains during the summer months, the scene would have appeared barbaric. Yule, however, did not mind people sneaking into the train. As a matter of fact, it was implicitly *encouraged*, as it meant one thing and one thing only: extra income. A passenger without a ticket was commonly called a *zayts,* rabbit, and would pay cash to the conductor for space on the luggage shelf underneath the ceiling, oftentimes paying far above the value of a standard ticket. Just one trip could potentially yield thousands of rubles, a rather substantial amount, but there were also expenses incurred by the custom: the train supervisor had to be paid as well as the inspectors who occasionally boarded the train and took their share based on the number of stowaways. After the first trip, Yule ended up with two hundred rubles, largely because Nechayev had refused to accept his share. By the end of the vacation season, Yule had put together enough money to get him through the subsequent year without any support from his father. In addition, he would be receiving an upgraded stipend of fifty-five rubles a month from the university. Life, he thought, was finally shaping up for the better.

An eye-opening event marked the beginning of the second year at the university, one that would inadvertently shape Yule's destiny and influence his decisions for a few subsequent years to come. At the end of September, Yaakov and a few other Jewish students had invited Yule to the only functioning Synagogue on Lermontov Prospect. Yaakov was an active participant in the movement to move to Israel, a movement that was rapidly gaining popularity among the younger generation of Jewish intellectuals. To facilitate the ultimate aspiration to make the transition to Israel, there were several underground schools organized so that the students could study Judaism and practice Hebrew.

"Come and join us in the celebration of the Simchat Torah," Yaakov told him. "It is a song and dance celebrating the end of reading the Torah." Although a lifelong atheist, Yule felt an unquenchable sense of curiosity well up within him. He accepted the invitation eagerly and, on the morning of the following Saturday, he took a lengthy walk to Lermontov Prospect, which was on the other side of the city. The synagogue was teeming with people, the human density further augmented by a large crowd of curious bystanders that had accumulated along the edge of the sidewalk. Yule managed to squeeze himself inside just in time to see a long scroll being carried around and around by dozens of evenly spaced people. Before Yule had a chance to understand the meaning of the somber procession, he was pushed further inside and the upper edge of the scroll was handed to him. Without even knowing how it had happened, he found himself wedged in between a Jewish man in a long black overcoat and black hat and a younger boy in yarmulke. The man looked at Yule angrily, as if invoking some kind of perdition, and pointed at his head. Yule realized that his head was not covered; he knew enough about Jewish customs to know that he was not even supposed to be inside of the synagogue without a hat. Yule muttered a quick curse to himself, highly embarrassed by his lapse of judgment. He quickly rushed outside, his face red. As he passed by the participants, he had the distinct impression that they were all looking at his head, which felt more exposed and bare than it had ever felt in his entire life. Outside, people were dancing and laughing, immersed in the festivities and seemingly oblivious to the world around them. Yule was upset with himself for being so uncouth and went home.

On the following Monday, during the first break between lectures, Professor Pankratov approached Yule.

"*What have you done?*" he asked, his voice quivering and nervous. "What could you have possibly done to make Litvak want to see you?"

Litvak, who taught the course on the History of the Communist Party, was the chairman of the Institute's Communist Party Committee, a position similar to that of a politruk in the military. Being called to his office was usually an indication of a serious infraction that would result in disciplinary action or even expulsion.

Yule merely shrugged his shoulders, not too concerned with the news. He had, after all, done nothing wrong. Thus, he headed for Litvak's office, which was located on the third floor. The massive wooden door was wide open, and the proverbial red carpet, about five feet wide, stretched from the door to Litvak's desk. He was sitting behind it in a large, plush chair, facing the door as if he was expecting his visitor to come in at any moment. The enormity of the desk and the chair was obviously a mechanism for intimidation, but Yule found the sight rather comical, for Mr. Litvak was a tiny man with a small hump, a pale face, and a full beard. The sight of him on that chair and in front of that desk presented a glaring mismatch. Mr. Litvak, it was widely known, had poor balance while walking and could not taste the difference between sweet and sour, a textbook case of the familial dysautonomia syndrome. The name Litvak implied that his family originally came to Russia from Lithuania and that he was an Ashkenazi Jew. The migration most likely took place when Poland and Lithuania were still one country sharing not only one government but also a rabid anti-Semitism that drove many Jews to escape. Some made the right choice by heading to the West, whereas others made the wrong one and headed east. Mr. Litvak, Yule observed, had red, dry, and unblinking eyes—he looked as if he could stare down an owl in the darkness. He apparently also suffered from what Dostoyevsky called a *revolutionary disease*, just like the Bolsheviks themselves who had killed the last Russian Czar and his family in cold blood. For people like Litvak, the zeitgeist of 1917 had never changed. In their minds they still carried Mousers in their side holsters, thoughts of bloody revolution and ideological justice dominating their singular minds.

"Come in, come in, Mr. Fine," said Mr. Litvak when he saw Yule through the open door. "Sit down, please." He pointed at the chair in front of his desk.

The distance from the door to the chair was about twenty feet, but the walk felt somewhat like Jesus's trip to Golgotha. Before Yule even reached his desk, Mr. Litvak flipped open a large binder and started to read. The binder looked suspiciously familiar. Whether it was the same dossier that had followed Yule for the past five years or whether it was just a copy of it was irrelevant; it contained the same incredibly detailed information.

"So, Mr. Fine," said Mr. Litvak, pulling his red eyes away from the binder and fixing them onto Yule's face in an unblinking, accusatory gaze. "How is it possible that a man with your outstanding military record, someone who has demonstrated his loyalty to defending the USSR, could attend a Zionist gathering?"

"A *Zionist* gathering?" repeated Yule in amazement. It took him an extra second to realize what Mr. Litvak was referring to. "I do not know any Zionists," he continued.

"Last Saturday, you and some other of our students were seen inside the synagogue, in the company of people who are known to us as Zionists." He paused, clearly savoring the magnitude of the moment, then added the punch line. "Some of whom were fresh out of prison, doing time for anti-Soviet propaganda."

"I did not know any person there who was in prison." Yule did not like the direction in which the conversation was headed.

"Nevertheless," continued Comrade Litvak, "there was a man by the name of Alexei Murzhenko…" Mr. Litvak paused upon mentioning the name, his eyes scanning Yule's face for any signs that would belie Yule's innocence. When he found none, he continued, "Who was locked up since he was eighteen years of age. He is being watched by the 'organs,' and you would do well to stay away from him."

Yule quickly realized that disputing the man would have been utterly futile; he knew the type from his previous encounters and decided to make the best out of the situation. "Yes, I was there, but only because I was invited by my classmates, not some Zionists."

"We know all about it, Mr. Fine. Some of those who you refer to as your… classmates will be expelled immediately. As far as *you* are concerned, I am letting you go, but not without a warning. Stay away from these people and from that synagogue," said

Mr. Litvak, piercing Yule with his burning eyes. "Is that understood?" He stood up, indicating the end of the conversation.

"Yes, Comrade Litvak," responded Yule, visibly relieved. He also stood up and turned around to leave the office.

"One more thing, Yule," said Litvak. His tone had altered to one that was much softer and not as mordant. "If I were you, I would seriously consider joining the Communist Party. I think you would make a good leader."

"I am very flattered and will definitely think about it, Comrade Litvak," said Yule as he left the office. Then, when he was certain that he was out of earshot, Yule muttered to himself, "Not a chance in this world." He made an attempt to picture the people he had met at the synagogue, trying to put a face to the name of Alexei Murzhenko. Nobody at the Synagogue looked particularly menacing or revolutionary.

Meanwhile, on January 1, 1968, an extraordinary event had taken place in the USSR—the minimum monthly wage was increased from forty to sixty rubles, a staggering fifty percent jump. The increase had arrived in the middle of a period of rapid decline in the rate of economic growth. It was also, however, a subtle reflection of the shift in the country's economic policies. Yule surmised that the fifty percent minimum monthly wage increase was not an act of governmental benevolence but, rather, an infusion of money into the economy. Yule's father had an entirely different take on the minimum wage increase; he thought that it was a purely political, not economic, move. Leonid Brezhnev just wanted to be liked by the people. Yule, however, did not view the two motives as being mutually exclusive.

Ever since Yule's return from the military and, in particular, after he had started his studies at the Gertzen Institute, his relationship with his father spiraled downhill. Efim and his wife were still cross with Yule for abandoning the potentially lucrative carrier in dentistry against their wishes. Efim, himself, was doing quite well as the assistant director of a top-secret chemical plant, working jointly with the Ministry of Defense. He was still slim and lanky, enjoying good health in his late forties thanks in part to his daily walks to and from work, covering a distance of about ten miles a day. Alex, who had become a dentist just like his mother, was also enjoying the fruits of his labor. His father, who was killed in the war, had two brothers, both of whom were also dentists. The relationship between the two stepbrothers could best be described as cold and guarded.

At the very beginning of the winter semester, Docent Kovshikov, the adjunct Professor that Yule had met in the beginning of his studies at the Institute, approached Yule.

"So, I have heard that you are doing quite well academically," he said, fixing his cold and colorless eyes on Yule. "Professor Pankratov has spoken very highly of you. As a matter of fact, he has recommended that I should get you involved in my research for the book that I am working on."

The offer was not entirely unexpected. Professor Pankratov, with whom Yule had developed a rather strong bond, had, on multiple occasions, alluded to the fact that he would like to see Yule continue his studies and to one day join the faculty.

"What kind of research?" asked Yule, intrigued by the prospect.

"It has to do with the abnormal perception of visual symbols in children and the consequences of it in syllable formation."

"That sounds like a book title."

"Indeed. It's the working title of my book," said Docent Kovshikov, the pride evident in his voice. It was, Yule knew, his first book, authorized by the Ministry of Education. As a member of the Communist Party of the Soviet Union, Kovshikov was pursuing the assignment with an ardent fervor, as if the wellbeing of the USSR itself depended on his research. Yule disliked the man. Whether it was due to his strange appearance or to his close affiliations with the Communist Party, he could not tell. The prospect, however, of working on potentially groundbreaking research intrigued Yule.

“When do I start?” he asked.

“Well, first I would like you to read a few books that are not part of your curricula. Please stop by my office after class.”

At five o’clock in the afternoon, Yule knocked on the heavy door that led into the faculty office. As expected, Docent Kovshikov was inside the room, accompanied by two female adjuncts. One of them, Yule knew, taught at the Typhlo-pedagogy Department, the education of the blind. She was in her mid-fifties, very tall, and wore glasses with thick lenses. The other woman was the French language professor. She was young and pretty, always dressed in crepe de chine, her radiant smile illuminating any room that she graced. Yule knew all about her famous daily walks to the auditorium, which was located at the end of a very long hallway. Male students dotted the walls of the hallway, awaiting the daily show. Their eyes always followed her callipygous figure as she strolled through the corridor, entranced by her exotic beauty.

“This,” said Kovshikov, “is Yule Fine. He is Pankratov’s favorite student and will be doing some research for me.” The older woman merely nodded politely, acknowledging Yule’s presence. The French teacher, on the other hand, came up to him, shook his hand, and introduced herself.

“My name is Maya Borisovna,” she said in a pleasant, almost operatic contralto. Her hand was slender and soft. “How come have I never seen you before?”

“Probably because I do not participate in the gauntlet that you must go through every day on our floor.”

She froze for a second, digesting the euphemism that had been thrown her way so unexpectedly. Being a learned person, however, she recovered quickly; the only subtle indication of her surprise was the slightly rosy hue of her cheeks.

"Oh, *you* are the one," she said, her laugh as melodious as her voice. Kovshikov was standing next to them, holding a book in his hands and watching the exchange with curiosity. Finally, when he realized that the show was at an end, he handed the book to Yule.

"Let me know when you are finished reading. And if you have any questions, please do not be shy," he instructed Yule.

The book that Docent Kovshikov had given to Yule was entitled *Posledovatelniye Obrazy*, Residual Images. It was a compilation of several studies dealing with the various degrees of the afterimages that one sees after looking at a bright light or when seeing a shape of a contrasting object for a few second after looking away from it. The research was not geared toward explaining abnormalities related to reading and writing skills, but Yule had already more or less figured out which way his research would be directed. His hunch proved to be correct; the next meeting with Docent Kovshikov was spent discussing the methodology of testing children with language acquisition problems, as well as discussing how to link those problems with the residual images. Throughout much of the next year, Yule spent most of his free time at the Petrogradski District Children's Hospital, painstakingly going through medical files and conducting speech and reading sessions with the dyslexic children. It was not part of his assignment to analyze the data, just to compile it. By the end of the first year, Yule had more than one hundred children tested and a plethora of detailed data compiled on each and every one of them.

Although the data did not point at a direct correlation between pronounced afterimages and reading abnormalities, there was a significant percentage of children who had both. Docent Kovshikov was very happy with the progress and, much to Yule's chagrin, was constantly praising him in public. It was, Yule thought, grossly overdone and felt utterly disingenuous. For some reason, Yule never completely trusted the man. Regrettably, his hunch proved to be correct. It had manifested itself at the end of his senior year, a time when many of the students were making decisions about what to do next in their lives. Yule had applied for a postgraduate study known as *aspirantura*. The Candidate of Science Degree was usually awarded based on original research, and Yule felt that the research he had already done was sufficient for a candidate of science dissertation. He was, however, wrong in his assumption. The day after the committee reviewed his application, he was summoned to the dean's office. When Yule approached the office, he saw Professor Ivanov nervously pacing back and forth in front of his desk and, as soon as Yule stepped through the threshold, Ivanov quickly escaped to behind his desk. He did not sit down, nor did he offer a seat to Yule. The pacing, the nervousness… Yule's heart sank in anticipation of the conversation. He knew that his application had been rejected; it was obvious from the mannerisms of the Dean.

"I have some rather unpleasant news for you," he said, avoiding direct eye contact with Yule. "Your application has been denied because we have already exceeded the quota for other nationalities." *Other nationality* was a euphemism for *Jewish*, and both of them knew it. To continue on with the conversation would have just prolonged the agony, so Yule merely thanked the dean and, much to the dean's amazement and relief, walked out of the office without uttering another word. As he walked down the corridor, Comrade Litvak emerged from around the corner, as if by sheer coincidence.

"I have heard," said Comrade Litvak, shaking his head as if pitying Yule. Then, without waiting for any kind of an acknowledgment or complaint, he went into a lengthy tirade centered around the fact if Yule had just followed his advice on becoming a member of the Communist Party, the fiasco would have been avoided.

To add insult to injury, Yule was not allowed to use his research outside of the Institute. One year later, Docent Kovshikov had successfully defended his doctoral dissertation using Yule's work and was awarded a doctoral degree in speech pathology. Was Yule's constant misery a product of some design, or was it just the result of mere circumstance, of the stars lining up in a certain manner and thus dictating his destiny? Time and time again, life seemed to throw an interminable amount of roadblocks toward Yule, especially during moments when everything seemed to be shaping up for the better.

Thus came the June of 1970, which brought with it events that had effectively changed Yule's world. The phone in Yule's apartment rang off the hook nearly all day long, shrieking for attention almost every time he put it down. The first call of the day was from Yaakov.

"Did you hear?" asked Yaakov in a very strange, uncharacteristic whisper, as if whispering would ward off any malignant listeners.

"Hear what?"

"The *samoletchiki*. The hijacking. My friends, they all got arrested," his speech was almost incoherent with excitement and came out in one continuous stream. "They came to my apartment, they also asked about you, they—"

Yule could not follow the incoherent rambling and quickly lost his patience. "Hold on a minute. Calm down. Now please, can we start from the beginning?" But in response, Yaakov told him to turn his radio on. Then, he hung up the phone. Yule wandered over to his radio, turned it on, and listened. The official version of the event was reported as if the world had effectively come to an end, the passionate voice of the reporter proclaiming the news in an excited, scandalous manner that conveyed the magnitude of the crime. Apparently, twelve people had been arrested for an "attempt to hijack a passenger plane." They were arrested before entering the tarmac to board a twelve-seat AN-2 chartered by the participants in advance. Their plan was to fly to Sweden and, from there, escape to Israel. The principal crime was the fact that they were trying to leave the country without legal authorization. Among the participants were ten Jews, one Russian, and one Ukrainian. The radio announcer, putting a not-so-subtle emphasis on each of their respective nationalities, solemnly read the names of the potential hijackers. One particular name made Yule jump: Alexei Murzhenko, the name that was emphasized by Comrade Litvak after Yule's visit to the synagogue a year before. Judging from the fact that the escape was foiled, it was obvious that the group had been watched all along, most likely by the KGB. In fact, it was Litvak who had alluded to the "organs." The group members were labeled with all kinds of derisive names, often referred to as *Zionists* and *recidivists*. It turned out that Murzhenko was really the only person with a previous conviction for "anti-Soviet" propaganda. Why these people were trying to connect Yule to a person he did not even remember was unclear. The answer, of course, came in the form of a Lieutenant Malashevski, during an interrogation that the KGB euphemistically called an "interview." An invitation to an "interview" was cordially delivered to Yule's apartment by a uniformed messenger the following day. The apparent invitation ordered Yule to report to the "Big House" on Liteyny Prospect, Building Number 4, Leningrad KGB headquarters the following morning.

And so, at nine a.m. the following day, Yule found himself standing in front of a grand-looking, classical style building. Pillars and high corner towers graced the structure; the beautiful granite face of the first floor's monumental façade was a clear and distinct departure from the constructivism normally used for governmental buildings. Yule was also told that there were several underground levels leading to the "cells of preliminary detention." One of the officers behind the counter in the lobby looked at Yule's summons, picked up the phone and said, "Yule

Fine is here." He replaced the receiver and told Yule to wait for a few moments. A few minutes later, a slim man of medium height, garbed in a KGB uniform, emerged from the staircase. "I am Lieutenant Malashevski," he said, shaking Yule's hand. His grip, Yule noticed, was firm, perhaps a little too firm for a conventional handshake. Rather, it was an open challenge heralding the beginning of a mind game that would plague Yule for the next several years. Yule had reciprocated with a hard squeeze of the lieutenant's hand, trying to remain within the realm of civility. He could not help but notice the wince on Malashevski's face. The lieutenant clearly did not like the fact that someone had a stronger grip.

"Follow me," he said as he started walking up the stairs. His office was at the end of a long and wide hallway lined with armless chairs along the walls. There were several tired-looking men in wrinkled clothing sitting in front of his office, doubtless the victims of many hours of persistent interrogations. None looked familiar to Yule. The lieutenant had a cozy office on the third floor facing the Neva River, a view as grand as the building itself. The first thing, however, that drew Yule's attention was the thick, familiar-looking file that sat open atop the desk, the book that had already chronicled so much of his life. He could not restrain his smile; the site of that file was becoming all too familiar, to the extent that it became almost comical.

"What is so humorous?" asked the lieutenant, clearly puzzled. People who entered his office did not normally smile. Rather, they usually begged with their eyes and their postures, remaining both humble and silent.

"It's just that... I've always wondered whether it's the same file that seems to follow me everywhere or whether everyone just happens to have a copy of it," responded Yule sarcastically. Lieutenant Malashevski gave Yule a long, hard look before answering. He was doubtlessly trying to figure out whether the arrogant young man standing in front of him was completely innocent or just plain stupid.

"*We*," said the lieutenant, "have the original." He pointed to an armless chair, similar to the ones in the hallway. Yule looked up and saw Leonid Brezhnev staring down from an oil painting that hung on the wall above the lieutenant's head. The Secretary General looked at least twenty years younger, when he still had human-sized eyebrows instead of the two rabid squirrels that he was currently sporting. "What is your relationship with Alexei Murzhenko?" he continued without pausing.

"I do not know him," said Yule. The lieutenant's eye assumed a *gotcha* expression. He opened his desk's drawer, pulled out a blown up, black and white photograph, and placed it on the desk, in front of Yule. It was a cropped out section of a panoramic photo of the scene in front of the synagogue. Yule immediately recognized Yaakov and several other classmates from the Gertzen Institute, but there were at least a dozen more people who looked completely unfamiliar to him. "Do you still maintain that you do not know him?" asked Malashevski with a sarcastic tone of voice endemic to provincial actors. "Even when the man is standing practically next to you?"

"So are many others whom I never met before," answered Yule, disregarding the sarcasm. "If you would be so kind as to point out this mysterious man to me."

"Here is what we'll do. Why don't you show me the people you *do* know and tell me their names," said the Lieutenant. He walked over to position himself directly behind Yule's back. There was, Yule knew, no harm in pointing out people that the KGB already knew about. Furthermore, it was the only way to establish some credibility with Malashevski and to end the ridiculous rendezvous. Thus, Yule pointed to his classmates, as well as a few others he knew from the Institute. Malashevski wrote their names down and then pointed at the man standing next to Yaakov. "What about this one?"

"I do not know him," said Yule firmly, guessing that it was Alexei Murzhenko. Malashevski was clearly disappointed, but there was nothing he could do to prove otherwise. He could, of course, hold Yule in preliminary detention for a while, but it appeared that he believed Yule. The only thing he *did* do, as practically all KGB people were wont to normally do, was attempt to recruit Yule to become an informant.

"You are free to go, for now," he said. "But I would like you to let me know as soon as you hear anything connected to this name, or if you receive any information from your friends who visited the synagogue with you regarding anything related to this case."

"Of course I will," said Yule, though both of them knew that it was a lie. Malashevski did not shake his hand.

It was a pleasure to leave the "Big House" behind and to take a walk along the river. It was a beautiful mid-June day, the beginning of the white nights, when the sky would stay a beautiful bright blue all night long. To Yule, it meant that he would be able to read even into the deep hours of the night without the assistance of an artificial source of light. For the rest of Leningrad, it meant that the mood of the people in the city would become greatly improved for at least one month. The white nights offered an ephemeral respite from the normally dark and dreary ambience. The people would enjoy it for that one, short-lived month, only to go back to the usual depression and drinking for the rest of the year. Yule, however, thought that the city of Dostoyevsky and Tchaikovsky would remain beautiful in any ambience, white night or not. As a matter of fact, he enjoyed Leningrad even more on rainy days in October, when the city looked gray and melancholy.

Throughout the next several days, there were numerous reports of mass arrests in Leningrad, Moscow, and the Baltic Republics, arrests usually followed by the notorious "process" that usually resulted in severe punishment, including two death sentences for the leaders and lengthy hard-labor terms for the rest.

That was also the summer that marked Yule's graduation; he had already received his mandatory job placement as a teacher and logoped at a special school for mentally retarded children. The place, a village called Lopukhinka, was about twenty miles east of Leningrad, reachable by the road running along the Gulf of Finland. He was to report there in mid-August. In the interim, there were still two remaining final exams to be taken, namely in psychopathology and the dreadful dialectic materialism. Distracted, Yule found himself reading the same paragraph many times over when studying for the latter.

Psychopathology was, as expected, smooth sailing. The exam afforded Yule an opportunity to show Professor Pankratov his gratitude by quoting Dostoyevsky in describing certain pathologies. Yule knew that the professor would, when grading the examination, appreciate the gesture. After the final had ended, Yule went up to Pankratov in order to say good-bye. They were alone in the auditorium—the other students escaped immediately upon finishing their exams, doubtlessly eager to enjoy the rare, breathable sunny day. Yule and Professor Pankratov merely looked at each other. Despite the forty-year age difference between them, the understanding was almost palpable. Yule looked around, as if to say farewell to the familiar auditorium. He looked at the oil portrait of Sigmund Freud, hanging directly next to Bekhterev on the wall behind the lectern.

"What are you going to do?" asked Pankratov, breaking the long silence. "It would be a shame to give up your research."

"I did not *give up* the research, professor. The system just discarded me like a piece of trash, like a used condom. And for what? Being Jewish?"

"I understand your bitterness, Yule. But at the same time, you would do a lot of disservice to defectology if you gave up your research." Professor Pankratov put his hand on Yule's shoulder and said, "I will recommend you to my colleagues in Moscow."

"Professor, you know as well as I do that the *Numerus Clausus* policy is valid in every corner of the country, *especially* in Moscow. But then again, you probably do not know that I am not allowed to use the research that I have completed," said Yule. "Professor Ivanov told me that my work is the property of the Institute."

Pankratov sighed. "No, I did not know that. Unfortunately, Ivanov is my superior, so I cannot override his decision." The professor moved away from Yule and walked over to the window, as he was wont to do every time he needed to collect his thoughts. Still facing the window, he finally said, "You are an intelligent young man and you will most likely come to the right decision. You not only have your life in front of you, Yule. The entire *world* is there as well. *That* is what I would have done if I were you." He turned around and said, in a sad, yearning voice, "I wish I could start all over again." He picked up his briefcase and walked out of the auditorium.

The message was clear.

Two days before the dreaded dialectic materialism exam, Yule left his apartment to air his head out. He strolled toward the Maltsevski Rynok at the end of Baskov Lane then turned right onto Vosstania Street. It was a beautiful summer day and, despite the heavy diesel fumes emanating forth from the exhausts of the passing buses and the loud screeching of the tramways turning onto Nekrasov Street, a mood of excitement permeated throughout the very air. As he strolled further along the street, his mind was renewed and invigorated with an uncanny sense of optimism. On the cusp of graduation and ready to finally accept his new fate and destiny, he was about to turn to a brand new page in the book of his life.

He was going to walk toward the Vosstania Plaza, where the Nevski Prospect began, but as he was passing a shoe store, something in the open door caught his attention. It was just the faintest of shadows, reflected in the large floor-to-ceiling mirror within the store but still visible through the wide-open entrance door. It was a pretty shadow, a shadow of a graceful, almost statuesque girl with blond hair tied into two pigtails. Yule was mesmerized. He could not explain what he saw, nor why he remained transfixed in that one spot by the open door. Suddenly, the shadow appeared in the mirror again, disappearing from view just as quickly as it had appeared as the woman quickly moved to the next counter and out of site. Uncannily and inexplicably intrigued, Yule walked into the store and looked around. There she was, dressed in a short skirt and a long, green jacket. She had beautiful, big chestnut eyes and full, red lips. For an instant, their eyes met. Yule's heart began to beat with a rapidity that he had never felt before, not even before his jumps out of an airplane or during his numerous fights. For a second, he was fearful that the drumming of his frenetic heart would become audible in the silence of the store. The woman quickly looked the other way and walked out of the shop, seemingly flustered by the eye contact.

The bus stop was right in front of the door and, in only a few seconds, a large city bus spewing black smoke and hissing with its pneumatic breaks had pulled up to the curb. She stepped gracefully into the bus and took a seat by the window. Yule began to panic. If he did not hurry, the opportunity would never present itself again. After the briefest of deliberations, he jumped into the bus right before the doors were slammed shut. Although she did not look directly at him, Yule knew that the woman saw that he had entered the bus. He took the seat facing her, but she was already deeply engaged in reading what looked like a textbook. When he attempted to read the title, he noticed that the book was upside-down. She finally righted the book, her cheeks turning crimson as she kept her eyes fixed onto a single page for the next fifteen minutes. The bus made several stops along Nevsky Prospect and made a wide, left turn onto the university embankment of the Neva River. Yule was almost certain that the mysterious, beautiful woman would get off at the university stop, but he was wrong; she got off the bus at the Academy of Fine Arts, and Yule lost site of her amid the magnificent neoclassical building of the academy, with its two Egyptian sphinxes guarding both sides of the grand quay that descended toward the river. As always, the sight of the structure had consumed his attention. He quickly recovered his composure, however, and saw the woman approaching the main entrance of the academy. Before she disappeared into the vast vestibule, Yule made two long strides and said, as if continuing an interrupted conversation, "I thought you were going to the university."

"No," she said with a tangible pride. "I am a student at the Academy of Fine Arts."

Her name, he learned, was Tatiana. She was eighteen years old and, in the April of the following year, they got married. During that first year prior to their marriage, Yule was working in Lopukhinka and Tatiana was a freshman living in the academy's dormitory on Izmaylovski Prospect. Thus, the two were far from each other and, as a consequence, they would meet regularly only on the weekends. Occasionally, Tatiana would take a bus to visit him at the school where he was teaching. In addition to his formal teaching career, Yule administered daily sessions of speech therapy in private, each session lasting for about two hours. The work was both challenging and enjoyable. A few months into the school year, however, the school principal had to leave for some unexplained reason. In his wake, Yule was appointed as the replacement. It was very unexpected, an eventuality that did not fit into his predetermined plans to leave the school after his completion of the one mandatory year following graduation. Against the vigorous protestation from his father, Yule quit the job at the end of his first year there.

Coincidentally, it was during that time when Yule started to seriously consider the prospect of leaving the USSR and immigrating to America. After one of his increasingly rare visits to his father, Yule decided to stop by Genna's apartment. His mother opened the door, a little apprehensive at first, but finally relaxed and told Yule that her son had left the country for Israel.

"Can you imagine," she said indignantly, "they stripped him of citizenship, and he had to pay eight hundred rubles for the 'right' to relinquish it." She dabbed her eyes with a handkerchief. "But we did not care. It was his dream to be free."

She stopped dabbing and her eyes suddenly lit up with pride. She looked at Yule in a motherly sort of manner and asked, "What about you? Are you planning to leave?"

"Eventually, but not for Israel."

She stiffened, obviously confused, and quietly asked, "Why not Israel?"

"It is a complex question, but in a nutshell, I do not think that, at least culturally, we are a good match."

"What is wrong with Israel's culture?" She was getting visibly upset. Yule began to regret his decision to engage in the sensitive topic, but it was already too late to recant what he said, so he had to answer. He had never shared his thoughts on the matter with anyone, never actually formulating them.

"There is nothing wrong with Israel's culture. It's just... just more *Middle-Eastern* than European. In addition, most of us are atheists, whether we care to admit it or not. It's just not a good match, I think."

There was a brief pause as Genna's mother contemplated Yule's perspective on the matter.

"Middle-Eastern," she repeated, looking at Yule and anticipating an explanation.

"I know it sounds odd, but you are forgetting that Russian Jews went to the entirely Muslim Ottoman Palestine even *before* the 1917 revolution."

She merely looked at him, trying to decipher the implications of what he had said. After another few moments of consideration, she asked, "So where would you go if you left the country?"

"America, of course."

Yule was not surprised by Genna's sudden departure. They had already discussed the possibility of leaving the country on multiple occasions, but never in truly concrete terms. Yule did know, however, that Genna studied Hebrew as part of an ever-growing underground movement to leave the country. That alone should have been a clear indication. The families of those who managed to leave the country were subjected to all kinds of punitive measures; losing one's job was the most common means of punishment for the crime of being a relative to a 'traitor.' Despite the repressions and substantial increase in KGB surveillance activities, the young Jews of Leningrad were risking everything to leave the USSR.

Yule's case, however, was rather unique. He feared applying to leave the country because of his military service in Spetsnaz, which could have easily been used by OVIR, a branch of the Ministry of Internal Affairs, as a pretext for denying him an exit visa due to reasons of 'national security.' There was, however, yet *another* serious problem that he had to resolve before even considering the application for a visa. One of the mandatory prerequisites was an invitation from a relative residing in the country of arrival. Those were the two most serious obstacles. In addition, there were also dozens of other forms, letters, and permissions to be obtained. Most of them made absolutely no sense and only served to make leaving the USSR as difficult as possible.

Despite Yule's constant trepidations, things were not all that bad. Little Vova, who was no longer that little, had just been honorably discharged from the military, where he had spent three years playing the drums in a band. After his discharge, he moved to Leningrad to live with Yule and to continue his musical education. It was a happy reunion.

KRESTY

I SHOULD PREFER EMIGRATING TO SOME COUNTRY WHERE THEY MAKE NO PRETENSE OF LOVING LIBERTY—TO RUSSIA

ABRAHAM LINCOLN

In the summer of 1974, during a ski trip to the mountains of Tsakhkadsor in Georgia, Yule met Norbert Kuchinke, a freelance West-German journalist, working for the *Der Spiegel* and *Stern* magazines. While gliding and slaloming down the slope, Yule had noticed a tall and slender man with long curls of red hair peaking out from his hat. The man, he noticed, was wearing distinctly bright Western ski attire and equipment. They were both going too fast, a run that ultimately terminated in a violent collision. Luckily, neither sustained any injuries. After the mutual apologies, they introduced themselves, fate bringing them together on the slopes of a Georgian mountain. Norbert was recently assigned to be stationed in Moscow; he spoke some Russian, though he was not yet fluent in the language. He did, however, speak Polish with ease, so they had quickly discovered a common language and a common interest in Russian history and religion. Naturally, the two struck up a friendship. After spending several days together and having a great deal of opinions exchanged on a variety of topics, they found that they indeed did have a lot in common. Thus, by the time Yule had to leave, they promised each other to stay in touch. While they were saying good-bye, Norbert pulled Yule to the side, beyond earshot of the departing skiers. In a hushed tone he said, "You should know that, as a Western journalist, I am being constantly watched by the KGB. The surveillance continues even when I am in the bathroom. What that means is that *you* will be under watch as well, especially now that they've seen us conversing. Actually, I won't be surprised if they start following you after we part."

"I do not care," said Yule, the determination and resilience clear in his voice. "I am *sick* of hiding and being afraid all the time. No, I *will* visit you in Moscow."

True to his word, they met several more times. Yule visited him in Moscow, staying in Norbert's apartment on Kutuzovski Prospect. Norbert picked him up at the Leningradski Rail Station and, as soon as Yule got into the car, he put his index finger to his lips, then pointed to his ears and to the ceiling. The gesture, Yule knew, was a means of indicating that the car was bugged. The same message was inaudibly conveyed to Yule when they had entered the apartment. The only time that they were truly able to talk freely was on the streets. They liked to take long walks, discussing various topics that both of them were interested in, namely religion and Jewish immigration. Despite the uncanny congruency of their opinions, they also had some minor disagreements. Norbert was in support of the fact that the Israeli government was trying to influence Soviet Jews to go to Israel only. He believed that by doing so, Israel was putting an unofficial pressure on the countries that were accepting Soviet Jews to limit the number of immigrants. Yule, on the other hand, felt that the choice should have been unrestricted and that it was not tenable for the Israelis to pressure other foreign governments. Norbert also reciprocated Yule's visit to Moscow by visiting him in Leningrad. There, he asked Yule to introduce him to his various friends. He was, he admitted, writing an article for his magazine about the Soviet dissidents and refuzniks.

One rainy September morning, Yule had left his apartment to go to a driving school, where he was taking a professional driver's course to be able to drive commercial trucks. He crossed Ivanovskaya Street and, as soon as he approached his bus stop, he noticed four men, dressed in black suits, emerging from a courtyard through a tall arch. There was something unnatural in their behavior—they walked very close to each other, their shoulders pressed together as if they were supporting one another. Their faces were tense, a nervousness also manifested in their almost goose-step walk The scene was downright ridiculous, but one of the four men looked oddly familiar; it had been three years since Yule last saw the man, and although he saw him only once and in a KGB uniform, he immediately recognized Lieutenant Malashevski. The lieutenant was clearly in charge of the operation. At that precise moment of realization, Yule had no doubt as to the intentions of those men, each dressed in black and parked in front of his apartment at eight o'clock in the morning.

As the group got closer, he heard Malashevski instruct his men. "Do *not* go in front of him. Approach from both sides." Yule did not offer any resistance and quietly went with the men into the courtyard from which they had emerged a minute before. There, they boarded a black car. It was a Raven, the same type of KGB vehicle used to transport Yule's first teacher to Lubyanka. Having done nothing wrong, Yule's only emotion was curiosity. *What kind of mutiny will I be accused of now*? he thought. After all, the times of the purges were long gone, as Ezhov was long dead and buried. Malashevski sat down in the passenger's seat, immediately next to the driver; the two other men had positioned themselves inside the van on both sides of Yule, looking at him with apprehension and some degree of fear. Malashevski, who had studied Yule's dossier three years ago, must have informed them about his Spetsnaz background.

There were no windows in the Raven but, after what seemed like only a few minutes, they had arrived at their destination. Yule stepped out and the first thing he saw was the familiar granite façade of the 'Big House' on Liteyny Prospect. The office of Lieutenant Malashevski, where Yule was escorted to, looked exactly the same as it had three years ago, with only one exception: there was an armed guard in the hallway by the office door. Malashevski displayed his usual cold and calculated courtesy, but he skipped the handshaking ceremony and immediately went down to business. He reached down into his desk's drawer and produced a thick, large envelope. He dumped its contents, mostly large photographs, onto his desk, spreading them out evenly and sorting them out in a certain order. He pointed at the first one and asked, "Who is this man with you?" It was a photograph of Yule standing next to Norbert, both in ski suits.

"His name is Norbert Kuchinke."

"Who is he?"

"He is a journalist. I met him in Zakhkadzor while skiing."

"What country is he from?"

"West Germany."

"Do you know what it is that he does here, in the Soviet Union?"

"He is a journalist. He does what journalists do."

"And what is that?"

"He writes articles for his magazine about the Soviet Union."

"And what is your role in all of this?"

"In addition to being his friend? I interpret for him."

"You had eighty Deutsche marks in you pocket. Where did you get them?"

"I borrowed the marks from Norbert." That was not entirely true. Norbert had exchanged some rubles for Yule, who wanted to buy a present for Tatiana in a store for foreigners, where the selection was much greater than in the regular Soviet stores.

The subsequent two hours were among the longest and most tiresome in Yule's life. The same questions were asked over and over again, arranged in different orders and each repeated at least five times. Yule, however, maintained his composure and remained calm. He continued to answer the increasingly familiar and repetitive questions, giving virtually identical answers time and time again. Malashevski, to Yule's delight, was getting visibly tired and frustrated. His plan to lure Yule into giving conflicting answers did not work. At around one p.m., he pressed a hidden button on his desk, and the armed guard immediately opened the door.

"Take him to the second level," he said angrily. "And give him *payku*, his food ration."

The second level was two full stories below the lobby. There, a very dimly lit corridor seemed to stretch on forever, curving to the left and disappearing into the abyss. There were massive doors that flanked both sides of the corridor. The guard opened one of the doors and showed Yule inside. An instant later, the door was slammed shut behind him. The containment cell was no more than ten square feet in size; it had no bed and was bare. Yule was optimistic; the vacuity of the room meant that his stay would be short.

The *payka* materialized through a small square opening in the door. It consisted of a mug of milk and a piece of black bread. Yule did not, however, feel like eating. An hour went by in that isolation. Afterwards, the same guard that had brought him to the room took him back upstairs into Malashevski's office. The same questions were asked again and again, the same answers given, word for word. During a brief moment of silence, Yule managed to ask Malashevski to notify Tatiana of his detainment.

"She knows," he said. "Our men are searching your flat as we speak, and your wife is there."

"What are you looking for?"

"I ask the questions, not you." The lieutenant was enjoying the display of power. "But, since you did ask, and since I'm in a benevolent mood, I will tell you. They are looking for the evidence of your connections with the West, especially with the Zionist movement. If we find what we are looking for, you will be put away for a *very* long time."

"I can tell you right now that you and your men are wasting time. My only connection with the West is my friendship with Norbert."

"Well, there's more too it than meets the eye. Under Article Eighty-Eight of the Russian Federation Penal Code, possession of foreign currency is punishable with up to five years of forced labor. Although the amount we found is teetering on the permissible minimum, it will be at the discretion of the court to decide."

The brief silence was interrupted by the ringing of the phone on the desk. It rang just once before Malashevski snatched the receiver from the cradle; it looked as if he was waiting for that call.

"Dah," he said and got quiet for at least a minute, listening very attentively. "Come back," he said. He slowly replaced the receiver, a look of disappointment painted across his face. Yule guessed that his people had not found anything incriminating within his apartment. He guessed correctly, for Malashevski, after a brief moment of hesitation, looked at Yule and said, "I will let you go home now, but you are to report to this office every morning at nine o'clock until further notice."

Yule gingerly entered his apartment, fearing what it would look like after being ravaged by the agents. Tatiana was sitting in the apartment amid the chaos left behind by Malashevski's people, crying. Even the grandfather clock did not escape the barbaric treatment; its face was ripped out and left to lie on the floor.

For the next three weeks, Yule reported to Lieutenant Malashevski's office religiously, though in many instances it was someone else questioning him. There was a young and relatively attractive junior lieutenant by the name of Maria Cherbak. She had peroxide-bleached blonde hair and wore her skirt above the knees, revealing her long legs. Her interrogation style was flirtatious and, occasionally, downright seductive. Maria moved around the office while questioning Yule, periodically leaning over the desk to point at a photograph, her back arched and her breasts clearly visible. On some other occasions, she would walk over to behind his chair, her high heels clicking against the floor. She would then lean forward in such a way that her breast squeezed against Yule's shoulder. While in that position she would breathe lightly onto his neck, seductively asking him questions such as, "Who is your contact at the Dutch Embassy?" She was clearly alluding to the Dutch Embassy in Moscow, which represented Israel in the absence of a diplomatic relationship between Israel and the USSR.

"I have never met anyone from the Dutch Embassy," Yule responded.

Maria Cherbak's strategy of seduction did not work. Finally, after her repeated attempts at coaxing Yule into an admission, she became very irate and loud, her normally sumptuous voice replaced by a screeching anger. The guard from corridor, alarmed by the increased volume, stuck his head into the office. "Is everything okay, Comrade Junior Lieutenant?"

"Yes," she answered, clearly irritated. The junior lieutenant, it seemed, was not used to being ignored by a man.

The second week of questioning had brought with it a somewhat pleasant surprise in the person of Lieutenant Mikhail Makoveev. He was young and prematurely balding, his eyes fixed in an expression of permanent helplessness. He kept Yule for more than four hours, reading from his dossier and asking about Spetsnaz and hand-to-hand combat techniques. It was, at least, a topic that Yule liked to discuss. Makoveev did most of the talking the following day. The interview, however, was less an interrogation and more a conversation. He was not married and lived with his mother on Suvorovski Prospect, near the Smolny Institute. He always wanted to be in Spetsnaz but was rejected due to his poor eyesight. "Can you teach me combat Sambo?" he asked Yule by the end of the day.

During his evenings and on most weekends, Yule attended a newly opened community gym on Rubinshtein Street named "Monolith," which also had a small dojo located within it. He worked out with weights and practiced the Shotokan karate style with several friends who were all at the black belt level. One day, Yule walked into the gym and bumped into Lieutenant Malashevski, dressed in a sweat suit.

"Yule!" said the lieutenant, as if they had been old friends. "So good to see you!"

"I'm sure it's mutual," said Yule, offering the lieutenant his hand and squeezing it as hard as he could. Lieutenant Malashevski's knees buckled slightly, but he did not make a sound because most of the people at the gym were looking directly at them. "I do not think," Yule continued in a whisper, "that *this* is an appropriate place for you to work out in," all the while looking straight into Malashevski's eyes. "And I promise that if you find another gym, I will pretend that I do not know who you are." Yule had no doubt that the lieutenant was doing undercover work, because the club was known to have refuzniks and people who were getting ready to apply. If Yule revealed the lieutenant's identity, some of the less forgiving members of the gym would probably take exception to his presence.

Although there was no additional incriminating evidence obtained from questioning Yule for the few subsequent weeks, the overzealous prosecutor still decided to bring charges. Yule was charged with the possession of foreign currency and, although the amount was below the punishable level specified in Article Eighty-Eight, they found some ambiguous line in the law and interpreted it to fit Yule's case. There were no witnesses or testimonies, no jury, only two deputies, one on each side of the judge, nodding agreeably with every word that came out of the judge's mendacious mouth. According to the judge, Yule's court-appointed defense attorney, Mr. Zorkin, represented the court, not the defendant. Within ten minutes, Yule was sentenced to three years of forced labor in a medium-security labor camp.

As Yule was being led by the guards from the court house, his attorney, Zorkin, walked up to him, looking very embarrassed, and whispered, "This verdict is illegal. I will appeal it right now, and it will be overturned. I promise you."

Yule was immediately placed into a Raven and driven away. The ride, however, was short, and when he stepped out of the black van, he found himself in the courtyard of *Kresty*, Crosses, a pre-trial detention center. Years ago, when Yule was engaging in his study of religious architecture, the Alexander Nevsky Cathedral was one of the churches he could not visit because it was located on the grounds of Kresty. During that time, he had learned that the prison was designed by Antony Tomishko, an Austrian national who was influenced by the Philadelphia prison system, only instead of building Kresty in the shape of a star with a central observation point at the center, he had built it as a cross. The general idea, however, was the same—to be able to control all wings from a single observation point. There were two identical structures, and the prisoners very quickly found an appropriate name for them: Crosses.

Yule surrendered all of his clothing and all of his belongings. Afterwards, he was ordered to take a cold shower, only to be garbed in a black prison suit with #784357921 embroidered in white on the outside of the left chest-pocket. Finally, he was escorted to a cell on the second level. The heavy metal door slammed shut behind him, a sound he had heard many times before.

The cell itself was dimly lit; it took Yule's eyes a few additional seconds to adjust to the ambience. The air was heavy, permeated by the stench of sweat and urine. He was standing with his back to the door, facing what appeared to be a large crowd stuffed into the confines of a small room. There were, he observed, no beds or chairs, but unlike the containment cell at the Big House, there was a small metal toilet located in the far corner. It was clearly a temporary holding cell. People were called out one by one, new prisoners flooding in to replace them at almost the same rate. Yule's name was called out in about half an hour, at which point he was escorted to a different wing, also on the second level. There, he was given a blanket, a towel, and a pillow. Yet again, the heavy door slammed shut behind him.

He looked around, taking in the surroundings. The new cell looked more permanent, as it housed two bunk beds, or *shkonka*, as they were referred to in the prison jargon, one on each side of the room. A small, barred window was located across from the door, and a metal toilet sat in the corner, the stench of its contents clearly wafting through the cell. There also was a small metal sink with a single, dripping faucet. In the immediate silence, each drop could be distinctly heard as it impacted the sink, the sound deafening in the muteness of the cell.

There were three zeks in the cell. Two of them were lying down on the bunk to his immediate left, one on the top bunk and the other on the bottom. The third was sitting on the toilet, reading a magazine. The man on the toilet had his pants down to around his ankles, and Yule could distinctly see a large tattoo on his thigh depicting a church with three onion domes. It looked like one of the domes was added recently, as it was darker and the skin around it was still red and thereby announcing the man's third *hodka,* his third time in prison. Thus, Yule christened him the Three-timer. The man on the toilet did not even look at the new arrival. There were no chairs within the cell, so Yule placed his bundle of linens on the bottom bed, where he sat down to try to figure out where to settle down. Suddenly, the man got off the toilet, pulled up his pants, and approached Yule. He was tall, lanky, and had a look in his eyes more dangerous than any other, the look of a man who had nothing left to lose.

"Your *shkonka* is up there," he said in an unexpectedly high voice. He patted the mattress of the upper bed.

Yule was not going to argue; he knew the unspoken law of the prisons, which was no different from the Gulag or the military. The man was right, so Yule got up without a word, placing his linens on the upper bed. "You are right," he finally said, making a step toward the toilet.

"Not so fast," said the Three-timer. "You have to apologize first."

"For what?" asked Yule, but he already knew that it was a rhetorical question. The man clearly wanted to assert his dominance over the newcomer, in order to maintain his place in the hierarchy of the inmates. Yule also knew, much too well perhaps, that the initial encounter would define his life within the penal system, in any prison located anywhere in the country. The magnitude of the situation weighed heavily upon him. He closed his eyes for a second, taking in a deep, calming breath. The days of interrogation and the actual trial left him exhausted and depressed, and the last thing he needed was a fight. But he had no choice; fighting was the only option.

"Listen, I respect you, with your three *hodki*, and I do not want to hurt you. So let us shake hands and end this."

Yule lifted his hands, palms facing the man, and made one last attempt to avoid a fight, offering the Three-timer a peaceful truce. The Three-timer, however, took the gesture as a sign of weakness and made his move. He reached behind his back and produced a *peaka*, a sharpened, half-foot long metal wire. The gesture made Yule feel slightly less guilty about what he was about to do. A simple deterrence, such as kick in the shin, would not do, as the man clearly had the intention of hurting Yule with the *peaka*. The

Three-timer moved his hand, aiming the *peaka* squarely at Yule's face. At that precise moment, his reflexes, sharpened by years of training, subconsciously kicked in. Yule's hands shot down, knocking the hand with the weapon toward the floor. He drove his right knee hard into the man's groin, then darted the fingers of his left hand into his Adam's apple. To the observer, the entire sequence would appear to be one continuous, short motion. The Three-timer went down, grasping his throat with both hands. The *peaka* rolled into the corner, behind the toilet. One of the two men, the older, shorter, and balder one, immediately jumped off of his bunk and walked over to the *peaka*, picking it up.

"Would you like to drop that, or do you need my help?" asked Yule, making a step toward him.

"No, no, no," said the bald man emphatically. "I am just picking it up for you. Here."

He handed the *peaka* to Yule. Meanwhile, the third man was pounding on the door, trying to attract the attention of the guards. Finally, the door burst open and two guards poured in. In a span of only a few minutes, the Three-timer was carried out on a stretcher while the remainder of his cellmates were taken into separate rooms for questioning. Yule, of course, was led to the underground level, locked up in a tiny cell with a cement floor. There were no windows and no toilet within the new cell. Due to the lack of windows and the absence of artificial light, the room was also pitch dark. As a consequence, he had not the slightest idea of how much time had passed. Thus, Yule used the rare opportunity to rest, somehow knowing that he would need all of his strength if he was to survive. Completely exhausted, he fell asleep in the corner, his back against the wall.

The cell door flew open, the light from the corridor blinding him for a few seconds. Within ten minutes, Yule found himself sitting inside the office of the Senior Political Officer, Captain Shcherba, who was, of course, reviewing the seemingly omnipresent dossier. The captain was young and good looking, with long, combed-back dark hair and big brown eyes. It took him just a few minutes to grasp the essence of Yule's background.

"Spetsnaz Sergeant, outstanding student, teacher, and school principal." He looked at Yule, a sense of incredulity painted across his face. "How the hell did you end up here?"

"I made a mistake."

The Captain seemingly liked the answer, although Yule was certain that he did not grasp the true meaning of the explanation. There was no mention of the fight that had just taken place. Instead, Yule divined that the true purpose of the meeting was an offer to take over command of the service brigade, a bunch of *zeks* that were assigned to maintain the prison and distribute food for at least four thousand inmates on a daily basis. Yule needed a few moments to digest the offer. It was, he thought, quite a turn of events, a journey that began at the court house, continued onward to solitary confinement, and finally ended in an offer for becoming the second most powerful man in Kresty. The position would effectively give him charge over about three hundred zeks that roamed free throughout the entire prison complex. Thus, the brigadier, or *bugor* in the prison lingo, had an enormous amount of power within the system.

"It looks like someone is protecting you from Liteyny," said Captain Shcherba. " I am also aware of the fact that your case has a lot of irregularities and is currently under judicial review. However, it will take at least six months to get the results and, until then, you might as well help me organize the men." He hesitated for a moment then said, "The previous *bugor* was… he was corrupt and is now awaiting trial. Unfortunately for him, he got into a fight with someone who was more skilled and now is in the prison hospital with a crushed windpipe." He looked at Yule, as if expecting some kind of a reaction, but Yule remained absolutely silent. "You wouldn't know anything about that, would you?" the captain continued.

"No, of course not."

"That's what I thought," said Captain Shcherba, smiling. "In any case, this position opens up a lot of possibilities, anywhere from an early release to getting additional hard-labor time. It all depends on you choices."

"It is a dubious honor, but I accept it," said Yule, who had quickly calculated the great advantage being offered to him.

"It's all settled, then," said the captain cheerfully. He pressed an intercom button and said, "Get the room and the uniform ready for Yule Fine."

The early stages of Yule's assignment as *bugor* were rough, to say the least. Despite the private room and free access to anywhere on the grounds, his life was greatly complicated by the former *bugor's* loyalists and stooges who were, prior to his unfortunate departure from the prison, helping him run his illegal drug distribution operation. Furthermore, they resented the fact that Yule was not a *vor-v-zakone*, a thief-in-law, like the previous *bugor*, who was apparently a high-class yegg. The thorn in Yule's side was a small but very nasty cluster of criminals who had, on several occasions, unsuccessfully attempted to set Yule up. Finally, when each feeble attempt proved futile, they went for a more direct approach by attempting to ambush him one early morning, the time when Yule habitually drove his truck to pick up the containers of food. Although there was an official driver, he liked to do the job himself because, in the past, some of the food containers would occasionally end up outside of the prison gates. The planned ambush also failed. Yule later found out that two security guards were involved in the ambush, the same two who were also involved in the drug and food smuggling activities. Both, of course, were arrested. Despite those difficulties, however, the majority of the *zeks* in the service brigade were happy to be led by someone who treated them in a fair, impartial manner. He learned that *Grob*, or Coffin, which was the nickname of Yule's predecessor, regularly took to beating up the *zeks*. Thus, things had settled down to something bordering on normalcy and, by the February of 1975, Yule was informed by his attorney that the case had been reviewed and the result would be known in just a few days.

As expected, Yule was released from Kresty just as quickly as he had been sentenced. There were no apologies or explanations; Captain Shcherba merely summoned Yule into his office and broke the news.

"Congratulations," he said, looking at a legal-sized sheet of paper. He stuck the document into a thick binder and said, "You are free to go home."

"Does it say why I was kept here?"

"No, it does not. All it says is *nemedlenno osvobodit*, to release immediately." He obviously knew the true story, but despite being a decent man at heart, he was still an intricate part of the MVD machine, and there were boundaries he would not cross.

"You have to speak with your attorney," he added. They shook hands. It was a firm yet friendly handshake, a manly affirmation of mutual respect. Downstairs, by the KPP, the security checkpoint, Yule exchanged his uniform for his civilian clothing, along with the rest of the items that were confiscated from him upon arrival. At long last, he put his foot through the threshold that separated Kresty from the world. A strange sensation permeated throughout his being, a mixture of euphoria and relief overwhelming his senses. Although it was a long distance to Yule's apartment on Ivanovskaya Street, situated on the other side of the city, he elected to walk the full distance, breathing in the moist and cold air so deeply that his head began to pleasantly spin. He was getting high off his freedom.

There were, Yule learned, some developments that had occurred while he was kept incommunicado at Kresty. Tatiana, who had graduated from the academy, started her job at the Museum of Urban Sculpture. His brother, the *no-longer-little* Vova, had gotten married to a lovely girl named Svetlana and had started a very successful rock-band named *Zemlyanye,* The

Earthlings. But the greatest, most significant surprise had arrived via the mail a few weeks after his release: a letter of invitation from unknown-to-him people living in Israel who claimed to be his relatives and guaranteed him financial support in the event of him leaving the USSR. Apparently, the numerous requests that Yule had made through Norbert, Yaakov, and many other friends had finally materialized, but the invitation was only the beginning of the long and arduous path to receiving the exit visa. Many other documents and letters had to be gathered and sent before he could even dare hope for an exit via. For example, he needed a letter from his parents and letters from multiple community organizations. One of the prerequisites was also a letter of recommendation from his previous employer. He would, of course, need letters from the utility companies stating that he was completely debt free. Just thinking about all of the requirements was agonizing. Furthermore, there was always the looming and distinct possibility of refusal, even after successfully gathering all of the required information. His service in Spetsnaz would, he knew, pose a problem. Nevertheless, Yule refused to abandon his optimism. It took another eight months for the decision to reach Yule after the application had finally been submitted. The wait was even more painful than the actual process.

The response arrived in the mail. Much to Yule's amazement and beyond all expectations, he had received an exit visa. At first, he couldn't believe it. He merely stared at the acceptance letter, dumfounded and speechless. He thought that the longer he stared, the more likely it would become that the letter was a hoax or a figment of his imagination. Alas, it contained nothing but the truth. Whether it was the KGB's way of acknowledging his unlawful imprisonment, or if the KGB simply did not want someone who could potentially embarrass them through his Western connections to stay in the country, it was impossible to say. The latter, he thought, was probably the answer.

Yule took one last look at his little apartment, standing in the door with his pullman suitcase and oversized duffle bag sprawled out on the floor. He could not accurately describe his feelings at that precise moment. He felt as if he was living vicariously through someone else, as if every step, every thought, and every breath was the work of some higher being, manipulating and controlling him like a puppet-master would his puppet. It was perhaps the strangest sensation that he had ever felt. Part of him was in-tune with the reality around him, the other stuck in a surreal, intangible state of being. His heart was racing, although he could not say why. And so, he looked at his apartment one last time, the apartment that served as his life in the USSR incarnate. He shut the door and went down the stairs, to his wife and the awaiting taxi.

His last day in the Soviet Union, that fateful 16 May, 1979, would not pass without incident. The USSR would not, of course, relinquish its stranglehold on Yule without at least one more fight. And so, feathers were flying all over the customs area at the Leningrad-Pulkovo Airport. The overzealous customs officer had assumed that the pillows Yule and Tatiana were bringing along with them as part of their luggage had valuable fur sewn inside. He cut the pillows open and flung out their contents. The area had been transformed into a shaken Christmas snow globe as goose-down feathers spewed out of the pillows. The customs officer was young and nasty, obviously hardened by his many fights with departing Jews who were no longer considered citizens of the Soviet Union. Naturally, the thought was that the Jews were trying to purposefully weaken the national security of the USSR by smuggling out of the country their valuables and heirlooms. Yule's family photographs were apparently very valuable to the government, because after carefully reviewing his baby pictures and wedding album, the officer added them to the pile of discarded items. Perhaps the most painful, however, was the confiscation of Yule's watch. The watch, a sliver Omega

Seamaster with a stunning blue face, was a gift from Vova, one that held much sentimental value to Yule.

After the farce in the customs area had passed, the time to say good-bye had finally arrived. There was a group of about a dozen friends and relatives who came to give their blessings and to say farewell. Vova, however, was not among them.

And so, at long last, Yule boarded the Aeroflot TU-104 headed to Vienna. He sat down at the designated seat, Tatiana sitting directly next to him. He gave her a lingering look, the faintest of smiles on his face. He then closed his eyes, blocking out the world around him until the only thing that he was aware of was the white muteness of his mind. Somewhere off in the distance, he felt the plane jerk as it took to the tarmac. The sounds and sensations of the world around him were becoming more and more distant with every passing second. He heard the roar of the engines as they came alive, preparing for takeoff. As the plane lifted off the ground, the last page of the saga of life behind the iron curtain had been turned, the book finally closed. The sequel of his life was yet to be written, but the bridges to the past had been burned down forever. What lay ahead, he did not know, but he found comfort in the fact that his life was about to begin anew.

EPILOGUE

He opened his eyes as the plane dipped mildly, a sign that the aircraft was about to make its final descent. Looking out of the window, he could see the landscape below getting larger as the plane swooped downwards in a gentle, effortless motion.

It was the 7th of September, 2007. The Lufthansa flight from New York via Frankfurt, Germany, had just touched down at the Moscow Sheremetyevo II International Airport. Twenty-one of the twenty-two members of the US Developmental Disability delegation went through passport control without any significant problems or complications. One member of the delegation, a middle-aged man dressed in a grey pinstriped suite, blue shirt, and parsley tie, was held up for questioning by a burley uniformed woman with hay-colored hair slicked back so tightly that the corners of her eyes appeared to be pointing upwards, thereby making her look somewhat Asian in appearance. She stared at the man's passport for a long while. Finally, she pulled her eyes off of the passport and stared intently at his face. Then, after another brief pause, she addressed him in Russian.

"It says here that you were born in Russia."

"I was," answered the man calmly, without giving off any signs of being intimidated or nervous.

"And what used to be your name then, when you were still living in Russia?"

He wasn't particularly surprised by the question and, maintaining his unperturbed demeanor, responded, "The same as it is now. Yule Fine." Yule focused his blue eyes straight onto hers and added, "They call me Doctor Fine back in America."

"*Doctor*, huh," said the woman, a not-so-subtle trace of sarcasm penetrating her voice. "In what discipline?"

"Let's just say that I work with people who have serious attitude problems and are wont to abuse their power over others. Among other things, of course."

The woman's face turned red with anger. She opened her mouth, as if in rebuttal, but did not have a chance to say anything in response. A uniformed man approached the two hastily. His lapels contained regalia that was indiscernible to Yule, most likely signifying some degree of importance in the hierarchy of airport security. He approached the burly woman and showed her a sheet of paper, pointing at a particular line in the lengthy document. They both looked at Yule somewhat nervously, and the man whispered something into her ear.

Yule was able to discern only one word, but that one word was enough to explain their reaction – *Kremlin*. In a heartbeat, the woman's facial expression turned from one of contorted anger to a strange mixture consisting of equal parts curiosity and fear. She quickly handed Yule's passport back to him and, without saying a word, turned to the next person in line.

"What was *that* about?" asked the delegation leader when Yule joined the rest of the group, clearly somewhat confounded by the brief spectacle.

"They might not call themselves the USSR anymore, but the spirit of Communism clearly lives on," said Yule easily, laughter creeping into his voice. "I'll explain later," he added, realizing that his response only served to puzzle his colleagues even further. Of course, he never got the chance to explain to them what had happened back at the airport; a plethora of new impressions and sights made them forget the incident entirely. Yule, however, was absolutely positive that the paper shown to the uniformed woman was a copy of his visa application, where he listed his brother Vladimir as a relative in Russia. Vladimir Vladimirovich Kiselev, one of the Russian President's close friends, had an office in the Kremlin and was in charge of the cultural affairs of the Russian Federation. He was, to put it bluntly, not one to mess with. His black Mercedes-Benz 500 had a green government permit which read VSUDU, *Everywhere*, displayed prominently on the windshield. He could have driven against traffic *backwards* if he wanted to, and the traffic cops would merely salute him as he passed by. Russia, after all, always loved and respected her "strongmen."

After navigating through customs, the group boarded a chartered bus to take them to the Marriott Tverskaya Hotel. It was an early and somewhat brisk September afternoon, but the traffic rivaled even rush hour in Midtown Manhattan. The number of foreign cars, predominantly Mercedes, Jeeps and various American-made SUVs, was overwhelming. Admittedly, Yule never liked Moscow with its hustling spirit and petit-bourgeois mentality; he always preferred the calmness and serenity of St. Petersburg.

Yule's international cell phone started playing *Volga Boatmen*, a ringtone designated for his younger brother. The song was performed by the Red Army Chorus, and its overwhelming power drew the attention of the other passengers. The phone's sudden outburst quickly brought him out of his reverie.

"Sorry," said Yule apologetically. "It's my brother calling."

"I've heard you encountered some unpleasantness at Sheremetyevo," said Vova.

Yule fell silent for a few seconds, trying to figure out how his brother already knew about the incident back at the airport. As if reading his mind, his brother interrupted the silence and said, "The Chief of Security called me to apologize for the misunderstanding. Pre-emptive strike, you know. Just in case you told me." They both laughed. Vova was clearly pleased with Yule's somewhat confounded reaction.

"I will pick you up at seven, at the hotel," said Vova. He hung up almost immediately, without so much as asking for the name of the hotel. There was, however, no surprise in that; it was obvious that he had no need to ask as he already knew all about Yule's accommodations, most likely from a KGB-style dossier on each member of the American delegation that had been delivered to the "proper" office and had been read by the "proper" person. Yule wondered whether or not his old file, that once ubiquitous folder that contained virtually his entire life, was still being circulated and read by the Federal Security department. It was an amusing thought, one that brought back a plethora of pleasant (and not-so-pleasant) memories of another life.

At seven o'clock sharp, there was a brief commotion outside of the hotel's main entrance facing Tverskaya Street as a black Mercedes, escorted by two rather substantial SUVs, stopped in the middle of the street, blocking off traffic. An impeccably dressed, well-tanned man sporting longish brown hair with a slightly receding hairline and grey temples had stepped out of the Mercedes and briskly walked towards the hotel entrance. *I can't believe it,* thought Yule. *My baby brother is going grey.*

Yule and Vova met in the middle of the street, and their hug was prolonged and tight. It had been almost five long years since they last met in person, and Yule had to hold back the tears that started to well up in his eyes. The members of the delegation rushed to the lobby's floor-to-ceiling windows, watching the unfolding events with evident curiosity. The two brothers got into the Mercedes and shut the door with an audible *thump.* Almost immediately, sirens started to blare and the cavalcade sped off, resuming the flow of traffic in front of the hotel. Yule spent the entire evening and almost the entire night talking to his brother, the two of them reminiscing about days long gone and times almost forgotten.

Yule was dropped back off at the hotel the following morning, only this time he was delivered by one black SUV that attracted far less curiosity. The entire delegation was already outside, boarding a bus destined for the Special Education Research Institute, a part of the Russian Academy of Education. It was, all in all, a very pleasant and professionally gratifying visit. Yule was happy to learn that autistic children in Russia were no longer considered "uneducable" as they had been when he left the USSR in 1979. His presentation about the state of autism in America was well received. The most memorable moment for Yule, however, was literally bumping into someone he had gone to college with back in St. Petersburg.

Maria Rusenkova was two years Yule's junior at the Hertzen Pedagogical Institute. She was a very serious, studious, and promising student who very quickly advanced through the academia rankings. Eventually, she earned her Doctorate and was invited to join the Academy of Special Education in Moscow. The two were very happy to see each other and to do some reminiscing. A café next door to the Institute was almost empty and afforded them some rare privacy.

"So, how is life in Russia?" asked Yule. "I hardly understand how this society works anymore."

She merely looked at him with a long, inquisitive look, as if trying to discern whether or not he was serious. After a momentary but awkward pause she said, "If you think any of us Russians can completely understand, you are dead wrong."

Sensing some discomfiture, Yule decided to drop the subject so as to not mar the unexpected reunion with petty politics. Instead, he asked, "Are you still with Naum, the guy you were dating back then?"

"No," she said, though not too angrily given the circumstances of their breakup. "Naum dumped me and married into a rich Jewish family from Sevastopol, but I met a wonderful man here, in Moscow. We have been married for twenty years and have three beautiful children."

Yule gave her a knowing look and said, "I could have told you that Naum was a scumbag, but you never asked, and I doubt that you would have listened anyway."

Maria shrugged it off and said, "I was twenty-one and in love."

Yule smiled and said, "Well, not that it matters much anymore. It looks like you have accomplished all your lifelong dreams – a doctor, a scientist, a mother of three and a great man in your life... who can complain?"

"Yep, that pretty much sums it up," said Maria jovially. "And I see that you are still as compendious as ever. You know, I've always admired that ability of yours."

There was an awkward pause. Yule broke the silence and asked, "Would you like to know what happened to me after I left the USSR?"

"No, don't bother, I know most of it already." She looked at Yule's puzzled expression and explained, "After we received the roster of the American delegation, I recognized your name and did a little research. I also read your dissertation and all about your work with the disabled."

"I am flattered," said Yule with genuine and sincere honesty. Then, in a not-too-harsh, almost playful tone, he said, "But I also remember that when I was leaving the country, you, as a member of the Institute's Student Association, were quick to condemn me as a traitor. Are you still of that persuasion?"

"Times have changed, and we all have changed with them," she said philosophically.

"Perhaps. But you must forgive me for not changing my feelings about Russia. I don't think I will ever forget how I was put in jail for no apparent reason and stripped of my citizenship when I was leaving."

"I understand," she said, looking straight into his eyes, "but this is still your *motherland.* We cannot choose where we are born, and that is as much a part of us as anything. Just as we cannot choose our parents."

"I agree to a certain extent," answered Yule, "but have you ever heard of adoption after parents have abused their children? We *can* choose where we live and what place we call home, and I chose the USA, the country that accepted me without asking for anything in return and gave me the means to achieve my current success. The only ingredient was hard work. I was never defined by my perceived religion or judged by my inclinations. In the USA, I defined *myself.*"

Maria looked at Yule, incredulity and amazement painted across her face. It was clear to him that the former Soviet and now Russian anti-American propaganda was still going strong. She had likely never heard anyone ever compare emigration with adoption, and the new perspective shed some light on her former opinions.

Afterwards, the conversation drifted towards more pleasant and trivial matters. The two parted as friends and promised each other to keep in touch.

14 September 2007. The Lufthansa flight from Moscow to New York via Frankfurt, Germany had arrived at JFK on time. The flight was uneventful and went relatively quickly as Yule spent most of his time answering the endless stream of questions from his colleagues who had crowded around his seat. They wanted to know about his connection with the Russian government and what his brother was doing at the Kremlin. Since they now knew all about Yule's connection with the Russian government, the

most pressing questions had to do with what would happen after the coming Presidential elections in Russia, specifically questions concerning a man named Medvedev, of whom no one had ever heard off.

Yule's brother had, of course, told him all about President Putin's ambitious plans for the future. Putin, everyone knew, had to step down because of the term-limit law. Vova, however, divulged that the President would simply run again after Medvedev's solitary term in office. Yule shared small tidbits of this information with his colleagues, but could not divulge the more intricate details because of the promise he had made to Vladimir.

The line to the JFK International Airport passport control for arrivals was mercifully short. A young, relatively handsome man behind the glass partition studied Yule's passport for just a few seconds and then slid the inside of its cover through the scanner. As he was doing that, Yule read his name tag. It read *Markeev*, clearly a Russian name.

Yule pointed at the name tag with his eyes and asked, "First generation?"

The officer knew exactly what Yule was referring to. He smiled a kind, tired smile and said, "Second generation, actually. My grandparents emigrated from Kiev in the sixties."

"Beautiful city," said Yule nonchalantly, remembering his visit from many years ago. He took his passport from the officer's hand and said, "Goodbye, Markeev."

"Welcome home," said Officer Markeev, smiling again.

"Indeed," whispered Yule to himself, holding back a tidal wave of heartwarming emotion. "My home."